Rethinking Research Methods in an Age of Digital Journalism

The digital infrastructure of media production, dissemination and consumption is becoming increasingly complex, presenting the challenge of how we should research the digital journalism environment. Digital journalism takes many forms – we therefore need to revise, improve, adjust and even invent methods to understand emerging forms of journalism.

In this book, scholars at the forefront of methodological innovations in digital journalism research share their insights on how to collect, process and analyse the diverse expressions of digital journalism, including online news, search results, hyperlinks and social media posts. As digital journalism content often comes in the form of big data, many of these new approaches depart from the traditional methods used in media research in significant ways. As we move towards new ways of understanding digital journalism, the methods developed for such purposes also need to be grounded in scientific rigour. This book aims to share some of the emerging processes by which these methods, tools and approaches are designed, implemented and validated. As such, this book not only constitutes a benchmark for thinking about research methods in digital journalism, it also provides an entry point for graduate students and seasoned scholars aiming to do research on digital journalism.

This book was originally published as a special issue of *Digital Journalism*.

Michael Karlsson is a Professor in Media and Communication Studies at Karlstad University, Sweden.

Helle Sjøvaag is a Research Professor in Media Studies at the University of Bergen, Norway.

Journalism Studies: Theory and Practice

Edited by
Bob Franklin, *Cardiff School of Journalism, Media and Cultural Studies, Cardiff University, UK*

The journal *Journalism Studies* was established at the turn of the new millennium by Bob Franklin. It was launched in the context of a burgeoning interest in the scholarly study of journalism and an expansive global community of journalism scholars and researchers. The ambition was to provide not only a forum for the critical discussion and study of journalism as a subject of intellectual inquiry but also an arena of professional practice. Previously, the study of journalism in the United Kingdom and much of Europe was a fairly marginal branch of the larger disciplines of media, communication and cultural studies; only a handful of universities offered degree programmes in the subject. *Journalism Studies* has flourished and succeeded in providing the intended public space for discussion of research on key issues within the field, to the point where in 2007 a sister journal, *Journalism Practice*, was launched to enable an enhanced focus on practice-based issues, as well as foregrounding studies of journalism education, training and professional concerns. Both journals are among the leading ranked journals within the field and publish six issues annually, in electronic and print formats. More recently, 2013 witnessed the launch of a further companion journal *Digital Journalism* to provide a site for scholarly discussion, analysis and responses to the wide-ranging implications of digital technologies for the practice and study of journalism. From the outset, the publication of themed issues has been a commitment for all journals. Their purpose is, first, to focus on highly significant or neglected areas of the field; second, to facilitate discussion and analysis of important and topical policy issues; and third, to offer readers an especially high quality and closely focused set of essays, analyses and discussions.

The *Journalism Studies: Theory and Practice* book series draws on a wide range of these themed issues from all journals and thereby extends the critical and public forum provided by them. The editor of the journals works closely with guest editors to ensure that the books achieve relevance for readers and the highest standards of research rigour and academic excellence. The series makes a significant contribution to the field of journalism studies by inviting distinguished scholars, academics and journalism practitioners to discuss and debate the central concerns within the field. It also reaches a wider readership of scholars, students and practitioners across the social sciences, humanities and communication arts, encouraging them to engage critically with, but also to interrogate, the specialist scholarly studies of journalism which this series provides.

Recent titles in the series:

(for full list, see: www.routledge.com/Journalism-Studies/book-series/JOURNALISM)

Journalism, Democracy and Civil Society in India
Edited by Shakuntala Rao and Vipul Mudgal

Photojournalism and Citizen Journalism
Edited by Stuart Allan

Entrepreneurial Journalism
Edited by Kevin Rafter

Rethinking Research Methods in an Age of Digital Journalism
Edited by Michael Karlsson and Helle Sjøvaag

Rethinking Research Methods in an Age of Digital Journalism

Edited by
Michael Karlsson and Helle Sjøvaag

LONDON AND NEW YORK

First published 2018
by Routledge
2 Park Square, Milton Park, Abingdon, Oxon, OX14 4RN, UK

and by Routledge
711 Third Avenue, New York, NY 10017, USA

Routledge is an imprint of the Taylor & Francis Group, an informa business

© 2018 Taylor & Francis

All rights reserved. No part of this book may be reprinted or reproduced or utilised in any form or by any electronic, mechanical, or other means, now known or hereafter invented, including photocopying and recording, or in any information storage or retrieval system, without permission in writing from the publishers.

Trademark notice: Product or corporate names may be trademarks or registered trademarks, and are used only for identification and explanation without intent to infringe.

British Library Cataloguing in Publication Data
A catalogue record for this book is available from the British Library

ISBN13: 978-1-138-07052-3

Typeset in Myriad Pro
by diacriTech, Chennai

Publisher's Note
The publisher accepts responsibility for any inconsistencies that may have arisen during the conversion of this book from journal articles to book chapters, namely the possible inclusion of journal terminology.

Disclaimer
Every effort has been made to contact copyright holders for their permission to reprint material in this book. The publishers would be grateful to hear from any copyright holder who is not here acknowledged and will undertake to rectify any errors or omissions in future editions of this book.

Contents

Citation Information ix
Notes on Contributors xi

Introduction: Research methods in an age of digital journalism 1
Michael Karlsson and Helle Sjøvaag

1 Taking Stock of the Toolkit: An overview of relevant
  automated content analysis approaches and techniques for
  digital journalism scholars 8
  Jelle W. Boumans and Damian Trilling

2 Tracing Online News in Motion: Time and duration in
  the study of liquid journalism 24
  Andreas Widholm

3 What Is the Meaning of a News Link? 41
  David Ryfe, Donica Mensing and Richard Kelley

4 Chances and Challenges of Computational Data Gathering
  and Analysis: The case of issue-attention cycles on Facebook 55
  *Niina Sormanen, Jukka Rohila, Epp Lauk, Turo Uskali, Jukka Jouhki
  and Maija Penttinen*

5 Word Counts and Topic Models: Automated text analysis
  methods for digital journalism research 75
  Elisabeth Günther and Thorsten Quandt

6 Quantitative Analysis of Large Amounts of Journalistic
  Texts Using Topic Modelling 89
  Carina Jacobi, Wouter van Atteveldt and Kasper Welbers

7 Googling the News: Opportunities and challenges in
  studying news events through Google Search 107
  Jacob Ørmen

CONTENTS

8 Grasping the Digital News User: Conceptual and
methodological advances in news use studies 125
Ike Picone

9 Same, Same but Different: Effects of mixing Web and
mail modes in audience research 142
Annika Bergström

10 Action Research: Collaborative research for the improvement
of digital journalism practice 160
Stephanie Grubenmann

11 Content Analysis and Online News: Epistemologies of
analysing the ephemeral Web 177
Michael Karlsson and Helle Sjøvaag

Index 193

Citation Information

The chapters in this book were originally published in *Digital Journalism*, volume 4, issue 1 (January 2016). When citing this material, please use the original page numbering for each article, as follows:

Introduction
Research methods in an age of digital journalism
Michael Karlsson and Helle Sjøvaag
Digital Journalism, volume 4, issue 1 (January 2016) pp. 1–7

Chapter 1
Taking Stock of the Toolkit: An overview of relevant automated content analysis approaches and techniques for digital journalism scholars
Jelle W. Boumans and Damian Trilling
Digital Journalism, volume 4, issue 1 (January 2016) pp. 8–23

Chapter 2
Tracing Online News in Motion: Time and duration in the study of liquid journalism
Andreas Widholm
Digital Journalism, volume 4, issue 1 (January 2016) pp. 24–40

Chapter 3
What Is the Meaning of a News Link?
David Ryfe, Donica Mensing, and Richard Kelley
Digital Journalism, volume 4, issue 1 (January 2016) pp. 41–54

Chapter 4
Chances and Challenges of Computational Data Gathering and Analysis: The case of issue-attention cycles on Facebook
Niina Sormanen, Jukka Rohila, Epp Lauk, Turo Uskali, Jukka Jouhki and Maija Penttinen
Digital Journalism, volume 4, issue 1 (January 2016) pp. 55–74

Chapter 5
Word Counts and Topic Models: Automated text analysis methods for digital journalism research
Elisabeth Günther and Thorsten Quandt
Digital Journalism, volume 4, issue 1 (January 2016) pp. 75–88

CITATION INFORMATION

Chapter 6
Quantitative Analysis of Large Amounts of Journalistic Texts Using Topic Modelling
Carina Jacobi, Wouter van Atteveldt and Kasper Welbers
Digital Journalism, volume 4, issue 1 (January 2016) pp. 89–106

Chapter 7
Googling the news: Opportunities and challenges in studying news events through Google Search
Jacob Ørmen
Digital Journalism, volume 4, issue 1 (January 2016) pp. 107–124

Chapter 8
Grasping the Digital News User: Conceptual and methodological advances in news use studies
Ike Picone
Digital Journalism, volume 4, issue 1 (January 2016) pp. 125–141

Chapter 9
Same, Same but Different: Effects of mixing Web and mail modes in audience research
Annika Bergström
Digital Journalism, volume 4, issue 1 (January 2016) pp. 142–159

Chapter 10
Action Research: Collaborative research for the improvement of digital journalism practice
Stephanie Grubenmann
Digital Journalism, volume 4, issue 1 (January 2016) pp. 160–176

Chapter 11
Content Analysis and Online News: Epistemologies of analysing the ephemeral Web
Michael Karlsson and Helle Sjøvaag
Digital Journalism, volume 4, issue 1 (January 2016) pp. 177–192

For any permission-related enquiries please visit:
http://www.tandfonline.com/page/help/permissions

Notes on Contributors

Annika Bergström is Associate Professor in the Department of Journalism and Communication at the University of Gothenburg, Sweden.

Jelle W. Boumans is Assistant Professor of Corporate Communication at the University of Amsterdam, the Netherlands.

Stephanie Grubenmann is a Senior Lecturer and Research Associate in the Institute of Mass Communication and Media Research, University of Zurich, Switzerland.

Elisabeth Günther is a PhD student in the Department of Communications at the University of Münster, Germany.

Carina Jacobi was a PhD student in the Department of Communication at the University of Vienna, Austria. Since graduating, she now works as an IT trainee for the Dutch Ministry of the Interior.

Jukka Jouhki is a senior researcher in the Department of History and Ethnology, University of Jyväskylä, Finland.

Michael Karlsson is Professor in Media and Communication Studies at Karlstad University, Sweden.

Richard Kelley is a Research Assistant Professor in the Department of Computer Science and Engineering, University of Nevada, USA.

Epp Lauk is a professor in the Department of Language and Communication Studies, University of Jyväskylä, Finland.

Donica Mensing is Associate Dean and Associate Professor in the Reynolds School of Journalism, University of Nevada, USA.

Jacob Ørmen is a postdoctoral researcher in the Department of Media, Cognition and Communication at the University of Copenhagen, Denmark.

Maija Penttinen is a MA student in the Department of History and Ethnology, University of Jyväskylä, Finland.

Ike Picone is Assistant Professor of Journalism and Media Studies in the Department of Communication Science at the Vrije Universiteit Brussel, Belgium.

Thorsten Quandt is a professor of Communication Studies at the University of Münster, Germany.

Jukka Rohila is a solutions architect at HP Indigo, based in Israel.

NOTES ON CONTRIBUTORS

David Ryfe is Professor and Director of the School of Journalism and Mass Communication at the University of Iowa, USA.

Helle Sjøvaag is a Research Professor in Media Studies at the University of Bergen, Norway.

Niina Sormanen is a PhD candidate in the Department of Language and Communication Studies, University of Jyväskylä, Finland.

Damian Trilling is an Assistant Professor for Political Communication and Journalism at the University of Amsterdam, the Netherlands.

Turo Uskali is a senior researcher in the Department of Language and Communication Studies, University of Jyväskylä, Finland.

Wouter van Atteveldt is Assistant Professor in the Department of Communication Science at the Vrije Universiteit Amsterdam, the Netherlands.

Kasper Welbers is based in the Department of Communication Science at the Vrije Universiteit Amsterdam, the Netherlands.

Andreas Widholm is Associate Professor of Journalism in the Department of Media Studies at Stockholm University, Sweden.

INTRODUCTION
Research methods in an age of digital journalism

Michael Karlsson and Helle Sjøvaag

The past 15 years have seen a steady decline in the news industry, while ironically there has been a great increase in journalism research (visible in, for instance, the emergence of specific journals and divisions within research associations). During this time period there has been a good deal of theorizing about changes in the journalistic profession, professional norms and routines, and on the role of journalism in society. While journalism theory has indeed been advanced, the same can unfortunately not be said about methodologies used in journalism research. Instead, the traditional concepts of sender, channel, message and receiver are still the most common starting points for much journalism research. This also holds true for most research on digital and online journalism, despite the many methodological challenges that follow from the characteristics of digital media and digital journalism. In order to assess contemporary journalism properly, we think that research methods must be assessed, adjusted, redesigned and perhaps even invented. This idea is far from novel as methodological innovation has previously been made, and more importantly, revitalized the field. Consider, for instance, the ethnographies of the 1970s (e.g. Tuchman 1972) that gave new insight into how news was constructed. Or how Lazarsfeld and colleagues, with content analysis, innovative use of panels and the invention of the "focused interview", lay some of the foundations that were to become the field of media and communications research (Katz 1987; Merton and Kendall 1946).

Yet, the challenges and, consequently, rewards for journalism studies and communication research might be even greater with the digitization of communications. We now face an ontological trial as some of the very categories, and their relationships, of journalism studies—producers, newsrooms, contents, channels of distribution and audiences—seem less certain than they did only a few years ago, becoming increasingly elusive when old boundaries, distinctions and demarcations dissolve. With a changing ontology come questions about a changing epistemology. The aforementioned discrete categories have typically been investigated using a fairly standard set of methods such as surveys, content analysis, interviews, ethnography and experiments. As our objects of study changes, our methodological approaches need to be considered as well, as it is unclear to what extent previously used methods remain feasible, need revision or if new methods have to be invented. The digital world of journalism is developing fast, and researchers need appropriate, stringent and viable methods for capturing and understanding these changes. So far, few systematic attempts have been made in this area. That is why this special issue of *Digital Journalism* is dedicated solely to digital research methods. In putting together this special issue, our aim was to encourage scholars to develop new and revised methods, take stock of old methods, discuss and propose innovative yet rigorous methodological approaches to the journalistic field, with a particular focus on digital journalism. The interest from the research community has been great. We received a total of 35 contributions for the special issue but were only able to accept 11, giving an effective acceptance rate of 31 per cent.

The contributions in this issue offer new and updated methods on how to view and measure the production, content, distribution and consumption of news. They discuss problems and possibilities, but also provide examples and guides that are easily understandable for the digital methods novice. This mixture of approaches considers not only methods using digital tools, but also pays attention to methodological innovation in doing research on journalism as a digital form of communication.

The promise of computational methods developed within the computer sciences is quickly emerging as methodological possibilities for journalism scholars to engage in the analysis of large amounts of digital new texts. Jelle Boumans and Damian Trilling's article "Time to Take Stock of the Toolkit: An Overview of Relevant Automated Content Analysis Approaches and Techniques for Digital Journalism Scholars", introduces methods established within computer science to study the content of blogs, social media and news websites. Boumans and Trilling demonstrate how these tools can be applied to the liquid character of the Web, and show how computational methods may account for the scale of data produced by digital journalism. They not only outline and exemplify what the methods do, they also discuss what to consider when applying them, raise caution concerning problems with these novel methods, and remind us that computational approaches to studies of digital journalism require a deep understanding of the data, first and foremost amplifying human abilities, not necessarily replacing them. Boumans and Trilling's overview provides an easily accessible, well-explained and encouraging entry point for scholars interested in computational approaches, without losing sight of how these tools can be appropriated to the study of digital journalism.

Studies are already emerging that are applying or designing computational methods for collecting and analysing digital journalism data. Using an automated data collection procedure, Andreas Widholm, in his article "Tracing Online News in Motion: Time and Duration in the Study of Liquid Journalism", addresses the problem of capturing the liquidity of digital journalism. Widholm describes a method designed for studying constantly evolving news flows online, the Regular-Interval Content Capturing method (RICC), adjusted to the dynamic character of online news. Designed to cope with news under constant alteration, RICC allows for the collection of reliable time series of data to identify variations in digital journalism over time. As an automated collection procedure, Widholm's RICC method demonstrates how computational collection procedures can open up possibilities for new theorization, broadening the analytical scale of studies of online news. Discussing both data collection and analytical results, Widholm's article is an example of how new tools can contribute to new knowledge about the processes of digital news production.

Designing new tools to encounter the challenges of collecting digital news data is a focus also in David Ryfe, Donica Mensing, and Richard Kelley's article "What is the Meaning of a News Link?" The authors describe how they develop an exploratory automated method—a computational tool, the journalism toolkit (Jot), for analysing large data-sets of news links. The tool not only collects links, it automatically classifies them based on their URL structure, according to four identified functions that links serve in news texts. Combining this new tool with established theory, machine learning principles also teaches the programme to filter collected links according to the five Ws: who is saying what, where, when, and to what purpose. The authors describe the largely hybrid nature of applying new computational methods to the study of digital journalism. While the collection and the initial classification are automated, the analysis also requires manual effort. Automated methods are used to discover the meaning of news links, in turn used to develop a taxonomy of the different meanings that links have. Ryfe, Mensing, and Kelley's article therefore not only provides an example of methodological development, but also presents an original contribution as to the meaning of news links on a theoretical level.

In many cases, tool development for digital journalism research requires a collaborative effort between journalism scholars and computer scientists. Niina Niskala, Jukka Rohila, Epp Lauk, Turo Uskali, Jukka Joukhi, and Maija Penttinen provide an example of a fruitful collaboration in this regard in their article "Chances and Challenges of Computational Data Gathering and Analysis: The Case of Issue-attention Cycles on Facebook". Here, the authors demonstrate a computational technique for gathering and processing large amounts of data from Facebook, analysing issue-attention cycles and news flows on groups and pages. The research tool analyses Facebook using Facebook's own application programming interfaces and public interfaces to capture new and emerging social media practices, in particular the cyclical nature of public attention in the digital news ecosystem. The authors describe the step-by-step approach taken in collecting and analysing the data, demonstrating how the method design widens the scope and quality of information at the researcher's disposal applied to new information environments. While technological thresholds in understanding technical aspects are described as helpful in the analysis, the authors also consider the ethical aspects of collecting data from social networking sites. Proven useful for analysing social networking sites, the technique applied by the Finnish research team to studying large amounts of social media data provides an example of the theoretical gains offered by multidisciplinarity in method designs for research on digital news flows.

In venturing into the digital methodological realm, certain thresholds do exist for the computationally uninitiated researcher. In their article "Word Counts and Topic Models: Automated Text Analysis Methods for Digital Journalism Research", Elisabeth Günther and Thorsten Quandt provide a useful entry point in this regard. Here, the authors outline a roadmap for analysing digital journalism using computational methods to perform text analysis of large amounts of documents. While these are tools borrowed from computer science and computational linguistics, Günther and Quandt demonstrate how semi-automated and fully automated methods can be used in the study of digital journalism. The authors present a roadmap—a practical guide describing the workflows involved—and discuss the different strengths that the methods entail that may enrich, if not replace, the manual content analysis. In order for scholars to embrace methods from such neighbouring disciplines, understanding what the techniques do and how they can be used in journalism research is paramount to lowering the threshold for application. Günther and Quandt's roadmap offers a helpful contribution in this regard.

RETHINKING RESEARCH METHODS IN AN AGE OF DIGITAL JOURNALISM

Carina Jacobi, Wouter van Atteveldt, and Kasper Welber's article provides an accessible and detailed addition to this effort. In "Quantitative Analysis of Large Amounts of Journalistic Texts Using Topic Modelling", van Atteveldt and colleagues provide a specific example of how automated methods—particularly topic modelling—can been used to study large sets of media texts. Focusing on one particular approach from computational linguistics—Latent Dirichlet Allocation (LDA)—the authors describe how the method can be applied to organize texts, demonstrated through a case study partially replicating the seminal study by Gamson and Modigliani (1989), applying the method to the *New York Times*' coverage of nuclear technology since 1945. Connecting to the hybrid methodological imperative present in many of the articles in this special issue, the authors emphasize that LDA is an unsupervised technique that also requires human interpretation of results. While applying computational methods such as LDA to the study of digital journalism can reveal patterns in large data-sets, the authors also offer suggestions as to how to advance automated studies of news text using additional methods borrowed from computer science.

Digital journalism research is, however, not only about journalistic texts. It is also about the production and use of news. These are areas that can benefit equally from applying digital methods to study the processes by which journalism is created and consumed. An important question in this regard is how audiences, and researchers, access digital journalism sources. Jacob Ørmen, in "Googling the News: Opportunities and Challenges in Studying News Events Through Google Search", addresses the issue of how to study news events through Google Search. Google functions as gatekeeper and mediator of news and information, and provides online traffic to online news sites. Ørmen in particular brings focus to the methodological and ontological issues in studying search results, building on the purposeful sampling of algorithmically generated content. Taking personalization factors into consideration—particularly the relationship between endogenous and exogenous factors influencing search results on website rankings, the article discusses the practical question of archiving search results, illustrated through a purposeful sampling of real-world participants and constructed profiles that work with the Google algorithm. Ørmen's article hence tackles the difficult question of black boxes in doing digital research, and how to establish a systematic approach to the ephemeral nature of digital data.

With the proliferation of digital journalism sources, people's news consumption has changed profoundly. Audiences are spreading across platforms, news sources, contexts and devices—fragmenting media use to the point where methodological expansion becomes necessary. Ike Picone's article, "Grasping the Digital News User: Conceptual and Methodological Advances in News Use Studies", discusses how to capture the news audience's changing practices. Picone here offers guiding principles for methodological innovation. First, research into audience activity requires a holistic approach in order to capture the magnitude of news consumption in relation to other media practices. Only when we understand people's entire media repertoire can we appreciate the role of news. Second, there is an increasing need, in light of mobile media, to know when and where news is consumed. Combining these principles provides a way to understand better the place of news in people's media repertoires. Picone therefore suggests that conceptualizing people as users of media, rather than as audiences, enables researchers to study the many capacities that media use entails—a framework that requires methodological innovation capable of capturing people's news experiences.

Gaining access to people's media use is the subject also of Annika Bergström's article "Same, Same But Different: Effects of Mixing Web and Mail Modes in Audience Research". Bergström here enters the debate about the effects of survey distribution platform on survey response. Research on online journalists and their audiences tend to be challenged when defining the population. Web surveys imply loss of sample control, requiring caution in data-set combination and survey design, especially with the proliferation of internet surveys and the subsequent concern for "professional respondents". Bergström's article questions how mixed survey modes affect research results, investigating how mode choice, item non-response and response distribution for habitual and attitudinal questions differ in Web and mail mode. While her findings indicate that item non-responses varied most across platforms, overall, differences were minor. Bergström hence finds that using different or mixing survey modes does not seem to affect the quality of data to any large extent. Thus, newsrooms, pollsters and policy-makers alike can continue to use Web and mail modes knowing that it will not affect responses that much.

Digital journalism research has also been largely concerned with the production of news, especially when switching to digital newsrooms. Stéphanie Grubenmann's article, "Action Research: Collaborative Research for the Improvement of Digital Journalism Practice", concerns the digital challenges in an editorial setting. Focusing on how academia and industry can work together to generate sustainable innovativeness and creativity in digital newsrooms, Grubenmann details both what practitioners—in their opportunities for reflection, systematic improvement and inducing change—and researchers—through holistic inquiry and closing the relevance gap between academia and industry—can take away from such a collaboration. In describing a project that employs action research aimed at fostering implementation of digital journalism in the newsroom, Grubenmann's article provides insight concerning both the journalistic processes involved in switching to digital platforms, the potentials inherent in industry–academia collaboration and the application of action research to study journalism's digital future.

When researchers strive to access the news produced by digitized newsrooms, the platform specificities of online and mobile—their underlying technologies—present new challenges to the methodologies of analysing content. Michael Karlsson and Helle Sjøvaag engage with these dilemmas through a discussion of the epistemology of three different forms of content analysis in "Content Analysis and Online News: Epistemologies of Analysing the Ephemeral Web". Taking the different ontologies of analogue and digital media as a point of departure, the authors juxtapose established content analysis with two emerging forms of content analysis—big data and liquid content analysis. The reach, strengths and weaknesses of the methods are discussed, both in application and in relation to the established methodology of content analysis as it is presented in standard textbooks within the discipline. The differences and similarities between these approaches are illustrated against nine dimensions: mode of analysis, variable design, scope/sampling size, sampling procedure, unit of analysis, recording/storage, generalizability, key coding agent and aim of analysis. Framed as a conceptual discussion rather than offering solutions to a methodology that finds itself in a "messy but productive" period, Karlsson and Sjøvaag encourage veracity in methodological experimentations based on the affordances of the digital journalism spaces where new, digital, content analysis methods can be applied.

Together the 11 contributions that make up this special issue on methods for digital journalism research speak to some of the challenges and opportunities that currently face journalism studies as a discipline. Digitization has taken place in all processes of the news ecology—in the production, content, dissemination and uses of news. While scholars have been apt at considering the affordances of digital technologies on the communication processes that journalism engages in, less attention has been given to the methods by which we engage with journalism in the digital age. Not only are the locations where data are accessed increasingly digital in nature—raising problems that analogue-designed research methods are partially limited at handling—methods in themselves are becoming more digital, i.e. they are becoming increasingly computerized. In this lies a realization of the threshold that faces research on digital media. Trained to access and comprehend data through methods that essentially require highly human efforts, computers are altogether different in this regard. Understanding and designing methods as objective interrogations of deductively obtained data is one thing, but designing and using methods performed by the logical ontology of computers is quite another. As tools of their own, computational methods require an understanding of the processes they perform, less they become black boxes of their own.

As many of the contributions here demonstrate, methods to access and analyse digital journalism products in many, but not all, cases require new skills. Some of the tools, protocols, methods and approaches appropriate to study journalism as text can be imported from other disciplines, particularly computer science and computational linguistics. These are not yet within the arsenal of the social scientific or humanities methodologies applied within the field, and seem largely absent from the curriculum applied in training students of journalism and communication. While the threshold for acquiring these skills may seem high, this should not deter scholars from actively trying out new methods. As some of the contributions show here, a productive vantage point to expanding our methodological arsenal is to collaborate with scholars from neighbouring disciplines. At least in the analysis of digital journalistic output—the texts produced by journalists—we appear to find ourselves in a particularly fertile field, where new computational tools may add to, if not replace, methods for studying digital journalism. Similarly, how we engage with the production and reception of journalism in the digital ecosystem find new venues when digitally based methods are applied, and when established approaches are tailored to studying digital objects at different points in the journalistic process. This is not to say that the established methods developed for studying news production, content and use in the analogue era are obsolete or irrelevant by any means. There is certainly merit in practising and refining methodology that does not require adjustment to the digital setting. While the digital is an important feature of journalism today, it is not the only, or necessarily defining, feature of contemporary journalism practice and consumption. What the scholars included in this special issue demonstrate, however, is that methodological innovation adjusted to the digital setting of journalism can be productive in terms of data access, data archiving and data analysis.

The digitization of journalism implies ontological changes that provoke challenges for journalism scholars to build an appropriate epistemology. Our hope is that this collection of articles offering new approaches to the production, distribution, content and consumption of news may serve as an inspiration for scholars within and without the journalistic field that can provide paths for future developments of methods and theory.

REFERENCES

Gamson, William A., and Andre Modigliani. 1989. "Media Discourse and Public Opinion on Nuclear Power: A Constructionist Approach." *American Journal of Sociology* 95: 1–37.

Katz, Elihu. 1987. "Communications Research Since Lazersfeld." *The Public Opinion Quarterly* 51 (4 PART 2): S25–S45.

Merton, Robert K., and Patricia L. Kendall. 1946. "The Focused Interview." *American Journal of Sociology* 51 (6): 541–557.

Tuchman, Gaye. 1972. "Objectivity as a Strategic ritual." *The American Journal of Sociology* 77 (4): 660–679.

TAKING STOCK OF THE TOOLKIT
An overview of relevant automated content analysis approaches and techniques for digital journalism scholars

Jelle W. Boumans[1] and Damian Trilling[1]

When analyzing digital journalism content, journalism scholars are confronted with a number of substantial differences compared to traditional journalistic content. The sheer amount of data and the unique features of digital content call for the application of valuable new techniques. Various other scholarly fields are already applying computational methods to study digital journalism data. Often, their research interests are closely related to those of journalism scholars. Despite the advantages that computational methods have over traditional content analysis methods, they are not commonplace in digital journalism studies. To increase awareness of what computational methods have to offer, we take stock of the toolkit and show the ways in which computational methods can aid journalism studies. Distinguishing between dictionary-based approaches, supervised machine learning, and unsupervised machine learning, we present a systematic inventory of recent applications both inside as well as outside journalism studies. We conclude with suggestions for how the application of new techniques can be encouraged.

Introduction

The current digital age brings about substantial changes to the field of journalism studies. Evidently more and more researchers from other fields have started analyzing journalistic content. Computer scientists, for instance, analyze data from journalistic websites, social media, or blogs (e.g., Mishne 2007; Morgan, Zubair Shafiq, and Lampe 2013; Stieglitz and Dang-Xuan 2012). The availability and volume of digital journalistic content make it interesting material for various academic fields, from behavioral finance (Uhl 2014) to wildlife studies (Houston, Bruskotter, and Fan 2010). Studies of journalistic content in these fields typically benefit from advanced computer-assisted methods that find their origin in computer science.

Given computer scientists' expertise in dealing with digital data, taking stock of their techniques can be very rewarding for journalism scholars. Automated content analysis (ACA) can identify patterns in journalistic data that traditional analysis would

---

[1]Both authors contributed equally to this work.

not, or only with greater effort (Flaounas et al. 2013). Additionally, it can provide "harder" evidence for what journalism scholars might already have suspected based on qualitative or small-scale quantitative research, help to sketch the bigger picture, and—last but not least—save time and money. Other fields testify to this potential: relevant applications of automated techniques are found in fields as various as linguistics (Schneider 2014), management studies (Illia, Sonpar, and Bauer 2014), behavioral finance (Uhl 2014), and political science (Grimmer and Stewart 2013). To a certain extent, journalism scholars do rely on the knowledge and insights from computer science. Examples range from assessing news formats (Sjøvaag and Stavelin 2012) to gender bias (Flaounas et al. 2013), and from sentiment analysis (Uhl 2014) to framing analysis (Hellsten, Dawson, and Leydesdorff 2009). But still, as noted in an earlier issue of this journal: "The introduction of computer science into the social sciences is still at an immature stage" (Flaounas et al. 2013, 102; similarly Freelon 2014, 71).

Becoming more familiar with the available ACA toolkit is increasingly necessary as our object of study changes. In addition to the traditional mass communication channels and their predictable, static content, journalism nowadays takes place via a variety of communication channels, including blogs, news aggregators, social media, apps, and news websites. It is not only the channels that have changed: technological advances have also created new quantitative forms including computer-assisted reporting, data journalism, and computational journalism (Coddington 2014). Yet, while scholars have paid ample attention to the increasing impact that computational applications have on the field of journalism (e.g., Carlson 2014; Fink and Anderson 2014; Flew et al. 2012), they rarely take advantage of the potential of these tools themselves.

Both the new channels as well as new journalistic practices require a critical inquiry into the methods that we use to study journalism. Traditional content-analytical tools generally cannot account for the dynamic and often interactive characteristics of the online news environment. In addition, the vast size of many digital journalism datasets make manual approaches unfeasible. Generally speaking, a discipline should strive for expanding its methodological toolkit when both the subject of study as well as the technological actuality changes. The journalism researcher's toolkit lags behind the state of the art of other fields that study journalistic content. To encourage exploring automated approaches, this article provides a systematic inventory of ACA approaches that have demonstrated their usefulness for the study of journalistic content.

Of course, automated methods also have drawbacks and this review will discuss them. Foremost, automated methods are not equivalent to manual methods. Because language is so multifaceted, automated methods will inevitably fall short on reducing a text to a model that represents the text in its entirety (Simon 2001). As Grimmer and Stewart (2013, 269) state: "All quantitative models of language are wrong—but some are useful." While human coders are not flawless either, they are generally better able to recognize the various meanings that words and phrases can have.

In the remainder of this article, we propose a classification of such techniques along a continuum ranging from deductive to inductive. Deductive techniques, as we propose to call them, define some coding criteria in advance (e.g., lists of relevant words), while inductive techniques rather seek to identify patterns in the data, without prescribing in advance what to look for. One could therefore also call the deductive techniques "top-down approaches" and the inductive techniques "bottom-up approaches."

Sorting Out the ACA Toolkit: From Deductive to Inductive

The approaches that are most easy and straightforward to apply are typically deductive. These are based on predefined categories or rules. The researcher has a large—theoretically motivated—say in deciding what content features the technique should extract. *Visibility analysis*, applied when the researcher is interested in how many times a specific actor or event occurs in the media, is a common example of a deductive type of research.

At the other end of the continuum, where we find the inductive techniques, one could say that it is the computer rather than the researcher which makes the decisions about what is meaningful in the dataset. Following the rationale that for some tasks, computers are better equipped than humans, it is up to the analytical technique to extract meaningful features from—often large—datasets. Implicit *framing analysis*, where the computer seeks patterns of co-occurring words that convey meanings in a collection of texts, is an example of such an application (Hellsten, Dawson, and Leydesdorff 2009). To structure our overview, we distinguish three general methodological approaches that can be arranged along this continuum: *counting and dictionaries*, *supervised machine learning*, and *unsupervised machine learning*. Figure 1 presents these approaches and provides examples of related research interests and statistical procedures.

Before we describe the methodological approaches and the types of problems they typically address, it is necessary to understand that most of them do not analyze the original, but pre-processed versions of the texts. Such pre-processing can include normalizing the text in terms of spelling and punctuation, *stopword removal* (removing words that are not meaningful, like "the," "a," "an"), and *stemming* (reducing words to their stem, so that "voting" and "vote" are recognized as the same concept). While these techniques are fairly simple, more advanced options like *named entity recognition* —where an algorithm tries to detect named actors in a sentence, or *parsing* (to include only specific parts of speech) can also be applied.

Methodological approach

	Counting and Dictionary	Supervised Machine Learning	Unsupervised Machine Learning
Typical research interests and content features	visibility analysis sentiment analysis subjectivity analysis	frames topics gender bias	frames topics
Common statistical procedures	string comparisons counting	support vector machines naive Bayes	principal component analysis cluster analysis latent dirichlet allocation semantic network analysis

deductive → inductive

FIGURE 1
Proposed classification of ACA approaches.

Often, a so-called bag-of-words representation of each text is created, which is based on the frequency with which each word is occurring, disregarding the order in which the words appear in the text. Just as stopwords are regarded irrelevant for understanding a text's meaning, there are also words that are considered particularly relevant for a text. Therefore, it is common to attach a specific weight to words. The rationale behind this is that words that occur rarely in language are more informative than words that are very frequently used.[1] For example, one can then use measures like the log likelihood (which compares the actual frequency of each word with its expected frequency) to compare collections of texts (e.g., Rayson and Garside 2000). Mishne (2007), for instance, uses this measure to distinguish different genres of blogs. However, as we will show in the next sections, the ACA toolkit includes much more.

Basic Counting and Dictionary-based Methods

Many content analyses in the realm of journalism studies address questions like "how often is actor X mentioned?" or "what are the most frequent topics in outlets Y and Z?" Such studies involve coding tasks that come down to counting words from a pre-defined list. A large-scale analysis that manually counted references to the European Union and political actors in 52,009 news stories (Schuck et al. 2011) is just one of the many examples of studies that involve counting and that could benefit from an automated approach. When counting is automated, success or failure largely reflects a correct (excluding irrelevant data) and exhaustive (including all the relevant data) definition of the search criteria. Essentially, a given string of text (a pre-defined word or a search string, often a so-called "regular expression") is compared to another string (e.g., a paragraph of a newspaper article). Requiring only a searchable database and basic software like Excel, SPSS, or Stata, this very basic method can be employed by journalism scholars with no previous experience and can result in insightful visibility analyses. One can, for instance, show how often a topic or actor is in the news, and how this differs between outlets or evolves over time. Vliegenthart, Boomgaarden, and Boumans (2011) used such an approach to analyze the relative visibility of politicians in British and Dutch newspapers over time.

The basis of a visibility analysis is in essence an example of a dictionary in its most simple form: a list of key words, used to determine the category a document belongs to. The simple principle behind a dictionary-approach makes it easy to measure a variety of concepts. Within journalism studies, the approach has, for instance, successfully been applied to capture metaphors from news articles (Krennmayr 2014) or hostility in news comments (Ksiazek, Peer, and Zivic 2014). One of the most common research interests to which it is applied, is *sentiment analysis*. Sentiment analysis aims at assessing whether the tone of news content is positive or negative. The dictionary in this case consists of a manually constructed list of words with attached tone scores, which can be either dichotomous or measured on a detailed scale. Sentiment analysis is widely used in marketing and market research to inform organizations on how their brands are evaluated in (social) media (e.g., Mostafa 2013) and is applied to all types of text, including genres as idiosyncratic as movie reviews (e.g., Taboada, Brooke, and Stede, 2009) or suicide notes (Huang, Goh, and Liew, 2007; Festian et al. 2012).

Despite the wide application in both industry and other scientific fields, by comparison journalism scholars have barely used sentiment analysis (one of the few exceptions being Kleinnijenhuis et al. 2013). In the related field of political communication, measuring tone or sentiment in a computer-assisted fashion is increasingly common, for example to measure how parties are portrayed in the news (Junqué de Fortuny et al. 2012; Van Atteveldt et al. 2008) or to predict election outcomes (but see the critical review of such endeavors by Gayo-Avello 2013). Similar questions are addressed by computer scientists: Stieglitz and Dang-Xuan (2012), for instance, showed how emotions in a political tweet can be used to predict the number of retweets.

The level of sophistication of sentiment analyses varies (Young and Soroka 2012). The most simple, non-statistical approaches count the number of positive and negative words in a text. More powerful algorithms involve multiple features of the text and can deal with, for instance, negation or punctuation use, like the SentiStrength algorithm (Thelwall et al. 2010). In addition, while some algorithms only allow assessments based on a positive–negative dimension, others such as LIWC[2] (Pennebaker, Booth, and Francis 2007) offer additional dimensions like subjectivity or even affective components (i.e., anxiety, anger or sadness; a review of 121 studies using LIWC is provided by Tausczik and Pennebaker 2009).

A study published in *Human Dimensions of Wildlife* on the portrayal of wolves in print media illustrates the wide variety of fields that study journalistic content by means of a dictionary approach. It complements a dictionary with a set of "idea transition" rules, which specify how words and phrases together can create new meanings. For example, when the word "should" appeared near the word "protect," the paragraph was scored as an instance of the concept "wolves should be protected" (Houston, Bruskotter, and Fan 2010, 394–395).

Three remarks should be made concerning the use of dictionary-based techniques. First, it all starts with availability. Dictionaries are manually constructed, which is a very labor-intensive task. Having access to a predefined dictionary is thus of great value. Second, often the applicability of a dictionary is limited to the specific domain within which it is developed. Applying it to a dataset outside this domain can lead to erroneous results (see, e.g., Loughran and McDonald 2011). The development of reliable, freely available dictionaries that are valid across domains needs to be continued. A third issue is that, while internationalization efforts have been undertaken recently, dictionaries are often tailored to the English language, rendering them irrelevant for datasets in other languages.

Above all, however, these lexicons have to be tested and validated (see, e.g., Burscher et al. 2014; Monroe, Colaresi, and Quinn 2008). Obviously, approaches that come down to identifying specific words are deterministic processes and thus extremely reliable, but their validity can be low (e.g., Conway 2006): sometimes, a given word can have multiple meanings, resulting in wrongfully counting an item as relevant (false positive); and sometimes, an unanticipated synonym or a paraphrase might be used which results in not recognizing a relevant item (false negative). "Validate, Validate, Validate," as Grimmer and Stewart (2013, 271), stress, is therefore a key principle of successful ACA. An interesting solution has been employed by Mohammed and Turney (2010), who showed that even a platform like *Amazon Mechanical Turk* can be used to create valid emotion lexicons, with limited financial means.

Supervised Methods

In contrast to ready-to-use techniques that require little manual effort (like using existing dictionaries to measure sentiment), there are more advanced ACA methods that are highly useful for deductive coding of large-scale datasets, but that nevertheless require a relatively high degree of initial manual labor. *Supervised machine learning* is such an approach. It comes in various flavors (like *support vector machines* or *naïve Bayes classifiers*), which cannot be discussed within the scope of this article. Very broadly speaking, techniques under this umbrella are suitable for coding implicit variables in a large dataset, when a smaller sub-set can be (or already has been) hand-coded, but the dataset of interest is so large that it is not feasible to code each article manually. Journalism researchers might be interested in classifying a large amount of digital journalism texts according to their genre (e.g. to find out how a certain issue or actor is treated in editorials compared to news reports). For a human coder, this classification is a rather easy task, but it is difficult to specify an explicit rule for what constitutes an opinion piece. A supervised machine learning algorithm learns from a human coder's decisions and would allow the journalism researcher to solve the classification problem for a virtually unlimited amount of articles. These techniques can be employed for a wide range of research problems including the coding of readability, subjectivity, and gender imbalances (Flaounas et al. 2013), but also, as we will discuss below, frames and topics.

In contrast to simple automated coding, which we discussed above and where the researcher specifies some rules for coding (e.g., code as A if words X or Y are mentioned—which, obviously, is a good way to code explicit and manifest[3] variables), supervised machine learning does not require formulating explicit rules. In fact, the idea is quite the opposite: human coders classify a number of texts, and the machine learning algorithm tries to infer which characteristics of a text lead to which classification. For example, one could ask human coders to classify 1000 articles according to their genres. Then, one would use 500 articles to train a machine learning algorithm and test it by letting it predict the classification of the remaining 500 articles. If the classification of the latter matches the classification of the human coders, one can use the algorithm to classify an unlimited number of new texts.

In spite of the obvious promises of this approach (once trained, it can be used over and over again without any additional costs), journalism scholars have largely neglected this technique. One of the few exceptions is the work by Scharkow (2011), who relied on supervised machine learning to code the topic of articles from 12 German news sites. More recently, Burscher and colleagues have shown that supervised machine learning can be used to code frames in Dutch news articles (Burscher et al. 2014; Odijk et al. 2013) as well as policy issues (Burscher, Vliegenthart, and De Vreese 2015). One should note that there is no inherent limitation as to which classifications can be coded and which cannot. While topics and frames might be of particular interest, one could also think of coding the tone of an article based on supervised machine learning instead of using dictionaries only (e.g., Thelwall et al. 2010).

In the long run, using supervised machine learning does not only increase efficiency, but also transparency and reproducibility. In fact, for English news, there already exist manually annotated corpora that can be used to successfully train a classifier to automatically code the topic of news articles (Flaounas et al. 2013). In this case, researchers do not need to code the training material themselves, making the technique effectively a fully automated one (for more details, we refer to standard textbooks like Manning, Raghavan, and Schütze 2008). The researcher has to evaluate, though, how close the predicted probability (e.g., of an article being about a given topic) is to the empirical observed probability. A number of metrics are available for this, and it is also possible to graphically examine the reliability of the classifier. When assessing a classifier, the researcher has to make a tradeoff between precision and recall. In the case of a binary classifier (which has only two categories: an item either matches the criteria or not), precision signifies how many of the selected cases are truly relevant, while recall signifies the fraction of all relevant cases that have been identified. For example, a classifier can have a perfect recall (find all relevant cases), but a low precision (it incorrectly finds a number of irrelevant cases as well); or it might have a high precision (only relevant cases are found), but a low recall (many relevant cases are not found).

In political science, the machine learning approach is becoming increasingly common (see, e.g., Grimmer and Stewart 2013). For example, research on the coverage of political speeches has shown that hand-coding between 100 and 500 texts is sufficient to train an algorithm that can distinguish between articles opposing or supporting a policy or between letters to the editor and other articles (Hopkins and King 2010). Similar, in political communication research, supervised machine learning has been applied in the analysis of political tweets (e.g., Roback and Hemphill 2013; Vargo et al. 2014). Also within computer science it is a common approach to use supervised machine learning for classifying the content of blog posts (see, e.g., Husby and Barbosa 2012).

Taken together, supervised machine learning promises that journalism scholars will make more efficient use of the limited resource of human coders. While traditionally, the work of human coders only had value for one single study, their efforts now serve a purpose that extends over multiple studies. Once the discipline has trained solid classifiers, these can be used over and over again. It would also enable *ad hoc* studies on emerging topics to be conducted in a timely fashion, allowing researchers to contribute to recent public debates. To do so, however, the technique has to become more accessible. Fortunately, in the last years, tools have been developed that can help journalism scholars applying supervised machine learning. For example, several R packages have been developed to this end (e.g., Hopkins and King 2010; Jurka et al. 2013).

Yet, researchers have to keep in mind that as a consequence of being dependent on a training dataset, human annotation is still the "gold standard"—by definition, the classifier cannot perform better. In fact, many classifiers perform better than random, but still considerably worse than humans. In addition, they have a certain black-box nature: in contrast to simple dictionary-based methods, it can be difficult to fully understand why a specific classification was made or not. For example, an unobserved oddity in the training data could result in systematic erroneous judgments by the classifier.

Unsupervised Methods

The supervised machine learning approach, by design, is used to code pre-determined categories—and, in fact, is the best way to do so. However, as Grimmer and Stewart (2013, 281) note, "Supervised methods will never contribute to a new coding scheme." Where such an inductive approach is needed, *unsupervised methods* come into play. Unsupervised methods might be especially interesting for those who want to address questions in the realm of digital journalism that traditionally would have been researched using qualitative methods; researchers interested in questions that aim at describing discourses, frames, or topics in an open way, without having any predefined categories, but who struggle with the amount of data and are looking for tools to help them make sense of the material.

For example, where Burscher et al. (2014) aimed at deductively identifying pre-defined frames, other studies (which we discuss below) attempted to inductively identify and extract frames from text. Just as both approaches to framing analysis exist in manual coding (Matthes and Kohring 2008), there is also an automated equivalent to *inductive frame analysis*. Inductive frames are usually extracted based on the idea that the co-occurrence of words can be interpreted as a frame. This can be done by calculating similarity measures and/or applying statistical techniques like *principal component analysis* or *cluster analysis*. Often, these co-occurrences of words are then graphically visualized as networks of words (e.g., Vlieger and Leydesdorff 2012).

While to our best knowledge no studies that explicitly relate to the field of journalism studies have employed these techniques yet, a number of studies from related fields analyze journalistic coverage in this way. For example, within science communication, the journalistic coverage of artificial sweeteners has been analyzed (Hellsten, Dawson, and Leydesdorff 2009); and within crisis communication, the relationship between coverage of disasters and PR releases has been assessed (Jonkman and Verhoeven 2013; Van der Meer et al. 2014).

Although there is no need for manual coders, like in the case of supervised methods, inductive frame extraction still requires some manual efforts in setting up the analysis and making sense of the results. Comparing the method described by Vlieger and Leydesdorff (2012) with manual content analysis, De Graaf and van der Vossen (2013) state that considerable manual effort is still necessary, while at the same time, reliability problems arise. Yet these techniques have a lot to offer for journalism research, especially with the development of easier to use software packages that can import data from different sources. First of all, the possibility to quickly visualize coverage even when a huge amount of data is to be analyzed allows for a better and deeper understanding than manual methods alone. If the dataset consists of thousands of articles, it is not feasible to read a substantial amount of them to get a grasp of the patterns present in the data. Second, as this approach in fact transforms each text to a set of numbers, it allows the application of all kinds of statistical approaches. This means that questions can be answered that could not be asked before, including the quantitative assessment of similarity overlap between collections of texts.

Related to this is the field of *topic modeling* (e.g., Řehůřek and Sojka 2010). One of the most powerful techniques in this field is Latent Dirichlet Allocation (LDA), first described only 12 years ago (Blei, Ng, and Jordan 2003). For example, LDA has been shown to help identifying important news items (Krestel and Mehta 2010). Grimmer and Stewart (2013) give a detailed overview of the application of LDA topic models in political science.

The approaches to inductive frame analysis and to the assessment of document similarity discussed thus far largely rely on a bag-of-words approach, in which it is considered necessary for the computer to understand the function or meaning of each word. Mishne (2007), for instance, shows that the mood of blog posts can be accurately predicted by the occurrence of a few characteristic words. Some criticize such an approach as overly simplistic. Indeed, it is easy to point to cases where this modeling of the data would fail, for instance with respect to negation ("not good" is counted as "good") or with the incapability of distinguishing between different meanings of a word. For example, the word "Amstel" could refer either to one of the largest beer brands in the Netherlands, to a renowned hotel in Amsterdam, or to the river after which both are named.

In response to the limitations that arise from disregarding the syntactic structure of sentences, methods developed in the field of computer linguistics use more advanced representations of texts, in which the relationship between elements is modeled. Techniques used for this purpose include *part-of-speech tagging* and *named entity recognition*. To be able to understand which word is a proper noun, and thus refers to a potentially interesting actor, or to distinguish between "Israel attacked Hamas" and "Hamas attacked Israel" (Sheafer et al. 2014) can be of vital importance to a researcher. A possible application for journalism researchers could lie in studies that do not only measure whether actors are mentioned, but also precisely in what context they are referred to. Building on such ideas, Van Atteveldt (2008) presents a method called auto- mated semantic network analysis and shows that it is possible to use a computer to code semantic relationships and disentangle the syntactical function of the elements of a sentence (see also Van Atteveldt, Kleinnijenhuis, and Ruigrok, 2008). This can, for instance, be a powerful tool to assess the role in which certain actors appear in the news.

Even more than in the case of dictionaries (which in principle can be translated), fixation on the English language is a considerable limitation for advanced natural language processing techniques. Parsers do not exist for all languages, and some languages are much more difficult to parse than others. Other limitations of unsupervised methods include the potential openness for different interpretations by the researcher: they do not offer one and only one correct solution. Also, especially when the researchers do not carefully plan necessary pre-processing steps, they can be sensitive to peculiarities of the material that are irrelevant from a theoretical point of view.

Identifying and Overcoming Obstacles

From the previous sections it has become clear that automated approaches have much to offer scholars studying journalistic content and, indeed, the approaches are commonly applied in a number of academic fields. Oddly enough, as yet, relatively few studies within the field of journalism studies make use of them (but see, for instance, Günther and Scharkow 2014; Kleinnijenhuis et al. 2013; Krennmayr 2014; Ksiazek, Peer, and Zivic 2014; Sjøvaag and Stavelin 2012). Particularly inductive and more complex approaches appear to be hardly applied by journalism scholars (a notable exception being Flaounas et al. 2013). To understand why this might be the case, a number of observations can be made.

First, there is a tendency to use familiar methods. While methods are continuously improved and new approaches are created, scholars are human beings and stick to methods they once learned, both in research and in teaching—which implies that it takes a long time before a methodological innovation actually diffuses and becomes commonly accepted. The younger generation of scholars may very well already be more accustomed to automated approaches. Second, journalism scholars are unaware of each other's research. Journalism scholars may also often simply be unaware of new methods. The reference list of this article illustrates this point: often, studies of core value to journalism research are published in the proceedings of a computer science conference or other venues less familiar to journalism scholars. In addition, citation patterns show little to no overlap. Third, different fields speak different languages. Even if a scholar does read an article from another discipline, it can be difficult to understand the language and technical terms that each discipline applies. Several options can be considered to overcome these barriers, as follows:

- *Cooperations and interdisciplinary teams*: A lexicon to guide the journalism scholar through the computer scientist's world and their jargon would be a welcome start. But more valuable would be to increase cooperation between the fields. The fact that there are more and more research teams involving both computer scientists and journalism or communication scholars (such as Burscher et al. 2014; Flaounas et al. 2013; Morgan, Shafiq, and Lampe 2013; Stieglitz et al. 2014) indicates a growing awareness of the surplus value that such joint projects can offer.
- *Teach new methods*: Some communication and journalism departments have started offering courses on computer programming. While we do not believe that every journalism scholar has to be a programmer, we deem some *code literacy* to be more and more useful: already some basic knowledge of programming can help to get a grasp of the computer science literature. Familiarizing current journalism students with advanced automated approaches will ensure that lack of knowledge and skills are no longer obstacles for the next generation of scholars. The first textbooks on how to use Python and R for these tasks have appeared (e.g., Munzert et al. 2015).
- *Use custom-made tools*: Vis (2013), for instance, stresses the importance of first thoroughly defining the research questions before making any decision on the tools to use. Often, the tool has to be tailored to the task. Luckily, as we have outlined in this article, the building blocks for such an endeavor exist. Indeed, more and more content-analytical journalism research relies on custom-written programs, making use of, for example, the large variety of available Python modules (Lewis, Zamith, and Hermida 2013; Sjøvaag and Stavelin 2012; Trilling 2015).
- *Share not only results, but also code*: As a last measure, we advocate a culture of sharing and acknowledging code. Instead of reinventing the wheel again and again, tools should be accessible—and, even more important, the source code should be available, allowing the researcher to tailor the tool to specific needs. The increased transparency would also help a lot to increase reproducibility of our research. First steps in this direction have already been made in neighboring fields. For example, the journal *Political Analysis* now requires all authors to submit a replication package, including not only the raw data, but also all syntax files and any form of code necessary to reproduce the paper's results. While admittedly some of the above suggestions are more easily implemented than others, it may be clear that there are various opportunities for journalism scholars to become more familiar with automated approaches.

Conclusion

In this article, we have reviewed a number of new methodological approaches and tools that can offer substantial added value to journalism research. They could be applied selectively, but also combined or enhanced, so that they suit the demands of journalism scholars. We proposed to order techniques for ACA along a deductive–inductive continuum. By doing so, we hope to have illustrated the wide range of possible applications. It might help researchers to relate automated techniques to approaches they are familiar with. At the same time, it should have become clear that there is no such thing as "the" automated content analysis, but that ACA approaches are very versatile. While often developed outside the field of journalism studies, the techniques can be employed to answer a wide variety of journalism studies research interests: from visibility, representation, and evaluation to tone, subjectivity, and frames. We stress that using automated techniques is by no means in opposition to or in competition with manual content analysis. The entire research process, ranging from formulating research questions to making modeling decisions and interpreting results, requires a deep understanding of the data. Thus, rather than replacing humans, it is more correct to view computers as *amplifying* human abilities (Grimmer and Stewart 2013). As remarked by Günther et al. (2015, 5): "A manual topic analysis cannot simply be translated into a fully-automated approach," as "the manual analysis will yield a more specific result." Optimally then, one would combine "the best of both worlds" (Wettstein 2014, 16). Regardless of the type of approach, advantages and disadvantages have to be carefully assessed—and it is the researcher's responsibility to check whether the method actually performs well. The quality of the output of an automated system largely depends on the quality of the input data. If, for instance, the collected data do not match the expected structure (e.g., because a website changed its layout during the research period) and this remains undiscovered, this will lead to biased or inaccurate results. Finally, we want to stress that automated approaches are by no means a panacea to all the challenges that digital journalism research faces. The analysis of visual data is just one example where manual coding still outperforms automated alternatives. Yet to keep up with the ever-evolving nature of digital journalism, the ability to adapt our approaches accordingly is a virtue. Familiarizing ourselves with what the ACA toolkit has to offer is the least we can do, and we hope that this overview will serve as an inspiration to do so.

DISCLOSURE STATEMENT

No potential conflict of interest was reported by the authors.

NOTES

1. A common example is the *tf–idf* (term frequency–inverse document frequency) scheme, in which the frequency of a term in a given document is weighted by the number of documents in which it occurs.
2. The name of the program stands for Linguistic Inquiry and Word Count.

3. These are variables that are directly observable (like *number of words* or *is actor X mentioned?*), and, unlike abstract concepts as tone or frame, are not open to multiple interpretations.

REFERENCES

Blei, David M., Andrew Y. Ng, and Michael I. Jordan. 2003. "Latent Dirichlet Allocation." *Journal of Machine Learning Research* 3: 993–1022.

Burscher, Björn, Daan Odijk, Rens Vliegenthart, Maarten de Rijke, and Claes H. de Vreese. 2014. "Teaching the Computer to Code Frames in News: Comparing Two Supervised Machine Learning Approaches to Frame Analysis." *Communication Methods and Measures* 8 (3): 190–206. doi:10.1080/19312458.2014.937527.

Burscher, Björn, Rens Vliegenthart, and Claes H. De Vreese. 2015. "Using Supervised Machine Learning to Code Policy Issues: Can Classifiers Generalize across Contexts?" *Annals of the American Academy of Political and Social Science* 659 (1): 122–131.

Carlson, Matt. 2014. "The Robotic Reporter: Automated Journalism and the Redefinition of Labor, Compositional Forms, and Journalistic Authority." *Digital Journalism* 3 (3): 416–431. doi:10.1080/21670811.2014.976412.

Coddington, Mark. 2014. "Clarifying Journalism's Quantitative Turn: A Typology for Evaluating Data Journalism, Computational Journalism, and Computer-assisted Reporting." *Digital Journalism* 3 (3): 331–348. doi:10.1080/21670811.2014.976400.

Conway, Mike. 2006. "The Subjective Precision of Computers: A Methodological Comparison with Human Coding in Content Analysis." *Journalism & Mass Communication Quarterly* 83 (1): 186–200.

de Fortuny, Junqué, Tom De Enric, David Martens Smedt, and Walter Daelemans. 2012. "Media Coverage in times of Political Crisis: A Text Mining Approach." *Expert Systems with Applications* 39 (14): 11616–11622. doi:10.1016/j.eswa.2012.04.013.

De Graaf, Rutger, and Robert van der Vossen. 2013. "Bits versus Brains in Content Analysis: Comparing the Advantages and Disadvantages of Manual and Automated Methods for Content Analysis." *Communications* 38 (4): 433–443. doi:10.1515/commun-2013-0025.

Fink, Katherine, and C. W. Anderson. 2014. "Data Journalism in the United States: Beyond the 'Usual Suspects'." *Journalism Studies* 16 (4): 467–481. doi:10.1080/1461670X.2014.939852.

Flaounas, Ilias, Omar Ali, Thomas Lansdall-Welfare, Tijl De Bie, Nick Mosdell, Justin Lewis, and Nello Cristianini. 2013. "Research Methods in the Age of Digital Journalism." *Digital Journalism* 1 (1): 102–116. doi:10.1080/21670811.2012.714928.

Flew, Terry, Christina Spurgeon, Anna Daniel, and Adam Swift. 2012. "The Promise of Computational Journalism." *Journalism Practice* 6 (2): 157–171. doi: 10.1080/17512786.2011.616655.

Freelon, Deen. 2014. "On the Interpretation of Digital Trace Data in Communication and Social Computing Research." *Journal of Broadcasting & Electronic Media* 58 (1): 59–75. doi:10.1080/08838151.2013.875018.

Gayo-Avello, Daniel. 2013. "A Meta-analysis of State-of-the-art Electoral Prediction from Twitter Data." *Social Science Computer Review* 31 (6): 649–679. doi:10.1177/0894439313493979.

Grimmer, Justin, and Brandon M. Stewart. 2013. "Text as Data: The Promise and Pitfalls of Automatic Content Analysis Methods for Political Texts." *Political Analysis* 21 (3): 267–297. doi:10.1093/pan/mps028.

Günther, Elisabeth, and Michael Scharkow. 2014. "Recycled Media: An Automated Evaluation of News Outlets in the Twenty-first Century." *Digital Journalism* 2 (4): 524–541.

Günther, Elisbabeth, Ines Engelmann, Christoph Neuberger and Thorsten Quandt. 2015. "From Text to Topics: A Comparison of a Manual and an Automated Content Analysis." Paper presented at Re-inventing Journalism, Winterthur, Switzerland. http://www.amiando.com/eventResources/h/v/fSMcdpvvmsUWee/Presentations_C2_Elisabeth_Guenther.pdf

Hellsten, Iina, James Dawson, and Loet Leydesdorff. 2009. "Implicit Media Frames: Automated Analysis of Public Debate on Artificial Sweeteners." *Public Understanding of Science* 19 (5): 590–608. doi:10.1177/0963662509343136.

Hopkins, Daniel J., and Gary King. 2010. "A Method of Automated Nonparametric Content Analysis for Social Science." *American Journal of Political Science* 54 (1): 229–247.

Houston, Melanie J., Jeremy T. Bruskotter, and David Fan. 2010. "Attitudes toward Wolves in the United States and Canada: A Content Analysis of the Print News Media, 1999-2008." *Human Dimensions of Wildlife* 15 (5): 389–403.

Huang, Yen-Pei, Tiong Goh and Chern Li Liew. 2007. "Hunting Suicide Notes in Web 2.0: Preliminary Findings." Ninth IEEE International Symposium on Multimedia Workshops, 517–521. doi: 10.1109/ISM.Workshops.2007.92.

Husby, Stephanie D. and Denilson Barbosa. 2012. "Topic Classification of Blog Posts Using Distant Supervision." In *Proceedings of the 13th Conference of the European Chapter of the Association for Computational Linguistics*, pp. 28–36. France: Avignon.

Illia, Laura, Karan Sonpar, and Martin W. Bauer. 2014. "Applying Co-Occurrence Text Analysis with ALCESTE to Studies of Impression Management." *British Journal of Management* 25 (2): 352–372. doi:10.1111/j.1467-8551.2012.00842.x.

Jonkman, Jeroen, and Piet Verhoeven. 2013. "From Risk to Safety: Implicit Frames of Third-party Airport Risk in Dutch Quality Newspapers between 1992 and 2009." *Safety Science* 58: 1–10. doi:10.1016/j.ssci.2013.03.012.

Jurka, Timothy P., Loren Collingwood, Amber Boydstun, Emiliano Grossman, and Wouter van Atteveldt. 2013. "RTextTools : A Supervised Learning Package for Text Classification." *The R Journal* 5 (1): 6–12.

Kleinnijenhuis, Jan, Friederike Schultz, Dirk Oegema, and Wouter van Atteveldt. 2013. "Financial News and Market Panics in the Age of High-frequency Sentiment Trading Algorithms." *Journalism* 14 (2): 271–291. doi:10.1177/1464884912468375.

Krennmayr, Tina. 2014. "What Corpus Linguistics Can Tell Us about Metaphor Use in Newspaper Texts." *Journalism Studies* 16 (4): 530–546. doi: 10.1080/1461670x.2014.937155.

Krestel, Ralf, and Bhaskar Mehta. 2010. "Learning the Importance of Latent Topics to Discover Highly Influential News Items." In *KI 2010: Advances in Artificial Intelligence*, edited by Rüdiger Dillmann, Jürgen Beyrer, Uwe D. Hanebeck and Tanja Schultz, 211–218. Berlin, Germany: Springer.

Ksiazek, Thomas B., Limor Peer, and Andrew Zivic. 2014. "Discussing the News: Civility and Hostility in User Comments." *Digital Journalism*. doi: 10.1080/21670811.2014.972079.

Lewis, Seth C., Rodrigo Zamith and Alfred Hermida. 2013. "Content Analysis in an Era of Big Data: A Hybrid Approach to Computational and Manual Methods." *Journal of Broadcasting & Electronic Media* 57 (1): 34–52. doi:10.1080/08838151.2012.761702.

Loughran, Tim, and Bill McDonald. 2011. "When is a Liability Not a Liability? Textual Analysis, Dictionaries, and 10-Ks." *Journal of Finance* 66 (1): 35–65.

Manning, Christopher D., Prabhakar Raghavan, and Hinrich Schütze. 2008. *Introduction to Information Retrieval*. Cambridge, UK: Cambridge University Press.

Matthes, Jörg, and Matthias Kohring. 2008. "The Content Analysis of Media Frames: Toward Improving Reliability and Validity." *Journal of Communication* 58 (2): 258–279. doi:10.1111/j.1460-2466.2008.00384.x.

Mishne, Gilad A. (2007). "*Applied Text Analytics for Blogs*." PhD dissertation, University of Amsterdam. http://hdl.handle.net/11245/2.47196.

Mohammed, Saif M. and Peter D. Turney. 2010. "Emotions Evoked by Common Words and Phrases: Using Mechanical Turk to Create an Emotion Lexicon." *Proceedings of the NAACL HLT 2010 Workshop on Computational Approaches to Analysis and Generation of Emotion in Text*, 26–34. Stroudsburg, PA: ACL. https://www.aclweb.org/anthology/W/W10/W10-02.pdf.

Monroe, Burt L., Michael P. Colaresi, and Kevin M. Quinn. 2008. "Fightin' Words: Lexical Feature Selection and Evaluation for Identifying the Content of Political Conflict." *Political Analysis* 16 (4): 372–403. doi:10.1093/pan/mpn018.

Morgan, Jonathan Scott, M. Zubair Shafiq, and Cliff Lampe. 2013. "Is News Sharing on Twitter Ideologically Biased?" In *Proceedings of the 2013 Conference on Computer Supported Cooperative Work*, 887–897. New York: ACM.

Mostafa, Mohamed M. 2013. "More than Words: Social Networks' Text Mining for Consumer Brand Sentiments." *Expert Systems with Applications* 40 (10): 4241–4251. doi:10.1016/j.eswa.2013.01.019.

Munzert, Simon, Christian Rubba, Peter Meißner, and Dominic Nyhuis. 2015. *Automated Data Collection with R: A Practical Guide to Web Scraping and Text Mining*. Chichester, UK: Wiley.

Odijk, Daan, Björn Burscher, Rens Vliegenthart, and Maarten de Rijke. 2013. "Automatic Thematic Content Analysis: Finding Frames in News. Social Informatics." *Lecture Notes in Computer Science* 8238: 333–345. doi:10.1007/978-3-319-03260-3_29.

Pennebaker, James W., Roger J. Booth and Martha E. Francis. 2007. *Linguistic Inquiry and Word Count: LIWC*. Austin; TX: LIWC.net.

Pestian, John P., Pawel Matykiewicz, Michelle Linn-Gust, Brett South, Ozlem Uzuner, K. Jan Wiebe, Bretonnel Cohen, John Hurdle, and Christopher Brew. 2012. "Sentiment Analysis of Suicide Notes: A Shared Task." *Biomedical Informatics Insights* 5: 3–16. doi:10.4137/BII.S9042.

Rayson, Paul and Roger Garside. 2000. "Comparing Corpora Using Frequency Profiling." NAACL-ANLP 2000 Workshop: Syntactic and Semantic Complexity in Natural Language Processing Systems. http://acl.ldc.upenn.edu/W/W00/W00-0901.pdf

Řehůřek, Radim and Petr Sojka. 2010. "Software Framework for Topic Modelling with Large Corpora." In *Proceedings of the LREC 2010 Workshop on New Challenges for NLP Frameworks*, 45–50. Valletta, Malta: ELRA.

Roback, Andrew and Libby Hemphill. 2013. "How Constituents Lobby Members of Congress on Twitter." In *Annual Meeting of the American Political Science Association*. http://ssrn.com/abstract=2301133

Scharkow, Michael. 2011. "Thematic Content Analysis Using Supervised Machine Learning: An Empirical Evaluation Using German Online News." *Quality & Quantity* 47 (2): 761–773. doi:10.1007/s11135-011-9545-7.

Schneider, Gerold. 2014. "Automated Media Content Analysis from the Perspective of Computational Linguistics." In *Automatisierung in Der Inhaltsanalyse*, edited by Katharina Sommer, Martin Wettstein, Werner Wirth and Jörg Matthes, 40–54. Cologne, Germany: Herbert von Halem.

Schuck, Andreas R. T., Georgios Xezonakis, Matthijs Elenbaas, Susan A. Banducci, and Claes H. de Vreese. 2011. "Party Contestation and Europe on the News Agenda: The 2009 European Parliamentary Elections." *Electoral Studies* 30 (1): 41–52. doi:10.1016/j.electstud.2010.09.021.

Sheafer, Tamir, Shaul R. Shenhav, Janet Takens, and Wouter van Atteveldt. 2014. "Relative Political and Value Proximity in Mediated Public Diplomacy: The Effect of State-Level Homophily on International Frame Building." *Political Communication* 31 (1): 149–167. doi:10.1080/10584609.2013.799107.

Simon, Adam F. 2001. "A Unified Method for Analyzing Media Framing." In *Communication in U.S. Elections: New Agendas*, edited by Roderick P. Hart and Daron R. Shaw, 75–89. Lanham, MD: Rowman and Littlefield.

Sjøvaag, Helle and Eirik Stavelin. 2012. "Web Media and the Quantitative Content Analysis: Methodological Challenges in Measuring Online News Content." *Convergence: The International Journal of Research into New Media Technologies*, 18 (2), 215–229. doi:10.1177/1354856511429641.

Stieglitz, Stefan and Linh Dang-Xuan. 2012. "Political Communication and Influence through Microblogging: An Empirical Analysis of Sentiment in Twitter Messages and Retweet Behavior." *2012 45th Hawaii International Conference on System Sciences*, 3500–3509. doi: 10.1109/HICSS.2012.476.

Stieglitz, Stefan, Linh Dang-Xuan, Aexel Bruns, and Christoph Neuberger. 2014. "Social Media Analytics." *Business & Information Systems Engineering* 6 (2): 89–96. doi:10.1007/s12599-014-0315-7.

Taboada, Maite, Julian Brooke and Manfred Stede. 2009. "Genre-based Paragraph Classification for Sentiment Analysis." In *Proceedings of the SIGDIAL 2009 Conference on the 10th Annual Meeting of the Special Interest Group on Discourse and Dialogue*, 62–70. Morristown, NJ: ACL. doi:10.3115/1708376.1708385.

Tausczik, Yla R., and James W. Pennebaker. 2009. "The Psychological Meaning of Words: LIWC and Computerized Text Analysis Methods." *Journal of Language and Social Psychology* 29 (1): 24–54. doi:10.1177/0261927X09351676.

Thelwall, Mike, Kevan Buckley, Georgios Paltoglou, Di Cai, and Arvid Kappas. 2010. "Sentiment Strength Detection in Short Informal Text." *Journal of the American Society for Information Science and Technology* 61 (12): 2544–2558. doi:10.1002/asi.21416.

Trilling, Damian. 2015. "Two Different Debates? Investigating the Relationship between a Political Debate on TV and Simultaneous Comments on Twitter." *Social Science Computer Review* 33 (3): 259–276. doi:10.1177/0894439314537886.

Uhl, Matthias W. 2014. "Reuters Sentiment and Stock Returns." *Journal of Behavioral Finance* 15 (4): 287–298.

Van Atteveldt, Wouter. 2008. *Semantic Network Analysis: Techniques for Extracting, Representing, and Querying Media Content*. Charleston, SC: BookSurge.

Van Atteveldt, Wouter, Jan Kleinnijenhuis, and Nel Ruigrok. 2008. "Parsing, Semantic Networks, and Political Authority Using Syntactic Analysis to Extract Semantic Relations from Dutch Newspaper Articles." *Political Analysis* 16 (4): 428–446. doi:10.1093/pan/mpn006.

Van Atteveldt, Wouter, Jan Kleinnijenhuis, Nel Ruigrok, and Stefan Schlobach. 2008. "Good News or Bad News? Conducting Sentiment Analysis on Dutch Text to Distinguish between Positive and Negative Relations." *Journal of Information Technology & Politics* 5 (1): 73–94. doi:10.1080/19331680802154145.

Van der Meer, G. L. A. Toni, Piet Verhoeven, Hans Beentjes, and Rens Vliegenthart. 2014. "When Frames Align: The Interplay between PR, News Media, and the Public in times of Crisis." *Public Relations Review* 40 (5): 751–761. doi:10.1016/j.pubrev.2014.07.008.

Vargo, Chris J., Lei Guo, Maxwell McCombs, and Donald L. Shaw. 2014. "Network Issue Agendas on Twitter during the 2012 U.S. Presidential Election." *Journal of Communication* 64: 296–316. doi:10.1111/jcom.12089.

Vis, Farida. 2013. "A Critical Reflection on Big Data: Considering APIs, Researchers and Tools as Data Makers." *First Monday* 18 (10): 1–16. doi:10.5210/fm.v18i10.4878.

Vliegenthart, Rens, Hajo G. Boomgaarden and Jelle W. Boumans. 2011. "Changes in Political News Coverage: Personalisation, Conflict and Negativity in British and Dutch Newspapers." In *Challenging the Primacy of Politics*, edited by Kees Brants and Karin Voltmer, 92–110. London, UK: Palgrave Macmillan.

Vlieger, Esther, and Loet Leydesdorff. 2012. "Content Analysis and the Measurement of Meaning: The Visualization of Frames in Collections of Messages." In *Research Methodologies, Innovations and Philosophies in Systems Engineering and Information Systems*, edited by Manuel Mora, Ovsei Gelman, Anette Steenkamp and Manesh S. Raisinghani, 322–340. Hershey, PA: Information Science Reference.

Wettstein, Martin. 2014. "'Best of Both Worlds': Die Halbautomatische Inhaltsanalyse [Best of Both Worlds: The Semi-automated Content Analysis]." In *Automatisierung in Der Inhaltsanalyse*, edited by Katharina Sommer, Martin Wettstein, Werner Wirth and Jörg Matthes, 16–39. Cologne, Germany: Herbert von Halem.

Young, Lori, and Stuart Soroka. 2012. "Affective News: The Automated Coding of Sentiment in Political Texts." *Political Communication* 29 (2): 205–231. doi:10.1080/10584609.2012.671234.

TRACING ONLINE NEWS IN MOTION
Time and duration in the study of liquid journalism

Andreas Widholm

Over the latest decade, news production practices have undergone dramatic changes as a consequence of journalism's migration from offline to online platforms. While the linear news models of the past were characterized by delivery of static texts within strict deadlines, contemporary non-linear production practices are characterized by flexibility and constant delivery of "liquid" news. This article presents a method specifically designed for the study of constantly evolving news flows online. Methodologically, the approach entails new opportunities to systematically scrutinize the online news process, using time, duration and positioning of published materials as central variables. Based on an illustrative analysis of the online news flow of the Swedish Public Service Radio, the article gives examples of how such analyses can provide new knowledge about the processes of digital news production.

Introduction

During his time as editor of *The New York World* in the early 1900s, Joseph Pulitzer is said to have written three journalistic rules on the wall of his newsroom: accuracy, accuracy and accuracy. Pulitzer's view, that journalism is a truth-seeking cultural practice, governed by ideals of clarity, precision and objectivity, has come to be a compulsory theme in student handbooks in news writing (cf. Kershner 2012) as well as a vital part of journalism's professional ideology (Deuze 2007; Kovach and Rosenstiel 2001). However, accuracy and objectivity are also widely contested values of journalism, constantly negotiated in relation to other ideals such as immediacy and "newness", aspects which may work as a "counter force" to journalistic accuracy. Although this is a *historical* contradication—even Pulitzer must have felt the burden of immediacy—the present era of digitalization and platform convergence puts pressure on journalism's commitment to true story-telling in ways that would be unthinkable just two decades ago.

Journalistic production practices have undergone dramatic changes as a consequence of the on-going migration from offline to online publication platforms. While the linear news models of the past were characterized by delivery of static texts within strict deadlines, contemporary non-linear production practices are characterized by flexibility, elastic deadlines and constant delivery of "liquid" news (Karlsson and

Strömbäck 2010). Online news journalists often publish their texts in the form of drafts, borrowing stylistic and generic conventions from the breaking news genre of international news broadcasting (Saltzis 2012). The texts are thereby subject to constant alteration, meaning that the old idea of news texts as static "end products" must be abandoned in favour of processual approaches to journalism more generally (Kautsky and Widholm 2008). Thus, while accuracy may still be a central *goal* in news production, the long way journalists have to walk in order to reach this goal has been described as an increasingly open process that takes centre stage in the online news flow (Karlsson 2012).

The on-going liquidization of journalism has posed long-lasting methodological problems for media researchers as most analytical models are based on static rather than dynamic methods for data gathering, providing no or only minor possibilities to scrutinize the "essence" of online news, namely its immediacy and variability (cf. Deuze 2008; Redden and Witschge 2010). As Herring (2010) noted, researchers of the internet have too often been satisfied with traditional forms of content analysis, while ignoring prevalent key features of the Web such as multimodality, interactivity and immediacy. Establishing new research agendas and methods takes time and instead of going against the grain, a more comfortable way, it seems, has been to lean on existing analytical models. Thus, in a time marked by structural transformations of the media industry, where online journalism becomes increasingly central, there is a pressing need for methodological innovation, especially with regard to content analysis.

This article sets the focus on current methodological attempts to analyse online journalism's liquidity and immediacy, and presents a redeveloped version of Regular-Interval Content Capturing (RICC), a method specifically designed for the study of the dynamic and constantly evolving character of online news (Kautsky and Widholm 2008). The proposed method is a computer-assisted and automatic technique for data gathering, enabling researchers to collect and store different versions of Web pages based on a given interval from minutes to days depending on the overall research question. The approach creates new opportunities to scrutinize the online news process systematically and the article shows how news topics as well as news geographies can be studied in terms of liquidity, using positioning, time and duration as key variables. Analyses of the ways in which individual stories, topics or news geographies are positioned on the start page of a website can offer interesting insights into what types of news are considered most important and newsworthy by the news organization. However, the fact that online news is a constantly moving target makes it imperative also to study the "temporality" of these practices. The temporal approach suggested here includes a systematic exploration across two dimensions. This includes (1) an analysis of publication time, e.g. *when* specific topics or world regions are given a prioritized space in the news flow, and (2) an analysis of duration, e.g. for *how long* certain features appear in the news flow. Furthermore, such a processual approach to online news also opens up news possibilities to study how framing, use of sources and modes of reporting vary over time. With regard to news geography, e.g. how journalists "map the world and sketch the contours and connections of their communities within that world" (Gasher 2007, 299), a temporal approach can reveal how online news coverage of different world regions relate to geographical time zones. As I will show in the coming analysis, RICC can also be used to pinpoint how differences in the temporal distribution of news are related to online consumption patterns.

The present article includes an illustrative analysis based on a twofold research design. A content analysis of the online news flow of Sweden's public service radio (Sveriges Radio, SR) is carried out, using two sets of data gathered in 2012 and 2013. The focus here is on how we can study the changes that online news flows undergo more broadly, rather than how individual news texts are changing (bearing in mind that the method is widely useful also for that type of study). I begin with a short introduction to the concept of liquid news and provide some examples of how it has been studied previously. The section tries to synthesize the central theoretical claims of these studies as well as the methodologies that have been proposed in order to meet these challenges. The subsequent sections are devoted to a description of the proposed method, followed by an illustrative quantitative analysis. The article ends with some concluding remarks and suggestions for future research on liquid news.

The Ephemeral Character of Online News

Although the present article is mainly devoted to methodology, it is necessary to reflect briefly upon liquid news as a theoretical concept. The term "liquid journalism" has been used by Deuze (2008) in an attempt to summarize how journalism in the digital online era differs from its previous analogue offline versions. Increased user-participation and audience interaction, platform convergence, complex "external" connectivity through hyperlinks, and textual ephemerality referred to above are some of the examples that have been used to describe the increasingly unpredictable nature of journalism in the digital era. For Deuze, these features are also intimately bound to the broader social changes of "liquid modernity" (Bauman 2000) where uncertainty, flux, change, conflict and revolution appear as the "permanent conditions of everyday life" (Deuze 2008, 851). More recently, Karlsson (2012) has defined liquid news as an "erratic, continuous, participatory, multi-modal and interconnected process that is producing content according to journalistic principles" (Karlsson 2012, 388). While these broad characterizations are highly relevant in broader studies of online news, the present article has a more narrow analytical scope, namely the consequences of new publication routines, which enable journalists to constantly re-publish, edit and adjust news texts in real time and on a 24-hour basis.

Over the past few years, a number of scholars have started to problematize the consequences of such publication routines. One of the most common approaches has been to study liquid news in terms of immediacy and the growing "need for speed" characterizing contemporary news culture (Juntunen 2010). However, although liquid news is a relatively new object of study in journalism research, it is important to emphasize that a long row of studies from the 1970s and onwards have contributed with essential knowledge regarding how news is structured in terms of time by various professional routines. An interesting example is, for example, Schlesinger's (1987) classical study of production practices at the BBC where he found a "stop-clock culture" emerge where the *predictability* of deadlines was identified as a central structuration force in journalists' daily work. Gans' (1979) study from the same period identified in a similar vein the constant *lack* of both time and space as one of the main reasons why journalists seldom have been able to challenge established working patterns or news values. This *need* for structure has also been a key element in Tuchman's (1978) seminal work on the paradoxical relationship between news values and news routines. As Lewis and Cushion (2009) note, although rolling news is a relatively new phenomenon, rolling deadlines and the "thirst to be first" are not. More recently, a number of studies have documented both change and stability of these patterns after the arrival of the internet as a central publishing platform for journalism. As Quandt expressed it in 2008, journalists use "content management systems, agency news clients, word processors and web browsers much like the elder generation used the phone, the type writer, and the wire service (Quandt 2008, 95). Similarly, Domingo (2008) argued that change is sometimes seen as a threat to journalists' professional status, which may explain why new media technologies do not automatically lead to new working routines. The idea that online news to a great extent leans on traditional practices is also a bearing argument in Lim's (2012) studies of immediacy. For Lim, the prevalence of online immediacy is nothing but a socially constructed myth that reigns in the media sector as well as in academia. His systematic studies of online news services in South Korea indicate, for example, that they tend to follow the same publication cycle as the print media.

However, more recent studies rather suggest that journalism now has entered a new phase of expanding *differences* between traditional news making (print, radio and television) and that of online news. In a recent study of the *New York Times*, Usher (2014, 89) reveals that online news has brought an "ASAP" (as soon as possible) culture, where journalists are "living in a world of constant pressure to produce news". The ASAP culture of online journalism simply forces us to reconsider what journalism is, and how we should understand it as a product. Ever since CNN and other international broadcasters entered the news market in the early 1990s, news consumers and journalism scholars alike have been increasingly acquainted with the concept of "breaking news". The breaking news format is usually associated with highly dramatized news events, covered in real time as they unfold, and constructed by means of a specific set of televisual representational techniques (Widholm 2011). A similar genre has been identified as "event-driven news" which is stories that are based on immediacy but not necessarily on high drama and sensationalism (Saltzis 2012). The effect of this type of news production has been profound, and some scholars have argued that the press has been forced to shift its attention from news production to editorials, columns and analyses, genres that are less dependent on senses of immediacy (Harcup and O'Neill 2001; Brighton and Foy 2007). However, while the printed press has experienced this shift in focus, the rise of platform convergence has also challenged television's previous role as the self-evident master medium of immediacy. Today, live news reporting can be found in the online editions of newspapers, as well as television and radio, meaning that the obsession with immediacy characterizing contemporary media culture is no longer associated with a "CNN effect" (Bruno 2011) but with a broader set of opportunities available to practically all news organizations. Thus, breaking news and event-driven news have become "everyday" modes of online news.

The changes outlined above have also changed the traditional generic boundaries of journalism. News is increasingly published in the form of "packages" (Deuze 2005), which may contain several interconnected stories that utilize different modalities and interactive functions. In the coming analysis, I will problematize this feature of online news in more detail between analyses that focus on individual subject entities and analyses centring on news as a flow.

Liquidity as a Methodological Problem in Journalism Research

Although online news and the possibility to update news texts in real time have been with us for nearly two decades, the "liquid" practices that these opportunities entail have been largely understudied in journalism research. This is not due to a general lack of interest among media scholars, but a direct consequence of the fact that old methods for data gathering and different sorts of content analysis are unsatisfactory to use in online environments. However, there is no consensus among researchers about whether Web-based information needs special treatment in content analyses. The fact that the nature of mediated communication changes in accordance with technological innovation is hardly a new phenomenon. History tells us that media researchers have been able to do comparative as well as cross-media analyses over periods that involve comprehensive technological changes as well as professional developments of journalism. McMillan (2000), for example, has defended what we might call a form of methodological conservatism, arguing that it is important to stick with the standard procedures of content analysis in studies of online media in order to uphold quality and comparability in research. One aspect of specific significance for the theme of this article is sampling techniques. Traditional models for content analysis (e.g. Krippendorff 1980) usually advocate random sampling in order to get a trustworthy material, but as noted by Herring (2010), this is an ideal that few researchers actually have lived up to. Studies of liquidity cannot be solely based on random samples, simply because they often presuppose more specific strategic samples which include time series of data within a given time-frame. Given that liquidity is still to be perceived as a "new" phenomenon in media research, there are no consistent or universally accepted methodologies for studying liquid news, which is a growing problem not least in the field of digital journalism studies (Karlsson 2012). Thus, it may not come as a surprise that most of the studies that problematize the changing and ephemeral character of online news do it from a methodological perspective.

The first step in any analysis of liquidity is to decide a proper analytical strategy; how should we approach it, and where should we look for it? These questions relate, on the one hand, to what type of sample we want to base our analysis on and, on the other hand, on the types of variables and categories that will be used as indicators of liquidity. In an explorative study of Swedish online news, Karlsson (2012) distinguishes between analyses that focus on individual stories (story level) and those focusing on the front page (site level). On the news story level, one can, for example, collect different versions of individual news stories and thereby scrutinize how they develop over time. By closely monitoring 15 selected new stories manually on a 10-minute basis, Karlsson managed to document the central features of liquidity such as problems of accuracy and the use of user-generated content in the news. Another more recent example is Saltzis' (2012) exploration of online breaking news in a number of British news sites. In the study, Saltzis uses quantitative content analysis in order to examine "what kind of changes news stories undergo", by capturing the frequency and the types of change that could be found in a series of breaking news stories. The study, which is based on a selection of 44 breaking news stories and in all 252 updates, is particularly interesting in the sense that it manages to document how online breaking news develops over time across a number of different news sites and also how different stories are shaped in different production environments. The study leans on material which was collected manually, and "new" versions of articles were often, but not always, identified on the basis of the taglines provided by the news producers, containing information about when the stories were last updated. Thus, a central premise of this type of analysis is to consider every new update or "version" as the unit of analysis.

A similar study that has focused on online journalism and immediacy is Kammer's (2013) exploration of real-time coverage of the 2013 terrorist attacks in Oslo in Danish and Norwegian news sites. Like Saltzis, Kammer works mainly on the news story level, but his method for gathering online data differs in the sense that it is semi-automatic rather than strictly manual. By using a free software called WinHTTrack Website Copier, Kammer manages to download manually 56 versions of the entire news sites, resulting in 1542 archived pages dealing with the terror attacks (of which many could be considered articles caught in different stages or versions). While this seems to be a good way of finding rich empirical materials for qualitative analysis, it is less useful if we want to do quantitative analyses of the development of online news. Offline versions of entire news sites are time-consuming to scrutinize, and it might be difficult to navigate through the empirical material. Due to the fact that it also takes a lot of time to collect such thick data-sets, we can never be sure that the archived website is an identical copy of what the website looked like in a specific period in time. As Brügger (2009, 125) notes, an archived website is an "actively created and subjective reconstruction" and since the Web is under constant recreation it is difficult to "delimit temporally the archived website in a consistent manner".

Data Collection and Variables for an Illustrative Analysis Using RICC

The main idea behind RICC is simple. Online news is increasingly driven by immediacy and variability and therefore we need to develop analytical strategies that can cope with news texts that are under constant alteration. In order to do so, it is necessary to collect reliable time series of data, which enable the researcher to identify how news varies over time. Likewise, it is important that the researcher, independently of the companies who produce the news, can identify changes. A common method is, as we saw earlier, to trust the official "last updated" time stamps provided by many news outlets. In a previous study (Kautsky and Widholm 2008) this problem was solved using free screen-capture software together with a command script, which executed a "screen dump" at set intervals. The screen capture was then automatically saved as a PDF with a unique time and date stamp. While this method proved to be useful, it was also connected to a number of problems. Standard screen dumps only capture the information available on the screen, which means that it is only a minor part of the entire start page that is actually downloaded. In addition, the method was not reliable as many downloaded files were corrupt or missing due to software problems. In order to solve these problems I consulted a specialist on Web programming who provided valuable assistance with the development of a new application based on Ruby program language. The application was designed for Apple computers and operates as a hidden background process, which proved to be a very secure method. The application automatically saves entire URLs at set intervals, from minutes to hours or days, and stores the pages as either JPG or PDF versions at a given location at an internet server or the computer. For the project described in this article, I chose to save the pages as JPGs, mainly because it makes it very easy to browse the entire material. JPGs can also be used to create video reconstructions of the news flow, allowing the researcher to "consume" several days of online top news in just a couple of minutes. By merging the data into a long sequence we can, for example, forward and rewind the news flow, which makes it easy to document micro-level changes (headlines, angles, visual editing and linguistic corrections), meso-level changes (the adding of new narratives, perspectives, actors, sources and social functions) and macro-level changes (broader thematic prioritizations, news values, etc.). As such, it is most suitable for analysis at the news site level, but it can also be used to track changes in single news stories. In the coming analysis I focus on the latter, mainly from a quantitative perspective (which is also one of the least used approaches in the study of liquidity more generally). The analysis draws on two data-sets (see Table 1).[1]

The most obvious reason why we should bother about the first page of a news site is, of course, that it is the place where a news organization presents its most "newsworthy" and influential pieces of journalism (Bucy 2004; Karlsson 2012; Van der Wurff 2005). The start page can therefore be seen as a mirror of the journalistic ambitions as well as broader prioritizations of a specific news organization. In addition, the front page can be seen as the "grand stage" of immediacy; the place most people go to when they want to quench their immediate news thirst. It is also important to underline that a start page of a news site should not be confused with the front page of a printed newspaper. Although both summarize the finest, newest, most prestigious and sellable stories that an organization has to offer (at the time of publication), a Web page is widely dynamic and includes far more information and a more diverse set of representational techniques.

The first data-set was collected during an entire week of March 2012.[2] The start page of Sverigesradio.se was downloaded every five minutes during the week, resulting in 2016 downloading sessions. The five highest prioritized news blocks were then coded manually and saved in a database, resulting in 10,080 units in total. Thus, the unit of analysis is the news block as it appears (changed or unchanged) in the news flow. In order to avoid potential misunderstandings it is important to emphasize that the 10,080 units do not represent different article versions, but rather what the articles looked like at the time they were downloaded. As I will go into in more detail in the analysis, however, it is important not only to cover *changes*, but also the allocated time of various elements and themes in the news flow. This is also a feature that makes my approach different from the majority of previous studies on liquid news, as they tend to prioritize change on behalf of stability. Thus, the material opens up for very detailed

TABLE 1
Two strategies for data collection

	Downloading interval	Periods	No. of down-loading sessions	Coded items on each page	Total no. of coded items
Data-set 1	Every five minutes	12–17 March 2012	2016	5	10,080
Data-set 2	Every two hours	May, September, December 2013, February 2014	336	10	3360

analyses of micro changes, but also for broader analyses of "themed periods" (Brighton and Foy 2007) such as elections, crises events, media events, etc., where variations and airtime are key aspects to study.

The second set of data was gathered on the basis of a different strategy. The aim was not to analyse variations during an entire week, but instead to get a broader picture of the content variations. Journalism tends to vary greatly on weekends compared to ordinary weekdays. In a study of US newspapers, Hester and Dougall (2007, 814) note, for example, that Sundays have a higher average number of sports and entertainment stories but also a lower average number of stories devoted to science and business. In order to get a trustworthy sample, I started the data collection on April 25 2013 and the application downloaded the front page of Sverigesradio.se every two hours. After one month, I constructed a week sample based on a four-day interval: 25 April (Thursday), 30 April (Tuesday), 5 May (Sunday), and so on, until I had a full week. The same procedure was performed in September and November 2013 and February 2014, resulting in 336 downloads in total. In contrast to the first data-set, I also chose to expand the number of coded items on each page, from 5 to 10. As displayed in Table 1, the total number of analysed items is thereby 3360.

The material has been analysed on the basis of content analysis using the following variables:

- Time of publication (every page has a time stamp which is easily identified).
- Position of item: 1–5 (study 1) or 1–10 (study 2).
- Theme (politics, sport, culture, etc.).
- Geography (domestic versus foreign; world regions covered).
- Liveness: news framed as "live", "direct", "right now", etc. (used in study 2 only).
- New subject entity: the first time a new story appears in the news flow (used in study 1 only).

Since the results presented here should be seen as illustrative examples of the type of analysis that can be performed using RICC, I will not draw any conclusions across the two data-sets. The expanded number of coded items from 5 to 10 in data-set 2, together with the constructed week samples, provides a broader and more representative picture than a study of just one week of top five news (some themes, like culture and social issues, seldom appear among the top five, but further down in the news hierarchy). Data-set 1 can, on the other hand, provide for more detailed analyses since the material is significantly "thicker" in terms of size. However, I want to emphasize that it is not the results *per se* that should be considered most important in this article, but rather how the suggested strategies for data collection can open up for new sorts of theorizing regarding online news as a product as well as a process. In addition, it is worth reiterating that the two data-sets were downloaded with a year between them and with different strategies, limiting the possibilities of drawing more general conclusions.

Measuring Online News: From Static to Fluid Entities

In contrast to previous studies of liquid news, I want to underline that duration, or in fact *lack* of change in some parts, is an important feature to document if we want to understand the prioritizations behind online news, from the first draft of individual pieces to the final withdrawal of entire news packages. By duration, I mean the attributed time or "lifespan" of a specific object or a set of news themes. This duration can furthermore be attributed to either commercial or professional values of journalism. As news producers constantly track consumer activities in real time, they can adjust the news flow according to specific reading behaviours (Karlsson and Clerwall 2013). The lifespan of a news article or a specific area of coverage is, in that sense, a product of its immediate commercial value; as long as an item delivers "clicks" and "shares", it has a steady and prioritized position in the news flow. This is also one of the explanations why breaking news has become an increasingly common feature of online news: a high degree of variability attracts readers to come back, not just once but several times during the day until the story is "closed". Professional values, on the other hand, can guide journalists to work according to a different logic. News texts that are ascribed high *relevance*, for example, are not necessarily those that undergo a high degree of alteration. Differently put, news stories may "deserve" a long lifespan and a prioritized position, not mainly because they attract readers but because of their capacity to convey relevant and meaningful information. Duration and variability as well as "newness" and relevance can therefore be seen as constantly *negotiated* online news values, not least in a public service organization like the one studied here. The positioning or "ranking" of different news topics can furthermore reveal how news flows are adapted according to professional rules of newness and relevance.

News Topics and Allocated Airtime

Let me start with some of the results from data-set 1, which reveal how the method can be used to study content variations during a relatively narrow time-span. Figure 1 offers some interesting examples of how results can differ depending on whether we analyse news in terms of static entities or as a flow. The figure displays the thematic distribution of one entire week in March 2012 and during this period, 217 "subject entities" were identified (31 entities per day on average). As noted previously, a subject entity is defined as a single news story or a "package" of interrelated stories presented in distinctive sections of the start page. Already here we are confronted with important methodological questions. If the 217 entities should provide the basis for our analysis, which version or at what stage of their development should we "freeze" the news flow and collect the data? We can, for example, choose the first version that appears in the news flow. That would mean that to a great extent we will stick with the traditional procedure of content analysis (e.g. we identify and register the entity one time only, we start the coding process of these "static" entities, we continue by processing the data and then our results should be ready for analytical consumption). If we follow such a static approach and look at the first versions only, three news themes stand out as particularly central: politics (23.5 per cent), crime and law (21.7 per cent) and economy (15.7 per cent). Although this procedure certainly can give a reliable picture of the thematic distribution of the news stories produced by SR at the time, it does not say very much about the actual prominence of these themes more generally. Consider, for example, that some stories might be accessible for readers during a relatively limited time-span, whereas others can stay in the news flow for a whole day or

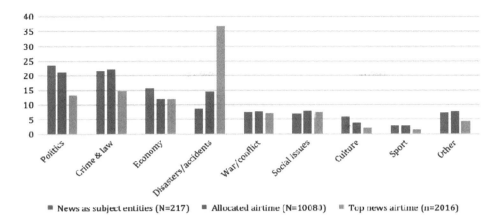

FIGURE 1
Distribution of news themes in terms of subject entities, allocated total airtime and top news airtime during one week of March 2012 (%)

longer depending on their ascribed news value. Is it a given that all entities should be regarded as equally important, or what happens if we complement the analysis with a temporal perspective, where we also take into consideration the relative lifespan of the entities? Instead of only looking at the 217 "frozen" subject entities, we can broaden the analytical scale and include all the collected materials into our analysis (that is 10,080 items in total). In essence, this means that we suddenly can base our analysis of, for example, news topics on percentages of allocated "airtime" (bearing in mind that we are working with a five-minute margin). As illustrated in Figure 1, however, there are no vast differences between the two approaches. The percentage shares for news topics are overall very similar, although slightly higher for crime news (22.2 per cent) whereas they are somewhat smaller for political news (21.3 per cent). A more striking difference can be seen for "disasters and accidents", a typical event-driven topic which constitutes 14.7 per cent of the airtime (compared to 8.8 per cent if we look at the static entities). Conversely, the figures for culture (3.8 per cent) and economy (12 per cent) illustrate that such stories, at least during the period studied here, seem to have a shorter lifespan than those centring on, for example, crime and law, social issues, or war and conflict.

The fact that event-driven news is prioritized in SR's online news flow becomes even more accentuated if we look at allocated airtime for each theme as top news (e.g. number one among the top five stories) during the studied week. Here, accidents and disasters constitute nearly 37 per cent. Given that these figures are based on one week of news coverage, it is important to emphasize that they should be understood as *examples* of how we can approach online news content in terms of liquidity. Since 2012, the online news service of SR has also changed significantly, both in form and content. Results from data-set 2, which give a more representative picture, reveal instead that sport has become a "grand theme" with 17.4 per cent of the airtime over the four periods. Culture constitutes as much as 10 per cent whereas, for example, crime news continues to be among the top three themes with nearly 15 per cent. However, even with these differences in mind, it is obvious that SR, just like the many commercial alternatives, operates in a news culture where fast and event-driven news is increasingly prioritized. This goes especially for sports, which is fruitful (and easy) to cover in terms of live reporting.

Publication Time and Content Variations: The Example of News Geography

I have thus far centred attention on how RICC can be used to broaden the analytical scale of online news in terms of duration. Before I go further into data-set 2, I also want to highlight how the method can be used to track another important dimension of the news, namely variation. Systematic studies of publication time, e.g. *when* news stories appear in the news flow, can give interesting insights into the actual routines of online news production, how news flows vary over certain periods and how journalists systematically prioritize between different type of news. One way of exposing such features is to look at content variation with regard to geographical focus. The concept of news geography has been coded on the basis of domestic versus foreign news, and on the basis of covered world regions.

If we first look at the distribution without a temporal perspective, we can conclude that domestic news constitutes the majority with 58.7 per cent. International news, on the other hand, focuses largely on European issues (51.6 per cent), whereas the Middle East (16.4 per cent) holds the second place followed by Latin America, Africa, North America and Asia, regions spanning from about 5 to 8 per cent each. The fact that SR centres the attention on domestic issues is hardly surprising since it is a national public service news broadcaster addressing a Swedish-speaking audience. However, what I want to highlight here is not the distribution as such. On the contrary, I want to argue that if we take the analysis a step further and also take publication time into consideration, we can show new aspects that previously have been left more or less unstudied.

In Figure 2, I have broken down the world coverage of each region into internal percentage shares using publication time as the independent variable. In other words, the figure reveals any connections between publication time and the coverage of a given region. A very crooked region line (as for Latin America) indicates a strong connection between publication time and the attention given to this region. Likewise, a straight line (as for Sweden) indicates a more constant attention.

Consequently, two major features stand out as particularly important here. First, that Sweden and Europe receive a steady and constant attention during all hours of the day. No matter when you access the site, you will face a large amount of news stories dealing either with Swedish news of local or national significance or with foreign news events that take place in Europe. A palpable result is also that the majority of the news from Latin America (68 per cent) is published and accessible for readers during night time between 00.00 and 06.00, a period when few news consumers are active. News events in North America follow a partially similar development and the region seems to be widely popular between 03.00 and 06.00, but in contrast to Latin America, North America also receives considerable attention during the most important "prime-time" hours in the morning. These results indicate that news values and selection practices work differently depending on time-specific features, something that has

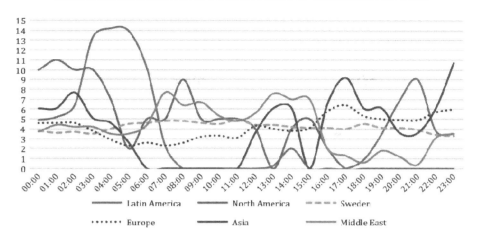

FIGURE 2
Temporal variations of news geography (%); N = 10,080

been studied to a very meagre extent in media research due to the lack of suitable methods. In an adjacent study of SR, which included interviews with journalists and editors at the Web desk (Widholm 2012), I concluded that the logic of FM broadcasting and listening figures are important factors that steer the online news output in specific directions during an ordinary workday at the Web desk. With the method suggested here, such features can be subject to systematic empirical investigations, and analyses can thereby go further than traditional content analyses have managed do to.

Going Live: Time Positioning and the Construction of Immediacy

As should be known by now, a striking feature of online news, which also distinguishes it from its offline versions, is the new possibilities for real-time reporting. This is at least what most studies of liquid news tend to focus on when discussing variability of published journalistic materials. Against this background, it is important not only to state the importance of immediacy on the theoretical level, but also ground these arguments in actual empirical investigations. Using data-set 2, I have examined the extent to which SR actually frames their articles in terms of immediacy. Immediacy is, I want to emphasize, not only a feature of online news, but also a defining rhetorical style. In other words, news is not always *the outcome* of immediacy but a product of specific *framing strategies* that foreground the dramatic uncertainty of on-going events. Labelling news stories as "breaking", "just in", "right now", "direct", and so forth, makes them more appealing, and these labels also encourage listeners and readers to stay tuned for new and fresh updates. By observing the actual usage of such framing strategies, we can thereby analyse how and to what extent they occur in the online news flow. In contrast to Lim (2012), who has successfully investigated immediacy in terms of newness, e.g. the extent to which new information is actually added to existing stories, I suggest that we also can explore immediacy as a discursively constructed feature of online news. An example of how that can be done is presented in Figures 3 and 4.

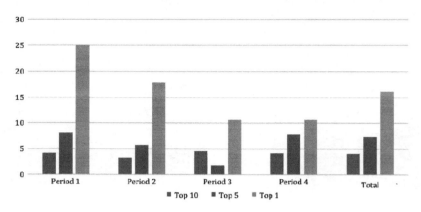

FIGURE 3
Immediacy in the news flow (%); $N = 3360$

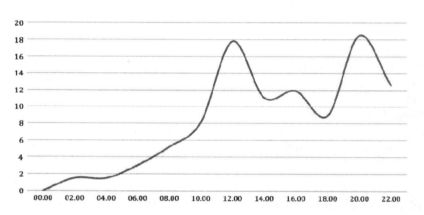

FIGURE 4
The temporal distribution of constructed immediacy (%, periods 1–4); $N = 137$

As illustrated in Figure 3, immediacy can be taken as a noteworthy but not dominant feature of SR's online news. If we look at the entire material (top 10 in the total column), live news reporting constitutes approximately 4 per cent, a number that is relatively stable over all periods examined. The limited number of stories using the breaking news rhetoric can easily be taken as evidence of the "mythological" status that immediacy holds within academia as well as in the media industry (Lim 2012). However, if we also take *positioning* into consideration, it quickly becomes clear that constructed immediacy first and foremost appear in the top news section of the news site. During period 1, for example, 25 per cent of all top news items analysed included signs of immediacy. Seen over all four periods, the number decreases significantly but it still reaches 16 per cent or almost every sixth story (see top 1 in the total column). It is also important to note that the analysis covers the news flow on a 24-hour basis, meaning that the figures would be significantly higher if we had focused purely on daytime news coverage.

Before I go to some concluding remarks, I want to return briefly to the question of publication time and provide a further example of how it can pinpoint the connection between immediacy and publication routines. In Figure 4, I have broken down the construction of immediacy into percentage shares using publication time as independent variable. In other words, the figure shows a highly important aspect that very seldom appears in analyses of immediacy, namely *when* it tends to occur in the news flow. One cannot of course expect a national public service broadcaster in a small country like Sweden to provide live coverage on a 24-hour basis, and the results are very clear on that matter. Immediacy is almost totally absent during night time and even during the prime-time morning hours it appears to be scarce. Live coverage starts instead during lunchtime, often in connection with follow-ups on the main stories presented earlier the same day. The most common period for live coverage is around 20.00, which is directly related to the prevalent position of live sport in the news flow. To sum up, the analytical models presented here suggest that time as well as positioning appear to be fruitful variables to use if we want to fully understand the role of immediacy in online news. In addition, it shows that there is a pressing need to do larger studies of immediacy as a socially constructed category of news. Together with systematic studies of actual updating frequencies, such analyses can provide more complex insights into the myth of online immediacy.

Concluding Remarks

The rise of a liquid ASAP culture of journalism, enabled by the new publication techniques and stronger competition from a wide array of digital sources, forces us to reconsider how we might analyse journalism as a product. How can we trace and understand online news flows in a time marked by flux, change and constant uncertainty? The central goal of this article has been to problematize the notion of news as a fixed entity from a methodological perspective, suggesting that scholars need to pay more attention to publication time and duration in the study of online news. Time has been central to this article for several reasons. First, in the more obvious sense, as news stories tend to look different depending on *when* we choose to consume, collect or analyse them. Previous studies of online news have mainly focused on liquidity from this perspective, scrutinizing the implications of "versionality" during specific periods or news stories when breaking news and immediacy reign in the news flows. The article has demonstrated that a key area for future studies of liquid news is to approach the relationship between time and news production on a slightly broader empirical scale. To a certain extent, this means that we need to analyse online news more like television and less like printed newspapers. One example is the possibility of measuring news themes both in terms of "subject entities" and in terms of duration or "allocated airtime". Although the illustrative analysis showed minor differences, I believe that this approach can be particularly fruitful to use in studies of, for example, election campaigns or during grand media events. Such analyses reveal not only how many and what type of stories journalists produce, but how these stories are exposed and for how long. Time series of data also allow us to analyse systematically the actual production practices of journalism and how they impinge on the character and quality of the news more generally. In the illustrative analysis, I showed for example how time impinges on geographical prioritizations and how the degree of immediacy varies during the different stages of the 24-hour news cycle. Finally, I have shown that *positioning* can work as a key to better understanding online news practices. The "ranking" of news stories is hardly a new phenomenon in journalism studies. On the contrary, it has been essential in classical studies of news selection and news values. However, without proper analytical tools including an increased sensibility for "liquidity", we can never fully understand how such practices are manifested in online news content.

ACKNOWLEDGEMENT

The author wishes to thank Fredrik Mårtensson at the Department of Media Studies (IMS), Stockholm University, who has contributed to the technical development of the method described in this article.

DISCLOSURE STATEMENT

No potential conflict of interest was reported by the author.

NOTES

1. The data were originally collected for a project I worked on as researcher in residence at SR. Some of the results presented here have been used for evaluation purposes at the company.
2. The data were collected 13–19 March 2012.

REFERENCES

Bauman, Zygmunt. 2000. *Liquid Modernity*. Cambridge: Polity.

Brighton, Paul, and Dennis Foy. 2007. *News Values*. Los Angeles, CA: Sage.

Bruno, Nicola. 2011. *Tweet First, Verify Later? How Real-Time Information is Changing the Coverage of Worldwide Crisis Events*. Oxford: Reuters institute for the study of journalism.

Brügger, Niels. 2009. "Website History and the Website as an Object of Study." *New Media & Society* 11: 115–132.

Bucy, Erik P. 2004. "Second Generation Net News: Interactivity and Information Accessibility in the Online Environment." *The International Journal on Media Management* 6 (1-2): 102–113.10.1080/14241277.2004.9669386

Deuze, Mark. 2007. *Media Work*. Cambridge & Malden: Polity.

Deuze, Mark. 2005. "What is Journalism? Professional Identity and Ideology of Journalists Reconsidered." *Journalism* 6 (4): 442–464.

Deuze, Mark. 2008. "The Changing Context of News Work: Liquid Journalism for a Monitorial Citizenry." *International Journal of Communication* 2: 848–865.

Domingo, David. 2008. "When Immediacy Rules: Online Journalism Models in Four Catalan Online Newsrooms." In *Making Online News: The Ethnography of New Media Production*, edited by Chris Paterson and David Domingo, 113–126. New York, NY: Peter Lang.

Gans, Herbert J. 1979. *Deciding What's News: A study of "CBS Evening News", "NBC Nightly News", News-week, and Time*. New York: Pantheon.

Gasher, Mike. 2007. "The View from Here: A News-Flow Study of the on-Line Editions of Canada's National Newspapers". *Journalism Studies* 8 (2): 299–319.10.1080/14616700601148895

Harcup, Tony, and Deirdre O'neill. 2001. "What is News? Galtung and Ruge Revisited." *Journalism Studies* 2 (2): 261–280.

Herring, Susan C. 2010. "Web Content Analysis: Expanding the Paradigm." In *International Handbook of Internet Research*, edited by J. Hunsinger, L. Klastrup and M. Allen, 233–249. London: Springer Science+Business Media B.V.

Hester, Joe Bob, and Elizabeth Dougall. 2007. "The Efficiency of Constructed Week Sampling for Content Analysis of Online News." *Journalism & Mass Communication Quarterly* 84 (4): 811–824.

Juntunen, Lara. 2010. "Explaining the Need for Speed: Speed and Competition as Challanges to Journalism Ethics." In *The Rise of 24-Hour News Television: Global Perspectives*, edited by Stephen Cushion and Justin Lewis, 167–180. New York, NY: Peter Lang.

Kammer, Aske. 2013. "Terrorisme I Realtid: 22. Juli 2011 I Danske Og Norske Netaviser." *Norsk Medietidsskrift* 20 (4): 292–310.

Karlsson, Michael. 2012. "Charting the Liquidity of Online News: Moving towards a Method for Content Analysis of Online News." *International Communication Gazette* 74 (4): 385–402.10.1177/1748048512439823

Karlsson, Michael, and Christer Clerwall. 2013. "Negotiating Professional News Judgment and "Clicks"." *Nordicom Review* 34 (2): 65–76.

Karlsson, Michael, and Jesper Strömbäck. 2010. "Freezing the Flow of Online News." *Journalism Studies* 11 (1): 2–19.10.1080/14616700903119784

Kautsky, Robert, and Andreas Widholm. 2008. "Online Methodology: Analysing News Flows of Online Journalism." *Westminster Papers in Communication and Culture* 5 (2): 81–97.

Kershner, James W. 2012. *The Elements of News Writing*. 3rd. edition ed. Pearson Education: Allyn & Bacon.

Kovach, Bill, and Tom Rosenstiel. 2001. *The Elements of Journalism: What Newspeople Should Know and the Public Should Expect*. New York, NY: Crown.

Krippendorff, Klaus. 1980. *Content Analysis: An Introduction to its Methodology*. Beverly Hills, CA: Sage.

Lewis, Justin, and Stephen Cushion. 2009. "The Thirst to be First." *Journalism Practice* 3 (3): 304–318.10.1080/17512780902798737

Lim, Jeongsub. 2012. "The Mythological Status of the Immediacy of the most Important Online News: An Analysis of Top News Flows in Diverse Online Media"." *Journalism Studies* 13 (1): 71–89.

McMillan, Sally J. 2000. "The Microscope and the Moving Target: The Challenge of Applying Content Analysis to the World Wide Web." *Journalism & Mass Communication Quarterly* 77 (1): 80–98.

Quandt, Thorsten. 2008. "News Tuning and Content Management: An Observation Study of Old and New Routines in German Online Newsrooms." In *Making Online News: The Etnography of New Media Production*, edited by Chris Paterson and David Domingo, 77–98. New York, NY: Peter Lang.

Redden, Joanna, and Tamara Witschge. 2010. "A New News Order? Online News Content Examined." In *New Media, Old News: Journalism & Democracy in the Digital Age*, edited by N. Fenton, 171–186. London: Sage.doi:10.4135/9781446280010

Saltzis, Kostas. 2012. "Breaking News Online: How News Stories Are Updated and Maintained around-the-Clock." *Journalism Practice* 6 (5-6): 702–710.10.1080/17512786.2012.667274

Schlesinger, Phillip. 1987. *Putting 'Reality' Together: BBC News*. London: Methuen.

Tuchman, Gaye. 1978. *Making News: A Study in the Construction of Reality*. New York: Free Press.

Usher, Nikki. 2014. *Making News at the New York times*. Ann Arbor: The university of Michigan Press.10.3998/nmw.12848274.0001.001

Van der Wurff, Richard. 2005. "Introduction: Impacts of the Internet on Newspapers in Europe." *International Communication Gazette* 67 (1): 5–7.10.1177/0016549205049175

Widholm, Andreas. 2011. *Europe in Transition: Transnational Television News and European Identity*. Stockholm: JMK.

Widholm, Andreas. 2012. Kontinuitet Och Förändring I Ekots Nyhetsuppdatering På Webben [Continuity and Change in Ekot's Online News]. Research report. Swedish Radio.

WHAT IS THE MEANING OF A NEWS LINK?

David Ryfe, Donica Mensing, and Richard Kelley

This paper investigates the meaning of news links in the context of a qualitative description of links on the home pages of six online news sites. Links are analyzed according to the following taxonomy: who is saying what, where, when, and to what purpose. This 5-Ws method for analyzing links yields four meanings: navigation, commercial, social, and citation. It is argued that the meaning of news links, while theoretically infinite, actually lies within the boundaries of these four meanings. Opportunities to use computational tools to analyze large datasets of news links are discussed in the context of a journalism tool (Jot), the author and colleagues are developing. Issues raised by this taxonomy of news links are several, but two in particular are highlighted for discussion: (1) the role of navigation links in determining the form of news; and (2) the fact that opportunities to share content via social links invariably are outsourced to social media companies such as Facebook and Twitter.

Introduction

Researchers have been studying news links almost since the emergence of online journalism (e.g., Karlsson, Clerwall, and Örnebring 2015; Peng, Irene, and Xiaoming 1999; Riley et al. 1998). Typically, the method used involves some combination of content and network analysis. Researchers crawl news websites collecting links, and then track how many links go to which destinations. This method raises an important conceptual and methodological challenge, namely that the mere counting of links in this way lends little insight into the meaning of the links themselves. For instance, is the meaning of a link made by a reporter in the text of a news story the same as an automated link to a topics page in the same story? Is the meaning of a link to a government database the same as the meaning of a link to a blog post? Do sidebar links mean the same thing as textual links? Sheer counts of links do not address such questions. Researchers have begun to recognize this problem (e.g., Coddington 2012; de Maeyer 2012). However, no one has yet taken the question head-on: what is the meaning of a news link?

To address this question, we begin with a comment made by Halavais (2008, 54): "In understanding what a hyperlink means," he writes, "we need to look at what a hyperlink does." To us, this seems exactly right. A hyperlink is a manifestation of intention. By linking one page to another, one piece of text to another, people intend to do particular things. To be successful—in other words, to get people to use links—these intentions must be recognizable to others: "Oh, the site (or the author) wants us to click here to do X." The meaning of links lies in the range of recognizable actions that can be accomplished through the practice.

To keep as close to these actions as possible, we conduct a descriptive, qualitative analysis of online news pages culled from a larger project we are conducting on local online news ecosystems (e.g., Ryfe et al. 2012). For the present paper, we have closely analyzed the homepage and next linked-to page on three sites, mercurynews.com, sfgate.com, and laurendo.wordpress.com. We have also examined their Twitter feeds and Facebook pages. For comparison's sake, we have checked results against a set of popular national news sites, including nytimes.com, andrewsullivan.com, and wonkblog.com.

To ascertain the meaning of links, we have used what we call a "5-Ws" method. A play on the 5-Ws theory of media effects, this method involves asking *who* is linking to *what*, *where*, *when*, and *to what purpose*. For present purposes, we applied the method manually to every link. However, as we will discuss, it is possible to write computer scripts to automate the process. Below, we describe a preliminary approach to doing so. At the end of this analysis, we learn that the meaning of links lies in a relatively small set of purposes. These purposes fall into four general categories, what we call *navigation*, *commercial*, *social*, and *citation*. Navigation helps users find content. Commercial involves linking practices for earning money from others. Social includes sharing content via social media feeds and/or offering users opportunities to share content. Citation directs users to information in an effort to establish the credibility of news reports. We have observed no linking practice that does not fall into one of these four basic categories. Herein, we believe, lies the meaning of news links.

The method we present is necessarily exploratory, as its worth will have to be demonstrated across a range of projects. Moreover, we are still in the early stages of developing an automated way to analyze large datasets using the method. We offer the taxonomy here as a way of helping scholars build knowledge across research projects, and also as a way of identifying important questions for future research. Two subjects seem especially worthy of greater reflection. The first has to do with navigation links. They are the most common kind of news link, yet to our knowledge they have received little to no scholarly attention. The second involves social links. Specifically, what should we make of the fact that news sites largely have outsourced the development of tools that generate social/share links? We end the essay with a consideration of these issues.

We begin, however, with a brief review of the extant literature, followed by a description of a link taxonomy.

A 5-Ws Taxonomy of News Links

Hyperlinking is the practice of linking an online document, or part of a document, to another document, or part of a document, through a small bit of HTML code, <a>href="[document to be linked to]"</a>. The idea of linking texts in this manner has a long lineage, stretching through ancient Talmudic commentary, Vannevar Bush's famous 1945 *Atlantic* article, "As We May Think" essay, Ted Nelson's Xanadu Project during the 1960s, and on to the creation of the HTML language (e.g., Halavais 2008). Today, it is basic to the architecture of any website—including news sites. Journalism studies researchers recognize as much, which is why they have studied linking practices almost from the emergence of online news. Over the last decade, the field of news link analysis has grown, but its continued success is threatened by the lack of a standard methodology for conducting analyses of links (e.g., Anderson 2010). Simply put, different kinds of links may mean different things, and the same link may mean something different in different contexts. Numerical counts of links fail to capture such subtleties.

We encountered these problems in a study of the regional online news systems that we conducted with several colleagues. We wanted to know how many news sites existed in the region around San Francisco, and whether and how they link to one another (and other sites). This led us to crawl 117 news sites in the region, a process that generated millions of links. Upon examining the resulting database, we realized that we had no good way of placing links into different categories. We knew how often site A linked to site B linked to site C, but without a way of making distinctions between links, we did not know what any of this meant.

Other researchers have come to the same realization (e.g., Anderson 2010). It has led de Maeyer (2012) to interview journalists in an effort to find out what they mean to do when they link; and it has led Coddington (2012) to closely examine a small number of links in the context of the content in which they are embedded. Neither strategy, however, provides what the field needs, which is a taxonomy useful for coding links across many different news sites.

Ideally, this taxonomy will do three things: it will account for the vast majority of links that appear on a news Web page; it will organize and categorize links according to their meaning; and finally, so as to allow large-N data analysis, it will be amenable to computational methods.

One immediate problem that must be overcome is to establish what we mean by the word "meaning." It is, as one might imagine, a fighting word among philosophers, and whole branches of the discipline focus on just this question. We have no interest in jumping off the deep end of this philosophical pool. Instead, we take the following tack. In the sense that we use the word, meaning refers to the purpose, motive, or intention of a link. Simply put, *what does a link intend for a user to do?* The answer to this question is, *ipso facto*, a link's meaning.

A Methodological Strategy

As to method, our strategy for discerning categories of meaning with respect to links was straightforward. First, we systematically inspected and clicked through every link provided on the home page, and the next-linked to page, on three news sites, mercurynews.com, sfgate.com, and laurendowordpress.com. We chose these sites because they are broadly representative of the 100+ others included in our database of Bay Area news sites. We then applied a "5-Ws" method to each link. The 5-Ws emerged organically out of the realization that the same kind of link can mean different things—that is, the user may be invited to do different things—in different contexts. For instance, consider a link to a news story. That link can mean something different if an algorithm generates and places it in an aggregation tool, than if it is generated manually in the context of a story written by a reporter. In the first instance, the meaning of the link is likely navigational, in that it is provided to the user to get from point A to point B. However, in the second the reporter likely includes the link because it is citational, that is, it is provided to a user as background information to support the story at hand. In this instance, meaning varies according to *who* generates the link, and *where* they place it on a Web page. This thought eventually led us to consider the range of variation across all links. It seemed to us that understanding the purpose of links required knowing something about who was linking to what, where on the page, and for how long (when). Different combinations of these criteria (who, what, when, where) led to different purposes. Out of this line of thinking emerged our 5-Ws. After much trial and error, we learned that what a link intends for a user to do—its meaning—varies according to *who* links to *what*, *where*, *when* (with *to what end* constituting the purpose of a link).

As a demonstration of how we operationalized these concepts, consider a hypothetical home page for a newspaper website. If this homepage is typical, it will have a navigation strip at the topic with words like "News," "Business," "Arts," and "Opinion." It will contain a photo or graphic associated with a story the editors wish to profile. It will contain a list of links to other stories. Suppose this home page includes 15 total opportunities for a user to click on a link. Given these circumstances, our method is straightforward. We click on each link and ask who is linking to what, where, and when. For instance, for the navigation strip, we may say that the designers of the site (whos) have placed these links in the page template (where), meaning that these links appear continuously (when) every time the page is loaded. Finally, each link takes a user to different sections of the news site, where specific kinds of content appear (what). Using our concepts, the following statement seems to hold: Web designers (*whos*) placed links to particular kinds of content (*what*) at the top of the home page (*where*), and embedded these links in the page template so that the links appear in perpetuity (*when*). This combination of attributes—designers embedding permanent links to content on a page template—imply an intended purpose, namely to help users navigate to particular content. Such links are, for this reason, navigational. Other combinations of these criteria intend other purposes. For example, suppose that a user is allowed to scroll over a link at the bottom of a photo, which transforms the link into various icons for email, Twitter, Facebook, and other social media sites. In this case, we may say that administrators of the site (whos) have dropped permanent (when) icons for social media sites (what) at the bottom of a photo (where). When administrators permanently fix social media icons next to content, we may conclude that they wish to provide users with an opportunity to share or comment on that content. The meaning of the link, in other words, is social. When thought of in this way, links weave together content via various intentions, and so lend order to the vast amount of information that may appear on a Web page.

The Taxonomy

In fact, we found that Web pages on news sites are *highly* ordered. Table 1 presents the range of answers we discovered as we set out applying our 5-Ws to each link. At the end of this exercise, we discovered that only four "*whos*" generate links on any news site we visited: algorithms, staff other than reporters (e.g., editors, Web producers), reporters, and users. *What* they link to includes a news section, news story,

TABLE 1
A 5-Ws taxonomy of news links

Question	Answers
Who	Algorithm Staff (other than reporter) Reporter User
What	News section News story Web page (general) Data Video Photo Government document Academic study Report (other) Blog post Social media content User comment

Where	Onsite
	  Template
	  Story
	  Post
	  Social media tool
	  Aggregation tool
	Offsite
	  Template
	  Story
	  Post
	  Social media tool
	  Aggregation tool

When	Permanent Weekly Daily Less than daily
To what end	Navigation Commercial Social Citation

data, video, photo, government document, academic study, think-tank report, blog post, tweet, and user comment. A link may be embedded in a number of places on a Web page (*where*), including on a template page, a Web page (not in the page template) in a story or blog post, and in a social media or aggregation tool. Also a link may be visible on the site (*when*) permanently, weekly, daily, or less than daily.

Let us pause here for a moment. It is important to recognize that this list is not necessarily exhaustive of the universe of possible links under each category. When we say that only four "whos" create links, for instance, it is possible that someone or something other than an algorithm, non-reporter staff member, staff member, or user might provide such links. We list these types as examples of the general category, and because in our limited dataset they were in fact the only "whos" represented. However, one of the advantages of the taxonomy is that it is flexible. Whatever else a linking practice does, it involves a "who" linking to a "what" some "where" on a Web page. Moreover, the meaning of the link arises from the relation between the whos, whats, and wheres of the practice. The 5-Ws method naturally accommodates additional types of linking practices as they arise, and additional meanings that journalists may assign links.

That said, once we sorted links according to the first four Ws, we noticed that links tend to vary consistently with one another. For example, algorithms generate most links on template pages, and most links in aggregation tools (editors generating the rest). Because algorithms pull information from underlying databases, they also make most permanent links, and they create a great number of links that appear and disappear on a site frequently (e.g., links that appear in scrolling social media feeds). Another pattern: reporters link to many kinds of content, but do so mostly in the context of their stories, which are usually visible on a daily basis. The connection between reporters, stories, and dailiness is especially strong. Even on their Facebook and Twitter feeds, reporters mostly link to stories that are published on a daily basis. Each new day brings new stories to write, and new links about those stories. A last pattern is that users are provided the fewest opportunities to link. Apparently, a division of labor has developed that assigns reporters the capacity to link and users the ability to click on those links. Finally, even when users are offered an opportunity to link, those opportunities are mostly provided by non-news organizations, that is, by social media tools created by companies like Facebook and Twitter.

As the categories of links developed, we realized that the variety of meanings on actually existing news sites was not infinite. For instance, most links generated by algorithms on template pages have the same purpose, namely they help users find content (navigational). The same can be said of links embedded in aggregation tools: algorithms generate most of them, and typically they are designed to help users find content (navigation). In the same way, links to advertisements are intended to generate revenue for the organization (commercial), and most links manually embedded by reporters in their stories are intended to enhance the credibility of the story (citation). A structure, this is to say, began to emerge.

As we began to sort the possible combinations, we determined that the meaning of links inheres in four basic purposes: they help users find content (*navigation*); they generate revenue for the organization (*commercial*); they allow users to share content (*social*); and they enhance the credibility of news reports (*citation*). Web pages of news sites are so uniform that coders rarely disagreed. In fact, we did not conduct a formal intercoder reliability test because it did not seem necessary. Two of the authors sat together and coded a small number of pages using the 5-Ws as criteria. They came to the same judgment in every case. A gray area did arise, but not in the context of manually coding links. Instead, it arose when we began the process of building a tool to automate the process.

Automating the Method

For the purpose of building our taxonomy, we applied our method manually. Admittedly, it was arduous and time consuming, and so could not possibly be done with a large dataset. However, because we believed the method is applicable to "big data" as well, we began to explore the possibility of porting links into a database and building a tool that will automatically classify each one. Because the issue of how to analyze large-N datasets is so central to the future study of news links, it is worth taking a moment to describe in more detail how we are approaching this problem. Doing so will also allow us to briefly discuss the one gray area of coding we have come across.

We have begun to build a tool capable of analyzing large datasets of news links using the 5-Ws method. We call the tool the "journalism toolkit," or Jot (https://github.com/RichardKelley/jot). At present, Jot is primarily an exploratory tool. It provides an initial classification for each link, which a human can then refine and extend. The basic unit of analysis for the tool is the uniform resource locator or URL of a link. URLs are highly structured objects. Each part of the structure of a URL contains clues that inform a reader (either human or machine) about the nature and purpose of the URL.

The (almost completely) general form of a link is: scheme://domain/path?query#frag. Each of the listed parts (scheme, domain, path, query, and fragment) contains information that can be used to classify the link. On a technical level, the *scheme* describes the protocol used by the link. There are dozens of scheme names that might appear in a URL, but the two most common (and the only ones we have observed in news sites) are http and mailto. The former is used for Web pages, and by itself contains little information to classify the link. But the latter, mailto, is used to provide contact information, and thus functions primarily as a kind of navigation.

The *domain* of a link describes the server that contains the page that is being linked to. This is most useful for determining if the link points to onsite or offsite content. However, it is worth noting that even this distinction may be hard to classify, even for a human. We discuss some details, and a specific example, below. The *path* in a link describes much of the hierarchical structure that can be found in a website. By examining the path of a URL, it is possible to determine much of the function of the link. For instance, on sfgate.com all national political news stories have URLs that begin with http://www.sfgate.com/news/politics/article/ and end with a story name. An example of such a name is Obamacare-dispute-sends-gov-t-to-brink-of-shutdown-4855268.php. In this case, the path component of the URL is /news/politics/article/Obamacare-dispute-sends-gov-t-to-brink-of-shutdown-4855268.php so that the path consists of both hierarchical information (an article about politics in the news sections) and article information (an article about the government shutdown). By examining each of these parts of the path, Jot can often identify both the purpose of a link and, through a process we describe more fully below, how long it is likely to be available for viewing.

The last two parts of a link, the *query* and *fragment* portions are optional and usually serve a specific purpose. The job of a query string is to pass information from the user's browser back to the Web server. A typical example is an onsite search engine. The query typed by the user is passed back to the website in the form of a query string (hence the name). On www.sfgate.com, an example would be: http://www.sfgate.com/?controllerName=search&action=search&channel=news%2Fpolitics&search=1&inlineLink=1&query=%22USDA%22.

In this case, there is no path component, but there is a query that consists of a number of "key-value pairs." So, for instance, we know that the "controllerName" key corresponds to the value "search," and that the "query" key corresponds to the value "%22USDA%22." The reason for the somewhat odd value is that URLs have special rules governing characters outside the digits 0–9 and the 26 letters of the US English alphabet. In this case, %22 is the symbol for a double quotation mark. The *fragment* portion is used entirely for navigation within a single page.

In addition to the structure and content of a link, we can also consider information in the body of the linked document, or information completely unrelated to the sites being analyzed. We have found two sources of information that are particularly relevant to our link analysis: historical information to determine the longevity of a link and crowdsourced information to identify advertising content.

To determine the lifetime of a link, we have little choice but to check the link repeatedly and see if it continues to exist. This allows us to determine if a link exists for minutes, hours, or days. To determine what links are permanent, we have settled on using snapshots of the Internet Archive, which allows users to see what a page looked like going back (in some cases) to the mid-1990s. Admittedly, like any archive, the Internet Archive is not complete. However, it provides a more or less accurate way of allowing us to determine which links on a page are likely to be permanent. Incidentally, we have found that navigational links tend to be permanent (or at least to be valid for several months).

After breaking apart a URL in this fashion, we may use machine-learning principles to "teach" a computer to accurately filter large numbers of links according to our 5-W categories. This process involves providing a computer with examples of types of links, and then, on the basis of these examples, allowing it to estimate the likelihood that a new link falls into one of those types. In preliminary run-throughs with news pages on sfgate.com, we attained an accuracy rate of roughly 50–55 percent. We forecast that over time we should be able to get that rate above 85 percent.

To be sure, the end result will never be perfect. In particular, we discovered one area where the machine had consistent difficulty. It concerns commercial links. When newsroom staff (e.g., Web editors) link to a story onsite, the link is most likely navigational. The same link to a story offsite may also be navigational, but it may be commercial as well. News organizations increasingly share content with one another as part of an underlying agreement. Moreover, they also contract with organizations to link to "native advertising," or content that looks and feels like a news story but is actually an advertisement for a product or organization. No matter how "teachable," our computer could not reveal such subtleties. It is likely, therefore, as argued, that some manual content analysis, and perhaps even additional methods will be required to firm up the data (e.g., Lewis, Zamith, and Hermida 2013). Still, we believe our overall approach to automating link analysis is sound. Jot shows that the 5-Ws method is amenable to use with large datasets, and in combination with other methods, may serve as a powerful tool for analyzing big data.

Overall, the value of the 5-Ws method lies in its flexibility. New uses of links are being invented all the time, which means that any proposed method for categorizing links risks quick obsolescence. The 5-Ws method avoids this fate by organizing links according to least common denominators. Whatever else they may do, links are embedded by someone (who), to something (what), in some place on a site (where). For this reason, our taxonomy should account for new linking practices quite easily. For example, at the time of this writing, the *New York Times* is in the midst of experimenting with a redesign of its website (see http://www.nytimes.com/marketing/prototype/). As described, the goal is to make content easier for users to find, and to make it easier for users to participate in conversations with one another about *New York Times* content. In practice, this means that the news site makes certain kinds of links more visible, and easier to use. It makes comments more visible by placing them in a sidebar next to stories, and it makes lists of "most popular" and "most commented" stories easier to see, and click on, by placing them in prominent positions on the page. Put another way, it rearranges the "whos," "whats," and "wheres" of linking—without changing these basic categories. Examples like this give us confidence that the 5-Ws method will accommodate future innovations in news links. New practices in linking may be created, but they will naturally fall within the basic units of our taxonomy.

The Purposes of News Links

When viewed most broadly, it is clear that navigation comprises the most common sort of link on news sites. By navigation, we mean any link that is purely designed to help users find content (whether that content is onsite or offsite). Among other things, these links include those to sections of the site (e.g., sports, entertainment, politics), links to stories (which often appear as lists), tag links (common on blogs), links that take a user to information about the day's weather, and links to the latest stock market numbers. Navigation links are so common because they are embedded in page templates. They are also common because there are so many kinds of them. As you scroll down the front page of most news sites, you will see a great variety of ways to navigate to content. Links are grouped together in boxes, and lists. They are organized according to user preferences (e.g., "most viewed" and "most comments" boxes). They appear in section links at the top of a page, and again in topics boxes down below, and yet again in section lists still further down. In fact, judged simply on the basis of variety, it appears that news organizations are devoting the most energy to innovating new ways for users to navigate to content. Another way to put this is to say that the primary intellectual problem news organizations have set themselves seems to be archival—how to make content findable by users. This in itself is revelatory. In their study of news links, scholars have mostly focused on the way, and the extent to which, journalists use links for citational and social reasons. In so doing, they have, in some sense, missed the forest for the trees, as these types of links are least common, and apparently of least interest to news organizations. Scholars may be interested in citation, but news organizations are much more concerned about navigation, or the simple problem of how to ensure that audiences can find their content.

In terms of basic purposes, we might stop here, because in some sense, all links are navigational: they direct users from one point on a site to another. However, as the use of links has increased, so have the purposes to which they have been put. For example, commercial links are navigational, but they also are clearly intended to generate revenue for a news organization. The most obvious type of commercial link is one to a display advertisement, but links to classified sections are also common. Interestingly, the number and kind of commercial links can vary by location of the user's ISP address. When we visited sfgate.com from Reno, NV, for example, very few display advertisements appeared on the home page. But when we visited from other locations, more advertisements appeared, and different combinations of advertisements appeared in different locations. Obviously, the news site drives advertising on the basis of user

FIGURE 1
The sfgate.com social media toolbar

location. Increasingly, links to advertising are also driven by user tracking. As these practices become more common, and websites are, at least to some extent, personalized to the user, it will be incumbent on researchers to take account of this fact. Along the way, it will be important to think about the roles location and user information play in a purportedly "spaceless" medium like the Web (e.g., Rogers 2010).

Providing users with an opportunity to share content is a third purpose of a link. For brevity's sake, we call this purpose "social." Such links connect users to content via social media feeds, or provide users with opportunities to share content through social media tools. By far the most common sharing opportunities come from the social media toolbar that appears on many news sites. This toolbar can take many forms. Figure 1 displays the toolbar of sfgate.com. It appears to the right of every news story posted by *Chronicle* reporters. On some sites, toolbars can be quite complex, providing as many as 20 different ways for users to share information. Others provide just a few. Whatever form it takes, it is quite ubiquitous, as it often appears on every page of a site.

Links may also provide users with opportunities to express themselves. This is typically done in the form of "comment" boxes (as in Figure 1). These boxes sometimes appear as just that—a box in which users type their comments. In this guise, comments may not be counted in a Web crawl. But often they also appear as a link to a separate "comments" page.

When this happens, comments are subject to being counted like any other link. It is also the case, of course, that users may be granted the freedom to embed links in their comments. Certainly, they have this opportunity on Facebook pages and Twitter feeds, and many blogs offer this function to users as well. We do not know how common the practice is on news sites, but it is one that we have witnessed, and so include it under the category of "social."

Citation represents a final purpose of links. We include under citation such practices as providing links to sources of information, establishing the authority of claims, and showing one's work. Consider, for example, the following excerpt from a blog post, "Paul Ryan Wants to Cut Income Taxes. Bobby Jindal Wants to Kill Them," posted by Dylan Matthews at wonkblog.com on March 20, 2013 (links are italicized).

> Most conservative policymakers at the federal level just want to sharply reduce the income tax, not eliminate it entirely. But more and more Republican-controlled states

are deciding to go big or go home. So far, Govs. *Bobby Jindal* (R-La) ... have announced plans to end their states' income taxes ... *Seven states* ... lack any individual income tax ... The Institute for Taxation and Economic Policy, a left-leaning think tank, *estimated* in its "Who Pays?" report.

In its entirety, the post contains 17 links to 13 sources of information, so many that it represents the very definition of "maximizing the value of the link" proposed by Jason Fry (2010). As the reader can see, Matthews uses these links primarily for citational purposes. In other words, he includes them to show his work. Other research shows that reporters do less of this in their news stories (e.g., Karlsson, Clerwall, and Örnebring 2015; Ryfe et al. 2012; Tsui 2008). Moreover, when they provide links in their stories, they mostly do so to pages internal to their own site. For example, a short sfgate.com article, "Long Sentences for SF Property Fraud," published by Vivian Ho on March 20, 2013 included just one link, which took users to a list of sfgate.com stories. Still, citational uses of links do appear in both news stories and blog posts. They are employed mostly be reporters, and typically for the purpose of showing their work.

Overall, these four purposes—navigation, commercial, social, and citation—account for all of the linking practices we encountered on the six sites under review. We suspect that the categories capture most, if not all, of the linking practices on news sites generally. We offer the taxonomy as a way for future researchers of news link analysis to gain methodological consistency.

While this paper focuses on a method of link analysis, it would not do to ignore completely the theoretical issues it raises. It is to these issues that we now turn.

Issues

As the practice of linking has proliferated on news sites, journalism scholars have focused attention on a relatively small set of questions. How do links contribute to the form of news reports? (e.g., Barnhurst 2010). How do linking practices differ between mainstream newspaper websites and blogging sites? (e.g., Herring et al. 2005; Leccese 2009; Tsui 2008). How do newspapers differ in their coverage of particular events or topics? (e.g., Dmitrova et al. 2003; Tremayne 2005). How are news stories disseminated through online news networks? (e.g., Chang et al. 2012; Himelboim 2010; Reese et al. 2007). How do links illuminate news frames? (e.g., Coddington 2012). How do links organize online news systems? (Ryfe et al. 2012).

The literature on these questions has made important insights. It has shown, for instance, that mainstream media still account for the vast majority of original reporting done in the news system. It has also determined that, while news sites generally link more than they did in the past, most links point internally to their own sites. Still, it is in some ways odd that the literature has invested so much attention to one of the least common kinds of news link, namely the link manually embedded by a reporter in a story, while more common kinds of links have escaped scrutiny.

In particular, we think the navigation link deserves greater attention. Despite the fact that they are the most numerous kind of link on any news site (by far), we have found no specific studies of these links. The first thing to say about them is that they quite literally organize the form of news on a Web page, and as Barnhurst and Nerone (2001) have demonstrated, the form of news illuminates deep assumptions about news, journalism, and public life. The second thing to say about them is that they largely generate the form of news through algorithms. This is to say, algorithms generate the great bulk of navigation links. A body of work is growing on the role algorithms play in digital society (e.g., Beer 2009; Galloway 2004; Gillespie 2014). This literature tackles questions like how algorithms constitute personal identity, and how they redistribute power in organizations and society. The conversations in this literature have only just begun to spill over into journalism studies (e.g., Anderson 2011; Annany 2013; Annany and Crawford 2014; Thurman and Schifferes 2012).

We suspect that part of the reason for this inattention is that few journalism scholars are technologically proficient. Yet, as Gillespie (2014) argues, many of the interesting questions raised by algorithms are social and political, not technological. For instance, who decides what goes into the set of instructions that make up an algorithm? How do these conversations take place? Who has a seat at the table? What issues are raised, and which are hidden? How do organizational and economic pressures shape the decisions that go into algorithms? Once in place, how do algorithms imagine, and reimagine, the journalist? The audience? Such questions require less technological proficiency than close scrutiny of the context in which algorithms are created and deployed.

Social links also deserve greater scrutiny. A striking fact about these links is that most news organizations have outsourced their production and management to third-party businesses, most obviously, to Facebook and Twitter, but also to a host of other companies that specialize in social media tools. For example, at the time of writing, the "Social Media Wire" that appears on mercurynews.com's website aggregates Twitter, RSS, and local media feeds from across the Bay Area. A company called "Crowdynews" created, and, we assume, manages the widget. Imagine for a moment a newspaper in the 1980s giving over prominent space on its front page to another information company. It is nearly inconceivable. Yet that is precisely what news companies of all kinds have done online. This fact raises a host of questions: Why have they done this? Who controls the information that is subsequently produced? Where is it archived (if at all)? Who is responsible for that information? What sorts of agreements, if any, have been hashed out between news companies and these third-party companies? If revenue is generated in this transaction, how so, and how is it shared? Does anyone in the news company monitor or in any way regulate the flow of links in these tools? If so, is this person a journalist, a technologist, or does she or he play some other role? Finally, what does it mean that news organizations—including blogs—have mostly given up being in the business of social media?

These issues related to navigation and social links are only the two most obvious we ran across as we developed this taxonomy. There are many others. Some of them involve the practice of reporting, but many do not. Scholars would do well to consider the full panoply of links on a news Web page. As they do, it is helpful to have a common methodological toolkit—including a taxonomy of links—with which to build knowledge across research projects. We hope that the taxonomy presented in this article goes some way toward filling that need.

DISCLOSURE STATEMENT

No potential conflict of interest was reported by the authors.

REFERENCES

Anderson, Chris W. 2010. "Textual Tunnel-Hops and Narrative Chutes-and-Ladders: The HTML Link as an Uncertain Object of Journalistic Evidence." Paper presented at the Yale-Harvard-MIT Cyberscholars Working Group, November 17.

Anderson, Chris W. 2011. "Deliberative, Agonistic, and Algorithmic Audiences: Journalism's Vision of Its Public in an Age of Audience Transparency." *International Journal of Communication* 5: 529–547.

Annany, Mike. 2013. "Press-Public Collaboration as Infrastructure: Tracing News Organizations and Programming Publics in Application Programming Interfaces." *American Behavioral Scientist* 57: 623–642.

Annany, Mike, and Kate Crawford. 2014. "A Liminal Press: Situating News Apps Within a Field of Networked News Production." *Digital Journalism* 3 (2): 192–208.

Barnhurst, Kevin. 2010. "The Form of Reports on US Newspaper Internet Sites, an Update." *Journalism Studies* 11: 555–566.

Barnhurst, Kevin, and John Nerone. 2001. *The Form of News: A History*. NY: Guilford.

Beer, David. 2009. "Power through the Algorithm? Participatory Web Cultures and the Technological Unconscious." *New Media & Society* 11: 985–1002.

Chang Tsan-Kuo, Southwell Brian, Lee, Hyung-Min Lee, and Yejin Hong. 2012. "Jurisdictional Protectionism in Online News: American Journalists and Their Perceptions of Hyperlinks. *New Media Society* 14: 684–700.

Coddington Mark. 2012. "Building Frames Link by Link: The Linking Practices of Blogs and News Sites." *International Journal of Communication* 6: 2007–2026.

De Maeyer Juliette. 2012. "The Journalistic Hyperlink." *Journalism Studies* 27: 1–10.

Dmitrova, Daniela, Connolly-Ahern Colleen, Williams Andrew Paul, Kaid Linda Lee, and Amanda Reid. 2003. "Hyperlinking as Gatekeeping: Online Newspaper Coverage of the Execution of an American Terrorist." *Journalism Studies* 4: 401–414.

Fry, Jason. 2010. "Maximizing the Values of the Link: Credibility, Readability, Connectivity". *Nieman Journalism Lab*. http://www.niemanlab.org/2010/06/maximizing-the-values-of-the-link-credibility-readability-connectivity/.

Galloway, Alexander. 2004. *Protocol: How Control Exists after Decentralization*. Cambridge: MIT Press.

Gillespie, Tarleton. 2014. "The Relevance of Algorithms." In *Gillespie, Tarleton*, edited by Pablo Boczkowski and Kirsten Foot, 167–193. Media Technologies. Cambridge: MIT Press.

Halavais, Alexander. 2008. "The Hyperlink as Organizing Principle." In *The Hyperlinked Society: Questioning the Connections in the Digital Age*, edited by Joseph Turow and Lokman Tsui, 39–55. Ann Arbor: University of Michigan Press.

Herring, Susan, Scheidt Lois, Wright Elijah, and Sabrina Bonus. 2005. "Weblogs as a Bridging Genre." *Information Technology and People* 18: 142–171.

Himelboim, Itai. 2010. "The International Network Structure of News Media: An Analysis of Hyperlinks Usage on News Web Sites." *Journal of Broadcasting and Electronic Media* 54: 373–390.

Karlsson, Michael, Christer Clerwall, and Henrik Örnebring. 2015. "Hyperlinking Practices in Swedish Online News 2007–2013: The Rise, Fall, and Stagnation of Hyperlinking as a Journalistic Tool." *Information, Communication and Society* 18: 847–863. doi:10.1080/1369118X.2014.984743.

Leccese, Mark. 2009. "Online Information Sources of Political Blogs." *Journalism and Mass Communication Quarterly* 86: 578–593.

Lewis, Seth, Rodrigo Zamith, and Alfred Hermida. 2013. "Content Analysis in an Era of Big Data: A Hybrid Approach to Computational and Manual Methods." *Journal of Broadcasting and Electronic Technology* 57: 34–52.

Peng, Foo-Yeuh, Tham Naphtali Irene, and Hao Xiaoming. 1999. "Trends in Online Newspapers: A Look at the US Web." *Newspaper Research Journal* 20: 52–63.

Reese, Steve, Lou Rutigliano, Hyun Kideuk, and Jaekwan Jeong. 2007. "Mapping the Blogosphere: Professional and Citizen-Based Media in the Global News Arena." *Journalism* 8: 254–280.

Riley, Patricia, Keough Colleen, Christiansen Thora, Meilich, Ofer, and Jillian Piersen. 1998. "Community or Colony: The Case of Online Newspapers and the Web." *Journal of Computer-Mediated Communication* 4.

Rogers, Richard. 2010. "Internet Research: The Question of Method—A Keynote Address from the YouTube and the 2008 Election Cycle in the United States Conference." *Journal of Information Technology & Politics* 7: 241–260.

Ryfe, David, Donica Mensing, Hayreddin Ceker, and Mehmet Gunes. 2012. "Popularity is Not the Same Thing as Influence: A Study of the Bay Area News System." *International Symposium on Online Journalism* 2 (2): 144–161.

Thurman, Neil, and Steve Schifferes. 2012. "The Future of Personalization at News Websites." *Journalism Studies* 13 (5-6): 775–790.

Tremayne, Mark. 2005. "News Websites as Gated Cybercommunities." *Convergence* 11: 28–39.

Tsui, Lokman. 2008. "The Hyperlink in Newspapers and Blogs." In *The Hyperlinked Society: Questioning Connections in the Digital Age*, edited by Joseph Turow and Lokman Tsui, 70–84. Ann Arbor: University of Michigan Press.

CHANCES AND CHALLENGES OF COMPUTATIONAL DATA GATHERING AND ANALYSIS
The case of issue-attention cycles on Facebook

Niina Sormanen, Jukka Rohila, Epp Lauk, Turo Uskali, Jukka Jouhki and **Maija Penttinen**

Digital and social media and large available data-sets generate various new possibilities and challenges for conducting research focused on perpetually developing online news ecosystems. This paper presents a novel computational technique for gathering and processing large quantities of data from Facebook. We demonstrate how to use this technique for detecting and analysing issue-attention cycles and news flows in Facebook groups and pages. Although the paper concentrates on a Finnish Facebook group as a case study, the demonstrated method can be used for gathering and analysing large sets of data from various social network sites and national contexts. The paper also discusses Facebook platform regulations concerning data gathering and ethical issues in conducting online research.

Introduction

Alongside the digital revolution and development of virtual environments, social scientific research is experiencing a paradigm shift towards computational approaches (Chang, Kauffman, and Kwon 2014, 67). Traditional qualitative and quantitative methods of social sciences appear to be limited in studying the phenomena of such rapidly altering environments as the internet or social media (Karpf 2012, 646). As social science research begins to use data-driven methods and novel tools for data gathering and analysis, a multidisciplinary approach is increasingly common (Chang, Kauffman, and Kwon 2014, 70). According to Steensen and Ahva (2014), we are living through the "fourth wave" of research about digital journalism, which following normative, empirical and constructivist waves, emerged mainly because of new practices related to social media. While arguing there is a need to reassess theories, they do not, surprisingly, identify any similar need for the new methodologies.

Internet and social media entail various platforms and social network sites (SNS) which have not yet been either sufficiently harnessed for research or have had their potential discussed, especially from the perspective of data gathering and analysis for social scientific or specifically journalism research. For example, Facebook generates a hybrid digital communication and news ecosystem where issues rise and fall in newsfeeds and on specific groups and pages, and news flows are continuously created by the users themselves, including sharing news generated by online news media.

Consequently, internet and social media enable the generation and access of massive data-sets ("big data") as sources for research material (Bollier 2010). Although there is a lack of common agreement and clarity concerning the definition of "big data" (cf. Boyd and Crawford 2012; Ukkonen 2013), the term has been widely adapted by media and journalism scholars (Couldry and Powell 2014; Lewis 2015; Lewis and Westlund 2015). Large digital data-sets used in data journalism are also being referred to as "open data" "that can be freely used, re-used and redistributed by anyone" (Coddington 2015; Mair et al. 2013; Open Knowledge Foundation 2012; Parasie 2015). Conventional journalism research benefits from using "big data" as a replacement for traditional representative sampling (Couldry and Powell 2014, 1). The current trend towards ubiquitous and mobile communications naturally increases the variety of "big data". The challenge is how to channel these data streams into knowledge, journalism or research (Lewis and Westlund 2015, 4).

The objective of this paper is to demonstrate the building procedure and possibilities of a new computational approach for gathering and processing online "big data" and to show how it can be used to detect issue-attention cycles and news flows in Facebook groups and pages. We use a case example from Finnish Facebook Community page "Valio Out of Fennovoima's Nuclear Plant Project" (2014). This is a group protesting against co-operation between the food-producing company Valio and the nuclear power company Fennovoima in building a new nuclear power plant in Finland. Facebook has, in Finland, become the main channel of the public's online activities and news consumption. A substantial majority of the population—about 86 per cent—regularly uses the internet, and Facebook is used by 95 per cent of all Finnish SNS users (Statistics Finland 2014). The case, as a topical issue in Finnish public debate, is particularly interesting from the journalism study perspective and will be used for detecting how the data gathered from Facebook can be used to compare and find synergy between the public's attention waves and media influence and operations.

Online News and "Issue-attention Cycles"

Online news is characterized as a revolutionary hybrid news medium (e.g. Allan 2006; Kautsky and Widholm 2008; Widholm 2015), which affects the role of journalists as mediators and moderators of information (Hermida et al. 2012) as well as changes the audience's behaviour. Social media platforms, such as Facebook and Twitter, form a digital news hybrid with traditional news media services. Facebook is acknowledged as one of the primary vehicles for news flows and exposure to news (Baresch et al. 2011; Bell 2014). News, via Facebook, is nowadays a mixture of Facebook users' posts, Facebook groups' and (fan) pages' posts, as well as advertisers' messages.

Consequently, in contrast to passive audiences, people can now also be considered as mediators and gatekeepers of news online. However, the audience's attention cannot be taken for granted. "Instead of a traditional push-model, users are free to navigate between sites to seek the information they desire and select their own versions of the daily news" (Weber and Monge 2011, 1063). Thus, in contrast to the traditional procedure of newspapers gathering their audiences, Baresch et al. (2011, 2) refer to "a new kind of news consumption strategy, a new kind of consumer, a 'stumbler' so to speak, who gets nearly all his or her news through incidental or socially selected exposure". Online news sites and portals fiercely compete to be the quickest at catching the audience's attention, thus publishing breaking news almost in real time. The same news criteria as in traditional media largely become irrelevant, since the virtual space is practically unlimited. Social media largely serves as a distributor of the news, but also as an independent news source. The dissemination of issues is unpredictable and uncontrolled, as everyone can at any time "share" a link, or news, to any number of SNS and other platforms. In addition, algorithms produce and distribute news online that can also be redistributed by social media users.

Moreover, the attention span of the media and the public on an issue is not unlimited. The cyclical character of public attention was noticed already in the pre-digital media era. More than 40 years ago, Anthony Downs outlined a concept of "issue-attention cycles" characterizing the rising and fading of public attention and concern towards major societal issues (Downs 1972).

Downs (1972, 39–40) suggests five stages of "issue-attention cycles", characteristic of the American society and media of the time: (1) the pre-problem stage, where only some experts or interest groups are aware of the problem; (2) alarmed discovery and euphoric enthusiasm, where the public becomes both aware of and alarmed about the evils of a particular problem; (3) realizing the cost of significant progress, which includes major sacrifices by large groups of population; (4) gradual decline of intense public interest and enthusiasm; (5) the post-problem stage, where the issue moves into a "twilight realm of lesser attention or spasmodic recurrences of interest". In the digital environment, issues rise and decline rapidly, but the attention cycles are not necessarily shorter than in traditional media as Anderson, Brossard, and Scheufele (2012) demonstrate.

In the pre-internet age, the traditional media governed the issue-attention cycle. The structure of the news flows in the traditional media is based on newsworthiness and the space the topical stories get in print and broadcasting outlets. However, before the era of computational approaches and data-driven methods, detecting and explaining the cyclical nature of public attention and major issues, which appear in the combined news flows of the digital news ecosystem, was not feasible.

Approaches to Computational Data Gathering for Research

Using semi-public data (data collected with a user account) to retrieve data for Facebook group and page content analysis research with a computational approach such as the one presented in this paper, i.e. a tool using Facebook's own application programming interfaces (API) to gather all available communication activity data from the platform's pages and groups and organizing it into a warehouse, is still very rare in social sciences. Semenov (2013) discusses many aspects of social media data analysis, implementation and repository designed for monitoring communities on social media sites (see also Semenov, Veijalainen, and Boukhanovsky 2011). In their working paper, Zlatanov and Koleva (2014) are using a software application called Opinion Crawler designed to extract data from open Facebook groups and use it for data analysis through people centric models and text network analysis connected to online originated protests. Nevertheless, the objectives of these studies are quite different from this paper's; they do not explain the software design specifics nor data organization procedures of Facebook data *per se* and are not done from the journalism study perspective.

Indeed, many Facebook data collection applications and technical platforms are available online for researchers (e.g. Digital Footprints, NodeXL, Netvizz, RFacebook, SocialMediaMineR and Facepager). For example, Netvizz (2015) is a ready-made application tool for retrieving data from Facebook, which asks for target users' permission to access their public profile and friend lists. Though quite similar in providing lists of posts and their likes and comments, in contrast to our approach it relies on the researcher to be a member of a group or liking a page, and is dependent on the tool creator's decisions on output data. The tool provides less data and analysis possibilities compared to independent data retrieval and building one's own data warehouse.

Another more technical and nearly identical data tool to ours in its data retrieval method is Facepager (2015), which fetches publicly available data from Facebook, Twitter and other platforms with an open standard format for transmitting data (JSON-based API) and stores it in a database. This tool can gather all the Facebook data, but in an unorganized form. Our approach is to transfer the data into the data warehouse in a specific model schema, which helps to organize and analyse the data.

Facebook and Data Collection

Privacy settings greatly impact on the results of data gathering on Facebook, especially the information the user has decided to hide from others (Giglietto, Rossi, and Bennato 2012). For example, analysing newsfeeds on Facebook could turn out to be more difficult than originally expected due to the general notion of only sharing the timeline with a limited list of "friends". Instead, focusing the research on Facebook pages could improve the results of data collection, because Facebook pages are regarded as public material with no limitations to its internal data (Giglietto, Rossi, and Bennato 2012, 152).

While conducting research on Facebook, it is important not to violate the common principles of the site. The general notion in Facebook's "Principles" and "Statement of Rights and Responsibilities (SRR)" about the data available focuses on the possibility of the users individually determining the information they are willing to share publicly. If users do not limit the availability of information, it becomes public data, and Facebook is not responsible for what information received from the site is used (see Facebook 2014a, 2014d).

Generally, access to SNS can be categorized into three data: *public data*, *semi-public data* and *dark data*. Public data can be retrieved from public interfaces without signing a user agreement with a service provider. Semi-public data can be accessed from public interfaces by signing a user agreement and using the user account to retrieve data. Dark data are obtained with techniques that the service provider has not intended for use or are against the user agreement of the service. For example, Facebook provides more data in their Web user interface than from their APIs. This difference has given rise to software tools like "scrapers" that instead of using machine interfaces use interfaces meant for human users to pool more detailed information from the network. Other "dark" tools, like harvesters, robots and spiders, gather data blindly in an attempt to remodel the social network. Facebook's RSS and "Automated Data Collection Terms" (ADCT) dictate terms of using automated tools, such as harvesting bots, robots, spiders or scrapers, and indicate a need to ask Facebook's written permission for using such tools or storing data, and forbid using any acquired data for business or advertisement purposes (Facebook 2014d, 2014h). Operators of Facebook's own Platform applications or websites, and users of Social Plugins must comply with the "Facebook Platform Policy" (FPP) (Facebook 2014g).

Below we discuss the collection of semi-public data from users and communication data from Facebook open groups and pages, and use the same data from a page in the case study analyses. During the creation of the data-gathering techniques, special emphasis was put on acting in accordance with Facebook's user agreements, principles, and any intent implied in the SRR, FPP and ADCT. Particular attention was paid to developer rules, protection of data, IDs and not selling or reproducing the data, applicable to our computational approach of semi-public data gathering, as we are not developing a specific platform app or website nor using the indicated automated data collection tools.

Building Data-centric Research Approaches for Studying Facebook

We describe here the path that was taken to create a research tool for studying Facebook. Facebook currently offers a readily available user interface data tool and a simple content search system, the Graph API Explorer. It is a software environment created for third-party developers, where it is possible to create applications to access data on Facebook by asking permission from users (Facebook 2014c). Instead of using the Graph API Explorer, we gathered semi-public data from pages and groups by using Facebook's own APIs and public interfaces, which allowed us broader freedom of research and more data to be obtained, still following the general (developer) principles and regulations of Facebook.

We will initially define key concepts and motivations behind using computational data gathering, then explore the possibilities of data organization, warehousing and analysis, and in the following section, demonstrate some basic case examples of the application of research data in studying issue-attention cycles and news flows in Facebook pages. While describing the building process of the tools, we have focused more on concepts and problem solving than on a direct hands-on approach. Our understanding is that conducting data-centric research and building computational tools is not purely technical work—it is more about thinking on what data we can obtain and what its meaning is from the point of research.

Automatic Versus Manual Data Gathering and Some Basic Concepts

The biggest drawback of manual data gathering is that this method is slow and prone to human errors. The Facebook page used in this article as a case example had 966 posts to its feed and 1921 comments attached to these posts. In addition, manual method makes only a limited amount of all data available. While Facebook shows the key information in a Web or mobile client, there is more data available from the system's APIs, such as metadata on how the system handled the content in question. Furthermore, during the lengthy manual data gathering, the information available can change or it can become unavailable. Although computational data gathering does not completely remove the risk of data being changed or going missing, it minimizes the window of opportunity where it can happen.

For an avid user, who has used Facebook public Web or mobile client, the concepts, terms and scopes might be self-evident, but not necessarily from their technical point of view. Depending on what API is in use, there are various terms for the underlying data and restrictions that are invisible for users when browsing the service. Some of the main concepts are explained in Table 1.

TABLE 1
Facebook's main concepts and their explanations

Concept	Explanation
API	Defines how a computer system can be accessed by another computer system, what data it can access and on what premises. Facebook has two different APIs, Graph API and FQL (Facebook Query Language), that allow other computer systems to access automatically Facebook. Both APIs allow the access to the same underlying system that runs Facebook (read more from Facebook 2014e, 2014f).
Feed	Central element of Facebook where posts including status updates and links are published. Individual users have their own personal feeds and so do groups, pages and applications. Another name for a feed is "stream". The Graph API uses the term "feed" whereas FQL uses the term "stream".
Post	Individual entry to a feed. It can contain text, image and video content, file, link, users associated with the entry, location and privacy settings. Users who can access the post can share, like and comment the post.
Comment	Entry that can be targeted on most types of content on Facebook. It can contain text, links and photos. Users can like a comment or reply to it.
Like	Action that a user can make to notify the creator of a post or a comment that the user has liked the entry. Everybody who can see the original entry can also see all "likes".
Share	Act where a user shares a post generated by someone else on their own feed, or posts it to a feed of a friend, group or page. Information about shares on Facebook is restricted. If a user has permission to read the entry, it is possible to read a list of users who shared the article if their privacy settings allow this.
User	Account of an individual user. Detailed personal information on Facebook is restricted. If the user is not a friend or the user has not chosen to relax their privacy policies, the only information that can be retrieved from the user are first name, last name, gender, age, friend count and subscriber count.

Searching and Retrieving Data from Public Interfaces

Both public interfaces of Facebook, the Graph API and FQL (Facebook Query Language), enable keyword search of selected data in the system. Currently, in version 2.2, it is possible by using the Graph API to make a keyword search according to names of users, pages, events, groups, places and locations (Facebook 2014e). Previously it was also possible to search posts with keyword search but unfortunately this feature is being removed from the system with the introduction of version 2.2 and the deprecation of the 2.0 version of the platform. With the same upgrade, Facebook is also removing support for FQL (Facebook 2014b).

After a search is made (for how, see Facebook 2014e), the system returns a list of matching results. Only users who have not removed themselves from public search are reached. When a researcher finds an interesting source of data and the data are publicly available, the data are retrieved by issuing calls to different endpoints of the Graph API.

There are, however, a few restrictions on which data can be retrieved. First of all, if the researcher is not the owner or administrator of a feed, no data about who has liked the page or group is available. Secondly, the biggest restriction is the API call limit. Currently Facebook only allows 600 calls per 600 seconds per authentication token, i.e. in simple terms one call per second can be issued to Facebook (see Mangobug 2012). While this restriction, for a human user, would not be a limiting one, for a computational data search and retrieval system this is a major hindrance and limitation. Also, while it takes only around 40 seconds to retrieve 1000 posts from a feed, it will take much more time to get other data, such as comments on the posts. In other words, while access to basic items is fast, being able to gather all data takes much longer. Thus, when designing an application to search and retrieve data, researchers should make an effort to classify the kinds of data they want before embarking on building a data storage and warehouse tool.

Push-stream and Pull-stream Views on Data Retrieve

Facebook's owners have access not only to what people do on their pages, but they also have information about who has viewed what and for how long. Such an overall *datascape* could be called *whirlpool*, where events external to the social network create internal actions in the system, which then can again create actions outside the network.

The "whirlpool" can be further broken down to two different ways of looking at retrievable data from Facebook. When a user makes a post, comment, like or share, they actually generate a messaging event to initiate different actions in the system. This view of retrievable data could be called the *push-stream*: user-generated events push the system to perform different actions. Another view of Facebook would be constructed on the basis of what it messages to a user. Individual users have their own event wall or feed that is filled by Facebook from the content generated by a particular users' network of friends and by advertisements displayed by the system itself. This view of the retrievable data could be described best as the *pull-stream* where individual users pull content from the system by browsing the content of their own or other users' walls.

However, Facebook sets restrictions on what is possible to retrieve from the system. Logged users can only access their own feeds, feeds of their own network, feeds of the other users who have set their feeds to public, and feeds of open groups and pages. In addition, Facebook does not give any information about individual visits to the content of a feed, besides for administrators of pages. These restrictions alone make it impossible to retrieve pull-stream data. In addition, Facebook does not give detailed information about "shares" and "likes". In the case of "shares", information about who shared and to whom is missing. The only statistic the system gives out is the total number of "shares". In the case of "likes", the system does not give the time of an individual "like". These restrictions hinder retrieving push-stream data, but do not make it completely impossible.

In conclusion, we can see that from the data that Facebook provides to third parties, the push-stream forms the most complete retrievable data. The pull-stream-based view is currently impossible to be reconstructed and the aggregated level is still heavily restricted. However, a limited "whirlpool" view could be constructed by combining push-stream data with aggregated pull-stream data as well as with external sources, such as traditional media. However, the recommendation based on our experience is to concentrate on retrieving data from the push-stream, looking at actions and their actionable effects.

The Necessity of Clarifying Data and Creating a Data Warehouse

When testing the computational data retrieval approach, we noticed multiple practical problems. Firstly, social networks, as other IT-systems, are under constant change where new features are developed and old techniques are terminated. Also, alongside changes in the official APIs, other changes, e.g. the privacy policy, could lead to alterations of available data. Thus, the research subject is a moving target that can suddenly change, in the worst case denying access or changing key functionalities and affecting the research results.

Another problem is that the APIs are intended to extend the functionality of their respected services. They are not designed for data analysis but for the day-to-day system operations. For example, each "post" retrieved via Graph API has 28 attributes that describe it and its relationship to other items and system metadata. Also, there are overall 31 endpoints in the system from where different data can be retrieved. Thus, there are too many different data objects and attributes to handle without any categorization or connection clues.

These problems evoked the idea that the data retrieved should be logically separated and isolated from the data format provided by the source system, and when moved into a different system for analysis, the data should be coded into a simpler form. Thus, a separate data warehouse was coded and constructed to manage the data.

Data warehouse in computing refers to a system that is used for saving data from one or multiple source systems into a single set for retrieving data reports and analysis. There are two different design philosophies regarding data warehousing. The first is the dimensional approach of Ralph Kimball's star schema where measurable and quantitative data are stored in fact tables, whereas descriptive attributes related to the fact data are stored in dimensional tables (Kimball 1996). The second design approach is Bill Inmon's 3NF model (Third Normal Form) where data are structured as much as possible in order to minimize data redundancy through normalization (Inmon 1992). It is also possible to make a combined approach of the two models. Hence, we decided to combine the idea of the star schema (storing the data into separate tables) with data normalization (simplifying and combining similar forms of data into the tables), thus forming a data model that is easy to search and analyse.

The data warehouse of this study was built on the basis of a *push-stream-based event data-centric model* modelled into a star schema, but structured and normalized as much as possible. "Event" was defined as a time-associated transaction in the system. Due to Facebook's restrictions on accessing data, only "posts" and "comments" could be defined as "events", and "likes" and aggregated data about "shares" were used to describe "events" to which they were tied. The data model used was based on a dimensional approach where "posts" and "comments" would be stored as "events" and all the other information describing and relating to them stored to dimensional tables (see Table 2; Figure 1).

The technical reason not to store "like" data to an "event" table was to make it smaller and simpler. Especially in feeds of groups and pages, every "post" and "comment" has multiple "likes" and thus, the size of the event table would grow immensely. Queries would also become more complex as "likes" would be treated as child events of "posts" and "comments" versus a direct relation linkage via the "like" table.

In addition to simplifying the form of the data, clarification and warehousing also enable using a single set of analytical tools to address multiple social networks via a common data warehouse. Although data from different social networks differ, their functionality in the conceptual level is similar (see Table 3). By identifying similarities between social networks, data from multiple systems can be brought into a single system and transcoded into a single format, enabling researchers to build and use exactly the same analytical tools for both networks.

TABLE 2
Titles and functions of the data warehouse tables

Table name	Table function
f_event	Fact table for storing posts and comments. The table has a parent–child structure, where posts act as parent events for comments.
d_event_type	Dimensional table for describing the event type. The event can be either a post or a comment. In case of posts, also information about the type of post will be saved: app story, event created, link posted, photos posted, post on wall, status update and video posted.
d_content	Dimensional table for storing content of an event. In case of a post not only text written by the user, but also possible file attachments, Web links and any caption content generated by Facebook are saved. The same is true about comments, although there are no files attached to them.
d_entity	Dimensional table for storing the information about an entity connected to an event. All different Facebook entities such as users, pages, groups and application are handled as entities.
r_like	Relation table between an event and an entity.

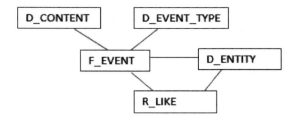

FIGURE 1
Event data-centric star schema of tables and their connections

TABLE 3
Key concepts of Facebook and their counterparts on Twitter

Facebook	Twitter	Functionality
Stream	@ or #-tag	Stream of content organized around certain user or specific subject.
Post	Tweet	Content that users send to their social networks.
Comment	Reply	Content that has a link to previous content to which it has follow-up relation.
Share	Retweet	Content that users have forwarded to their networks.
Like	Favorite	Shared sign between users of one user liking a specific content.

Possibilities of Analysing Data from the Warehouse

After the decisions and organization of data, the warehouse now stores the data in five tables (see Figure 1): f_events, d_content, d_entity, d_event_type and r_likes. From these tables both the d_content and d_event_type tables describe what was the content of an event, thus together forming the content-centric type of data. Tables r_like and d_entity deal with actors and their relation to events and each other, forming the people-centric type of data. The last type of data is the "event" based, consisting of "posts" and comments made in a feed.

The content-centric data are the most unrestricted from the three types. Content in general can be retrieved without hindrance. Analysis of the content of texts, photos and videos is still the major domain of qualitative research. Content can be, indeed, automatically analysed for example, with sentiment analysis, using word lists to calculate the content of a text, but these techniques are yet under construction and their usefulness is under discussion. However, the most useful function of storing the content along with other feed information is the ability to get the content out quickly and with additional information, such as time and date, number of likes, comments, users tied to a specific content, and so forth.

The people-centric data are a rather limited type, not only due to Facebook's restrictions to personal data, but because the user information available is tied to user-generated events. If a person has read a post or a comment but not done any other activity, there is no trace of that user. Thus, the user information is limited only to people who at least once were active in a feed. The information always available about the users includes first name and last name, used language version and user's profile picture. Gender information is available in 99.9 per cent of cases, friend count in 54.7

per cent and affiliation information in 2.9 per cent of cases. This is essentially all the information that Facebook gives about users directly, but it does enable making comparisons based on gender and on amount of friends a user has.

The event-centric data enable more data to be gathered and analysed. In a context of a feed, one can track a user's total number of "posts", "comments", "likes" and "shares", and commented, liked and shared posts and comments. Further information can be generated by taking into account the type of content and time of a post or comment in question. The problem with the event-centric data, as noted before, is that Facebook does not give information about individual shares and about the time when a "like" was made. Thus, analysis of the event data is analysis of actions and their responses. For example, a "like" is always a response, while a "comment" and a "post" can be both actions and responses to other posts and comments. With this data, we can generate a view of what has happened, what are the responses to it, and by combining this data with data about content and users, we can start to explain behaviour of a feed.

Using the Computational Approach in Journalistic Research: Case Facebook

To demonstrate potentials of Facebook data and its organization for journalistic research, we chose a page of a protest group called "Valio Out of Fennovoima's Nuclear Plant Project" (2014) with 3095 followers. The page was searched from Facebook with Graph API, all its available semi-public data were retrieved and directed to the organized data warehouse, which automatically saved the data to the assigned tables.

In the following, we use the concept of the "issue-attention cycle" for demonstrating the potentials and possibilities of computational data gathering. Our aim is not to attempt to explain exhaustively the ebb and flow of public attention on the issue of building a nuclear power station in Finland and all the activities of the respective Facebook group. Instead, we are trying to show how to discover and visualize the waves of attention using large data-sets, and indicate some possible basic ways of analysing them.

Detecting Issue-attention Cycles

Groups and pages formed to support or protest against an issue make it possible for journalism and media researchers to observe issue-attention cycles of certain societally topical issues. Our example consists of the above-mentioned group's data since its birth, from week 32 of 2011 to week 45 of 2014.

Focusing on the page's event-centric data of "posts" and related communication activity, such as shares, likes and comments, it is possible to observe the intensity of the group's attention. Table 4 shows a data table example that contains weekly downloads of the page's "posts" and post-related activities. It is also possible to take a daily download of "posts" for even more specific cycle evaluations.

Table 4 firstly shows the *year*, *month* and *week* of the "posts", then the total amount of *posts* grouped by time, and also by their producer: *post by source* indicating the page/administrator of the page as the source, *post by other* indicating any other actor as the source, and total number of *posters*, i.e. amount of individual producers of the posts. The table also shows the same total amounts and grouped information of post-related *shares*, *likes*, *comments* and *comment likes*.

TABLE 4
Excerpt of a data table of weekly posting quantities and posts' related activities

Year	Month	Week	Posts	Posts (source)	Posts (other)	Posters	Shares	Shares (source)	Shares (other)	Likes	Likes (source)	Likes (other)	Comments	Comments (source)	Comments (other)	Comment likes	Comment likes (source)	Comment likes (other)
2013	11	45	13	10	3	3	69	69	0	23	23	0	8	5	3	4	3	1
2013	11	46	18	18	0	0	197	197	0	64	64	0	19	19	0	28	28	0
2013	11	47	5	5	0	0	72	72	0	15	15	0	7	7	0	12	12	0
2013	11	48	5	4	1	1	16	16	0	10	8	2	4	4	0	3	3	0
2013	12	49	11	8	3	2	127	127	0	40	38	2	10	10	0	5	5	0
2013	12	50	11	11	0	0	109	109	0	27	27	0	18	18	0	14	14	0
2013	12	51	11	8	3	1	64	64	0	26	22	4	11	5	6	7	4	3
2013	12	52	5	3	2	2	17	17	0	7	5	2	6	5	1	4	4	0
2013	12	1	12	11	1	1	116	116	0	40	36	4	17	15	2	22	21	1
2014	1	2	4	4	0	0	7	7	0	8	8	0	5	5	0	5	5	0
2014	1	3	8	7	1	1	43	43	0	16	16	0	10	8	2	7	5	2

By categorizing the activity information according to each producer, one may find some interesting aspects. For example, in this short data excerpt we can see that in total 103 "posts" were made on the page wall, and most of them by the page/administrator, i.e. source ($N = 89$, 86 per cent). In addition, there are no shares made by the group "members" (i.e. other), only by the page and with large quantities, and nearly the same applies to "likes". This may give an initial indication of the group's internal dynamics and objectives.

From the issue-attention cycle perspective, the total amounts of posts, shares, likes and comments (see Table 4) give a good overall picture of the communication activities of a Facebook group. Figure 2 visualizes the overall data-set with a specific focus on total amounts of "posts" and their tied activities of shares, likes and comments, showing a synopsis of the amounts from approximately every other week from years 2011–2014.

By looking at Figure 2, we can make observations of the issue-attention cycle in the social media context. The total data figure shows how attention has been relatively steady and low-level immediately after the launch of the group (during 2011–2012) and only towards the end of 2013 and in 2014 have activities been boosted. The early phases of the formation of the group may reflect the "pre-problem" stage, as the initiators of the group must have been people who had enough information to be worried about the issue. Alongside the growing attention of the traditional media (close to the end of 2013), when Fennovoima made a deal with the Russian nuclear energy corporation Rosatom (Taloussanomat 2013), the group's activities reach the "alarmed discovery" stage. The activity increases even further at the beginning of 2014. At this time, media attention focused on the fact that the Fennovoima's plant project had, due to funding problems, been transformed into a Russian project (e.g. YLE 2014). During the "alarmed discovery" stage, the group actively shares information, which also gets significantly large quantities of "shares" and "likes".

To be able to give an exhaustive explanation of the actual reasons of the activity peaks, their relation with the public agenda and the group's inner development, qualitative analysis is also necessary. The most lucrative way of starting qualitative analysis is by uploading content-centric data of posts from the warehouse for content analysis.

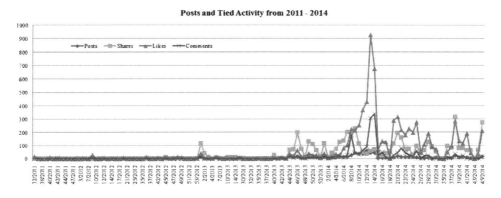

FIGURE 2
Weekly amounts of posts and tied activities of shares, likes and comments (2011–2014)

This would, for example, reveal the specific content of the posts and comments that created the high activity peaks of weeks 12–14, 2014. The quantitative data enabling activity visualization is, nevertheless, a good foundation for any further analysis.

News Flows as Escalators of Attention

Communication of groups and pages on Facebook includes links to online news articles and contents of other social media and websites, as well as other users' comments, shares and "likes" on the links, which all are components of social media's news flows. Examining these news flows by tracking, for example, articles on particular topics, changing patterns of the consumption and production of news can be described, as well as issue-attention cycles explained.

Focusing on content-centric data of the links attached to the "posts" shows what news articles or other content, and from which sources, have been linked. In addition, the event-centric data of related comments, likes and shares show how the news links generate activity and thus escalate their impact and create new news flows.

Table 5 shows a snapshot of one way of retrieving and organizing the data table that is formable by this focus from the warehouse. The complete data table includes 121 links to sources retrieved from the group's wall since the time the group was formed, from week 32 of 2011 to week 45 of 2014.

More specifically, by looking at the first *source* column row "www.facebook.com", the second column *referred* indicates the total amount that a link from the source "www.facebook.com" has been posted on the page ($N = 222$). The third column *referrers* indicates the total number of actors posting the link ($N = 9$), and the next three columns categorize the *referred* information according to the specific producing actor: *users*, i.e. individual people ($N = 6$), Facebook *page* ($N = 3$) and Facebook *group* ($N = 0$). The data table's final six columns show the *like count*, i.e. total number of likes made on the "Facebook" source links ($N = 3661$), their total *share count* ($N = 1279$) and total *comment count* ($N = 1038$), and the average frequencies each link has been *liked (average)*, *shared (average)* and *commented on (average)*.

The data output includes a lot of specific producer information, which offers interesting perspectives for interpretation, but also gives the basic total amounts of used "links" and their likes, shares and comment counts. The overall data offer vast possibilities of counting and correlations. For example, one simple option is to start by counting news source links in comparison to other used link sources (e.g. entertainment) to evaluate media influence, proceeding to the comparison of different media sources. Our study's results show that the most linked source on the page has been Facebook itself ($N = 222$), the second most used source has been YLE (Finnish National Public Service Broadcasting Company) ($N = 57$) and the third was *Kaleva* (a daily newspaper) ($N = 40$). Interestingly, Finland's most popular and authoritative quality newspaper, *Helsingin Sanomat*, appears only as the fifth source.

In addition, by focusing on the total amounts of attention and activity the posted links have generated, i.e. likes, shares and comments, one can measure the general impact of the links. Figure 3 shows the four most linked news sources and their escalated activity.

TABLE 5
Excerpt of data table with focus on links and their escalated activity

Source	Referred	Referrers	Referrers (user)	Referrers (page)	Referrers (group)	Likes	Shares	Comments	Likes (average)	Shares (average)	Comments (average)
www.facebook.com	222	9	6	3	0	3661	1279	1038	16.49	5.76	4.68
yle.fi	57	8	3	5	0	204	281	49	3.58	8.03	0.86
www.kaleva.fi	40	9	3	6	0	258	270	32	6.45	15	0.8
www.taloussanomat.fi	29	10	2	8	0	86	72	15	2.97	10.29	0.52
www.hs.fi	23	6	0	6	0	84	155	23	3.65	12.92	1
www.adressit.com	21	9	3	6	0	42	40	3	2	2.67	0.14
www.talouselama.fi	20	7	2	5	0	113	63	43	5.65	7	2.15
www.uusisuomi.fi	18	8	2	6	0	59	69	6	3.28	13.8	0.33
globalpost.com	16	1	1	0	0	0	0	0	0	0	0
www.iltasanomat.fi	10	7	1	6	0	9	4	2	0.9	2	0.2
www.tekniikkatalous.fi	9	2	1	2	0	18	13	5	2	1.86	0.56
puhutaanydinvoimasta.fi	6	3	1	3	0	105	125	18	17.5	31.25	3
www.kauppalehti.fi	6	4	1	2	0	6	3	5	1	1	0.83
www.greenpeace.org	5	2	1	1	0	11	1	1	2.2	0.33	0.2
www.mtv.fi	5	1	1	1	0	93	86	8	18.6	21.5	1.6

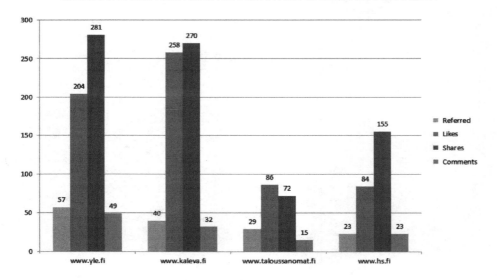

FIGURE 3
Four most linked news sources and their escalated activity of likes, shares and comments

One could continue by making more complex analyses and models of the way the amounts and content of posted news links affect the way they have gained attention among the public (likes, comments) and get to be forwarded to new publics (shares).

The described approach offers various possibilities for setting the research focus and analysing the data. Quantitative analysis can be combined with qualitative analysis, for example, by retrieving content-centric data with a focus on time and full content of the links, as the links can be opened and qualitatively analysed. When looking at the cycles of issue attention, one might, for example, choose links from the high-attention period, study their journalistic framing and narratives, and compare them to the low-attention periods.

Conclusions and Discussion

This paper reflects the paradigm shift in social scientific research towards a computational approach in data gathering and analysis. Our main conclusion is that the use of innovative research techniques of internet studies and analysis of large data-sets in studying digital and social media enormously widens the scope and quality of the information that social scientists can have at their disposal. The traditional methods of social sciences, such as surveys, various ways of text analysis and interviews, etc., are not sufficient for studying the new kinds of information streams of the new hybrid digital news ecosystem that combines online media, social media and other digital sources of information/news. They remain limited also in researching the consumers and producers acting in this ecosystem, as they, too, become increasingly combined (often called as "prosumers"). The altering subjects and foci of research also require enlargement of the variety of information available for researchers.

In this article, we introduced a new option for gathering and processing large data-sets for studying attention and information flows on SNS, specifically Facebook. Much of the data Facebook contains are not freely accessible, but there are healthy amounts of open data, for example on Facebook pages and open groups. One way of computationally accessing such data is to search and gather semi-public data by using Facebook's own APIs and public interfaces. This method allows more data to be obtained and freedom of data organization compared to specific applications asking permission or other ready-made online tools. In the approach we emphasized isolating the data from the source system and coding it to a simpler form in a separate data warehouse. Before building a data warehouse model, it is nevertheless important to understand the aspects of the available data and their connections, which are presented in this paper. Understanding the technical aspects is also helpful in retrieving and planning data analysis (beyond the case examples of this paper).

The case example analysis in this paper was kept quite simple and limited to the "issue-attention cycle" of one topical issue in the Finnish public debate and link flows on the group page. The analysis showed how large data-sets can be used to present time-scales of high and low waves of online activity and attention on an issue. By comparing them to real societal happenings and established media content analysis, various cycles and explanations of issue-attention are possible to outline. In addition, the process allows for tracking news flows on social media and their impact among the public both by quantitatively comparing how much shared news gets attention online and qualitatively by analysing, for example, comments on shared news articles. What news and how it gains the public's attention and becomes forwarded in social media provide journalists and media houses with valuable information regarding online news consumption and news flows.

The same data-gathering and processing technique can be used for studying various other journalistic aspects both quantitatively and qualitatively, including the integration of other SNS. For example, comparing traditional media content analysis with the online public's societal or political issue attention and framing may give new insight into who sets the agenda in todays' society—online publics or the media? In addition, the data can be used to detect how media use online topics as sources compared to the online public finding their topics from traditional/online media.

The ethical rules and views of collecting and using online data for research still remain under debate. However, by abiding by general laws and the rules of the platform or the SNS under scrutiny, using case-by-case reflection, and securing the anonymity and safety of individuals and data, a researcher should be able to conduct ethically acceptable online research.

DISCLOSURE STATEMENT

No potential conflict of interest was reported by the authors.

FUNDING

This work was in part supported by the Media Industry Research Foundation of Finland and Faculty of Humanities, University of Jyväskylä.

REFERENCES

Allan, Stuart. 2006. *Online News: Journalism and the Internet*. Maidenhead: Open University Press.

Anderson, Ashley A., Dominique Brossard, and Dietram A. Scheufele. 2012. "News Coverage of Controversial Emerging Technologies: Evidence for the Issue Attention Cycle in Print and Online Media." *Politics and the Life Sciences* 31 (1-2): 87–96.

Baresch, Brian, Lewis Knight, Dustin Harp, and Carolyn Yaschur. 2011. "Friends Who Choose Your News: An Analysis of Content Links on Facebook." Paper presented at the International Symposium on Online Journalism, Austin, Texas, April 1–2. Accessed November 15, 2014. https://online.journalism.utexas.edu/2011/papers/Baresch2011.pdf

Bell, Emily. 2014. "Silicon Valley and Journalism: Make up or Break up?" *The Reuters Memorial Lecture 2014 for the Reuters Institute in Oxford University*, November 21st. Accessed November 24, 2014. https://reutersinstitute.politics.ox.ac.uk/news/silicon-valley-and-journalism-make-or-break

Bollier, David. 2010. *The Promise and Peril of Big Data*. Washington, DC: The Aspen Institute. http://www.aspeninstitute.org/sites/default/files/content/docs/pubs/The_Promise_and_Peril_of_Big_Data.pdf.

Boyd, danah and Kate Crawford. 2012. "Critical Questions for Big Data: Provocations for a Cultural, Technological, and Scholarly Phenomenon." *Information, Communication, & Society* 15 (5): 662–679.

Chang, Ray M., Robert J. Kauffman, and Young Ok Kwon. 2014. "Understanding the Paradigm Shift to Computational Social Science in the Presence of Big Data." *Decision Support Systems* 63: 67–80. doi:10.1016/j.dss.2013.08.008.

Coddington, Mark. 2015. "Clarifying Journalism's Quantitative Turn: A Typology for Evaluating Data Journalism, Computational Journalism, and Computer-Assisted Reporting." *Digital Journalism* 3 (3): 331–348. doi:10.1080/21670811.2014.976400.

Couldry, Nick, and Allison Powell. 2014. "Big Data from the Bottom up." *Big Data & Society* 1 (2): 1–5. doi:10.1177/2053951714539277.

Downs, Anthony. 1972. "Up and down with Ecology: The Issue Attention Cycle." *The Public Interest* 28: 38–51.

Facebook. 2014a. "Principles." Accessed November 7, 2014. https://www.facebook.com/principles.php

Facebook. 2014b. "Platform Upgrade Guide." Accessed December 18, 2014. https://developers.facebook.com/docs/apps/upgrading/

Facebook. 2014c. "Graph API Explorer." Accessed November 21, 2014. https://developers.facebook.com/tools/explorer/145634995501895/

Facebook. 2014d. "Statement of Rights and Responsibilities." Accessed November 7, 2014. https://www.facebook.com/legal/terms

Facebook. 2014e. "Using the Graph API." Accessed November 21, 2014. https://developers.facebook.com/docs/graph-api/using-graph-api/v2.2#fieldexpansion

Facebook. 2014f. "Facebook Query Language (FQL) Overview." Accessed March 16, 2015. https://developers.facebook.com/docs/technical-guides/fql

Facebook. 2014g. "Facebook Platform Policy." Accessed March 16, 2015. https://developers.facebook.com/policy/

Facebook. 2014h. "Automated Data Collection Terms." Accessed March 20, 2015. https://www.facebook.com/apps/site_scraping_tos_terms.php

Facepager. 2015. Accessed March 18, 2015. https://github.com/strohne/Facepager

Giglietto, Fabio, Luca Rossi, and Davide Bennato. 2012. "The Open Laboratory: Limits and Possibilities of Using Facebook, Twitter, and YouTube as a Research Data Source." *Journal of Technology in Human Services* 30 (3-4): 145–159. doi:10.1080/15228835.2012.743797.

Hermida, Alfred, Fred Fletcher, Darryl Korell, and Donna Logan. 2012. "Share, like, Recommend: Decoding the Social Media News Consumer." *Journalism Studies* 13 (5-6): 815–824. doi:10.1080/1461670X.2012.664430.

Inmon, William H. 1992. *Building the Data Warehouse*. NY: John Wiley & Sons Inc.

Karpf, David. 2012. "Social Science Research Methods in Internet Time." *Information, Communication & Society* 15 (5): 639–661. doi:10.1080/1369118X.2012.665468.

Kautsky, Robert, and Andreas Widholm. 2008. "Online Methodology: Analysing News Flows of Online Journalism." *Westminster Papers in Communication and Culture* 5 (2): 81–97.

Kimball, Ralph. 1996. *The Data Warehouse Toolkit. Practical Techniques for Building Dimensional Data Warehouses*. NY: John Wiley & Sons.

Lewis, Seth C. 2015. "Journalism in an Era of Big Data: Cases, Concepts, and Critiques." *Digital Journalism* 3 (3): 321–330. doi:10.1080/21670811.2014.976399.

Lewis, Seth C., and Oscar Westlund. 2015. "Big Data and Journalism." *Digital Journalism* 3 (3): 447–466. doi:10.1080/21670811.2014.976418.

Mair, John, Richard Lance Keeble, Paul Bradshaw, and Teodora Beleaga. 2013. *Data Journalism: Mapping the Future*. Suffolk: Abramis academic publishing.

Mangobug. 2012, January 3. "Re: What's the Facebook's Graph API Call Limit?" [online forum comment]. Stackoverflow. Accessed December 19, 2014. http://stackoverflow.com/questions/8713241/whats-the-facebooks-graph-api-call-limit

Netvizz. 2015. "Instructions". Accessed March 18, 2015. https://wiki.digitalmethods.net/Dmi/ToolNetvizz

Open Knowledge Foundation. 2012. "Open Data Handbook Documentation. Release 1.0.0." Accessed December 19, 2014. http://opendatahandbook.org/pdf/OpenDataHandbook.pdf, retrieved 19.12.2014

Parasie, Sylvain. 2015. "Data-Driven Revelation? Epistemological Tensions in Investigative Journalism in the Age of 'Big Data'." *Digital Journalism* 3 (3): 364–380. doi:10.1080/21670811.2014.976408.

Semenov, Alexander. 2013. "Principles of Social Media Monitoring and Analysis Software." PhD diss., University of Jyväskylä. https://jyx.jyu.fi/dspace/bitstream/handle/123456789/41559/978-951-39-5225-9.pdf.

Semenov, Alexander, Jari Veijalainen, and Alexander Boukhanovsky. 2011. "A Generic Architecture for a Social Network Monitoring and Analysis System." In *The 14th International Conference on Network-Based Information Systems*, edited by Leonard Barolli, Fatos Xhafa, Makoto Takizawa, 178–185. Los Alamitos, CA: IEEE Computer Society. doi:10.1109/NBiS.2011.52.

Statistics Finland. 2014. *Use of Information and Communications Technology by Individuals 2014: One Half of Finnish Residents Participate in Social Network Services.* Accessed November 10, 2014. http://www.stat.fi/til/sutivi/2014/sutivi_2014_2014-11-06_tie_001_en.html

Steensen, Steen, and Laura Ahva. 2014. "Theories of Journalism in the Digital Age: An Exploration and Introduction." *Digital Journalism* 3 (1): 1–18. doi:10.1080/21670811.2014.927984.

Taloussanomat. December 21, 2013. "Fennovoima Ja Rosatom Sopimukseen Ydinvoimalasta" [Fennovoima and Rosatom make a deal of nuclear power plant]. Accessed January 1, 2015. http://www.taloussanomat.fi/kotimaa/2013/12/21/fennovoima-ja-rosatom-sopimukseen-ydinvoimalasta/201317748/12

Ukkonen, Antti. 2013. "Big Data Ja Laskennalliset Menetelmät [Big Data and Computational Methods]". In *Otteita Verkosta. Verkon Ja Sosiaalisen Median Tutkimusmenetelmät* [Excerpts from the Web: Research Methodology for the Web and Social Media], edited by Salla Maaria Laaksonen, Janne Matikainen, and Minttu Tikka, 274–304. Tampere: Vastapaino.

Valio out of Fennovoima's nuclear plant project [Valio pois Fennovoiman ydinvoimala-hankkeesta]. 2014. Facebook. Accessed December 19, 2014. https://www.facebook.com/pages/Valio-pois-Fennovoiman-ydinvoimala-hankkeesta/175916569145235?ref=ts&fref=ts

Weber, Matthew S. and Peter Monge. 2011. "The Flow of Digital News in a Networkof Sources, Authorities, and Hubs." *Journal of Communication* 61 (6): 1062–1081. doi:10.1111/j.1460-2466.2011.01596.x.

Widholm, Andreas. 2015. "Tracing Online News in Motion: Time and Duration in the Study of Liquid Journalism." *Digital Journalism*. doi:10.1080/21670811.2015.1096611.

YLE. March 27, 2014. Fennovoiman Ydinvoimalan Varma Suomalaisosuus Putosi Alle Puoleen [Fennovoima's secured Finnish finance share dropped under a half]. Accessed January 3, 2015. http://yle.fi/uutiset/fennovoiman_ydinvoimalan_varma_suomalaisosuus_putosi_alle_puoleen/7160093

Zlatanov, Biser V. and Maya F. Koleva. 2014. "Networks of Collective Power: (Non)Movements and Semantic Networks." Paper presented at the ECREA 2014 European Communication Conference, Lisbon, November 12-15.

WORD COUNTS AND TOPIC MODELS
Automated text analysis methods for digital journalism research

Elisabeth Günther and Thorsten Quandt

With digital journalism and social media producing huge amounts of digital content every day, journalism scholars are faced with new challenges to describe and analyze the wealth of information. Borrowing sophisticated tools and resources from computer science and computational linguistics, journalism scholars have started to gain insights into the constant information flow and made big data a regular feature of the scientific debate. Both deductive (manual and semi-automated) and inductive (fully automated) text analysis methods are part of this new toolset. In order to make the automated research process more tangible and provide an insight into the options available, we provide a roadmap of common (semi-)automated options for text analysis. We describe the assumptions and workflows of rule-based approaches, dictionaries, supervised machine learning, document clustering, and topic models. We show that automated methods have different strengths that provide different opportunities, enriching—but not replacing—the range of manual content analysis methods.

Introduction: The Need for Automated Text Analysis Methods

Many changes have altered the face of journalism research in the past decades: as technological developments paved the way for digital journalism and social media, huge amounts of digital content are produced every day and can easily be accessed from locations all over the world. In our information society, "big data" offered the promise of a bright future for journalism research, with vastly improved possibilities for content analysis.

But does potentially easy access equal easy analysis? And does so-called "big data" lead to more insights into agenda-setting processes, news flows, and the portrayal of specific topics in the media? After the first excitement, there came disillusionment—the enormous amount of heterogeneous information calls for radically new approaches, new methods—and potentially new questions as well. To be able to describe and analyze this wealth of information, journalism researchers feel the need to adapt to the rapid advancements and turn to research methods that originated in unfamiliar disciplines such as computer science and computational linguistics. In this interdisciplinary research area, there is a variety of options available that can assist scholars to analyze hundreds of thousands of documents efficiently. This article provides a practical guide, largely based on the authors' own experiences—and indeed, sometimes failures—of exploring and applying these new techniques.

Typically, we can divide text analysis methods into two groups: deductive methods that are based on a pre-defined codebook with a set of relevant categories, and inductive methods that share an explorative character aiming to identify certain attributes of the text content. Automated methods enrich our methods repertoire on both sides: previously established categories can be translated in a way that enables the computer to do (part of) the coding process for the researcher. Fully automated approaches, on the other hand, assist researchers to explore text collections that are beyond the capacity of a manual analysis. In the following, we go through the research process step by step, presenting common deductive and inductive automated text analysis methods. All approaches belong to the research area of natural language processing, which aims at the machine-based information extraction from human language. This information can be at various levels of granularity: methods target singular words or groups of words, relations between them or aim to reveal latent structures that connect words and documents invisibly. Given the challenge that document collections are often too big to read, these automated methods are a necessary extension to the traditional methods repertoire of journalism research and a logical first step—not only for fully automated analyses, but also for primarily manual analyses of textual content. Even in cases where the codebook is already set, inductive tools can be helpful to get to know the text corpus (i.e. the document collection) in case researchers have little prior knowledge about its content. In order to reduce manual workload or increase reliability, they also offer ways to subset the data by identifying relevant documents for a following (manual) in-depth analysis.

While automated methods minimize the costly manual coding phase or might even make it redundant, the research process also requires certain additional steps. Preprocessing, for example, is an essential foundation for the application of most natural language-processing algorithms and includes data cleaning and transformation—as computers process natural language in a fundamentally different way than human coders do, the computer science mantra "garbage in, garbage out" is key to avoid misleading results. In order to make the research process in this innovative area more tangible, we start with a description of common preprocessing tasks.

We proceed with a description of deductive text analysis methods that require the researcher to manually define the categories prior to the analysis (see Figure 1 for a roadmap). [1] *Rule-based approaches* are a toolset mostly used to extract text. With

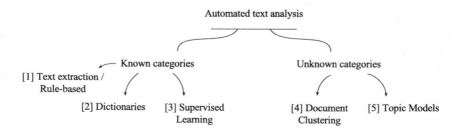

FIGURE 1
Overview of common text analysis methods

the help of logical operators and regular expressions (Friedl 2006), researchers can exploit recurring patterns within a text collection to retrieve relevant information, such as the name of the author or the title of a text. [2] If researchers can translate the respective categories directly into lists of elements that they want to identify within the text, hand-crafting a *dictionary* might be the appropriate solution. Sentiment analyses are a well-known example of this approach, evaluating the occurrence of positive and negative terms in a document based on a specific list (= dictionary). [3] *Supervised machine learning* also works with a built-in dictionary, but takes the demanding task of constructing it manually off the researchers' hands. Human coders only have to process a sample of the documents, providing the computer with classification examples to derive machine-readable rules. By then automatically applying these rules to the additional documents, the workload of human coders can be reduced considerably.

Following these options that work in a deductive manner, we describe two fully automated approaches. These methods are especially useful when a researcher has little knowledge on the contents of a document collection. When crafting a codebook for a manual content analysis, setting up a dictionary, or specifying rules to extract text features are not feasible, fully automated approaches are a valuable aid to get to know more about the documents' contents. [4] *Document clustering* is one of the options to detect the topic structure of a document collection: basically also built on word frequencies, this method allocates documents into thematic groups by means of a cluster analysis. As there are no pre-defined categories, the researcher has to interpret the clusters to find the link between the grouped documents and make meaning of the results. [5] *Topic models* such as the Latent Dirichlet Allocation (LDA) also aim to discover links between the documents, but work with a statistically more sophisticated model. Based on a multi-level probability model, this approach describes each document as a mix of several latent topics and provides a thematic representation of the text collection.

Preparing the Data

Before turning to the actual analysis, researchers have to take a close look at the condition of their dataset. Just like in any traditional text analysis, the first step in the automated content analysis is to prepare the input material. Given that we might look at the analysis of hundreds of thousands of documents, this cannot be done by hand. In the following, we describe common techniques that can be applied to automatically clean and normalize the dataset before the actual analysis. Which steps are necessary depends on the condition the text is currently in (e.g. language and textual form) and the analysis strategy researchers plan to apply.

As a basic principle, natural language is not easy to analyze automatically: for a human coder, it is obvious that "write", "writes", and "written" refer to the same verb and activity, but a computer does not possess this knowledge by default. Words can be inflected, in plural, contain special characters, be synonyms, or be ambiguous. Even deciding which part of the text is relevant for the analysis, and which is advertising, is a challenge. To ensure a high quality for the results of the automated text analysis methods, preparing the set of documents for the analysis is essential. It is not unusual that the preparation for the analysis demands most of the effort invested in the whole process (Witten, Eibe, and Hall 2011).

Removing Boilerplate

The first step in the preprocessing stage is to remove parts of the text that are irrelevant for its content. Online sources offer a wealth of information that is of interest to journalism scholars—very often, however, we get more than we wanted. When a Web crawler is used to retrieve the data, it does not distinguish between "good" and "bad" content, but by default simply downloads the complete Web page. This is due to the fact that, in contrast to human coders, a computer is not naturally equipped with the necessary reading literacy to identify relevant text parts (LaBerge and Samuels 1974). As a result, archives of online contents are often messy and contaminated with HTML markup, advertorial content, navigation elements, or user comments. This so-called *boilerplate content* is at best useless for the analysis, but increases computational costs for the following analyses and might even distort the results. Researchers can rely on several algorithms that remove the undesired data automatically (for an overview of state-of-the-art techniques, see Kohlschütter, Fankhauser, and Nejdl 2010).

Normalizing Text

The next step in the preprocessing is to normalize the data: when combining documents from different sources, different styles and formats have to be adjusted. News websites, for example, vary vastly in the way they manage their data and present their content. A major obstacle can arise from the fact that organizations choose different encodings to store text data on their local servers. If this is not taken into account when downloading online content, the text will be distorted with meaningless combinations of special characters. Websites with dynamic features can also pose a problem, as they reveal certain parts of the content only upon interaction with a user; due to the fact that, for example, a Web crawler does not interact with the website in the same way, this can create missing values. If metadata such as the date, title, or author of an article are of interest for the following analysis, this information can already be extracted when retrieving the documents; by accessing news articles via a website's RSS feed (Greer and Yan 2011), metadata can be accessed in a standardized format. Nonetheless, unexpected problems might arise, such as different time zones within the publication dates and times, and require careful inspection.

Normalization is also needed at the level of individual words. At this point, it is important to introduce the concept of *terms*: some words convey meaning only in combination with another ("United States") or share the same meaning with another ("U.S.A." and "USA"). Terms are the result of the normalization that is needed to preserve these units of meaning. Common steps in this process include the normalization of accents and diacritics ("Sao Paulo" and "São Paulo"), capitalization and case-folding (setting all words to lower case; exceptions such as "Turkey" and "turkey" might apply), British and American spelling, and foreign names ("Cologne" and "Köln"). Usually, numbers and punctuation are also removed at this step. Depending on the language of the text and the aim of the research project, additional processing steps might be necessary (Manning, Raghavan, and Schütze 2009, 26–30).

Removing Stopwords

In most text analysis methods, the importance of words in a given text differs greatly—not all are equally relevant for the analysis. To the contrary, removing non-selective function words ("do", "with", "until") from the text is even a way to improve functionality and efficiency of many approaches. So-called *stopwords* are generally the most common words across the document collection and can therefore be filtered based on their frequency. Ready-made *stopword lists* are also available for many languages.

Stemming

Another common preprocessing step is to remove the inflectional endings from words, so that "laugh" and "laughs" are trimmed to the same word stem. This can be an appropriate way to remove information that is only necessary within a given sentence or document. Stemming efficiently reduces complexity in a large dataset, but comes at a price in individual cases: as stemmers are based on language-specific rules, they do not necessarily normalize synonyms ("woods" and "forest") or homonyms (groups of words that share the same spelling but differ in meaning, such as "bank" as a financial institution and land alongside a river) correctly. If a stemmer acts too aggressively, it can furthermore be difficult to recognize the original meaning of overly truncated words.

Getting to Know the Data

Automated methods are especially useful when working with large datasets. While it is mostly not an option to look at every text in detail before the analysis, getting a basic understanding of the content of the collection is key to appropriately applying a text analysis method and to being able to interpret its outcome. To this means, simple frequency-based descriptions and visualizations are very effective. While some of the approaches presented in this section can also work as independent categories (e.g. readability parameters), they are included here as parts of a toolset to explore the context of a text collection when reading the documents is not an option. It is important to keep in mind that patterns found in a first exploratory step do not necessarily hold true in the following analyses; it is therefore recommended to carefully cross-validate before drawing conclusions. One goal of this step is to check for missing values or cases that have not yet been normalized. Especially when working with different sources, it can be difficult if not impossible to include all necessary preprocessing steps at the first attempt. Graphical visualizations such as a histogram for documents' text lengths are great to identify outliers and preprocessing mistakes.

Text statistics

Text statistics are key parameters to display the characteristics of a document collection. These shallow text features are easily calculated, but, like a document's fingerprint, can provide background information and even reveal document authorship

(Abbasi and Chen 2005). Lexical features such as word, sentence, and text length, for example, give indications on style, genre, and type of text, but can also show irregularities and problems within the dataset. Furthermore, they can be combined to form an indicator of text readability (DuBay 2004). As it is difficult for a computer to read and understand a text as it was intended by the author, complexity can be reduced by breaking it down to a list of words: the most frequent words, for example, can help to get an impression of the document's vocabulary. There are also several options to study keywords in context: instead of calculating the frequency of single words, the most frequent *n*-grams can show which two (bi-grams), three (tri-grams), or four words (four-grams) are most often jointly mentioned (so-called *collocations*). A *concordance* analysis is conceptually very similar, but requires a specific term as a starting point. For this term, surrounding text passages in all the documents are extracted to display the context in which it is mentioned. *Co-occurrence* analyses, on the other hand, do not require words to be mentioned in sequence; they are based on a co-occurrence matrix that denotes the number of times two words are mentioned in the same paragraph or document.

Visualizations

Next to text statistics, visualizations are a key to showcase patterns: basic text parameters can be plotted in order to get an overview of their dispersion across the document collection or over time. If metadata such as the date of the documents is available, the words with the highest frequency might be transferred into a word trend diagram to investigate changes in language over time. Even simple visualizations such as word clouds, a popular representation of word frequencies, can be helpful at this step.

Corpus Comparison

In order to explore a text collection, it is also worthwhile comparing the corpus against another one. The distinct features of the documents become apparent most easily when contrasted against those from another collection. While researchers are usually interested in the differences between the documents within a collection, this step aims to find common characteristics and derive knowledge about the data collection as a whole. Kilgarriff (2012) describes a simple yet efficient way to get to know a document collection by comparing a list of its top 100 keywords. Possible applications include comparing texts from different genres (commentary versus interview), types of text (tweets versus Facebook posts), sources (different countries or media outlets), or time periods (news articles before and after an election).

Automating the Analysis of Pre-defined Categories

When all necessary preprocessing steps have been conducted, researchers can finally turn to the actual analysis. In this section, we describe text analysis methods that are based on a pre-defined codebook; the main challenge therefore consists in the translation of the known categories into machine-readable tasks. While there are also other useful methods, we focus on three of the most common ones: *rule-based* methods, *dictionaries*, and *supervised machine learning*. Which one is best depends on the characteristics of the category and the task to be completed.

Rule-based Approach

Realizing a classification task with a *rule-based approach* is a very versatile option and commonly used for text extraction. As rules exploit recurring patterns, they are suitable for many variables that share a repetitive characteristic. To establish a rule set, researchers have to identify these patterns and translate them into machine-readable tasks. This can be thought of as creating a map for the computer that details starting point, junctions, distances, and destination—providing turn-by-turn instructions on how to navigate to the points of interest within a text. Both formal (retrieving the sixth word in the third line of every document) and textual properties (retrieving the words before every instance of "Obama") of a document can be helpful in this process and help to translate diverse interests of journalism research. Sjøvaag and Stavelin (2012), for example, use a *rule-based approach* in order to select and count metadata (publication date stamps, geographical location, news agency, and author) and Web-specific attributes (audio/video media players, flash games, polls, questionnaires, hyperlinks, and commentary sections) of online news. For each attribute, the authors set up a specific rule. Tailored to the given dataset and variables, rules are often domain- or even project-specific. For this reason, drafting them can be a trial-and-error process and might feel hacky, yet constitutes a valid option. There are also standards that can be applied without (much) adjustment. One of the classics in this section is the extraction of hyperlinks based on the source code of a website (which includes both the article text and the boilerplate content we discussed above): here, the HTML markup can be thought of as road signs within the text, guiding the Web browser to correctly display the content of a Web page. Every time there is a hyperlink, this is announced by the sign "href=", so that the Web browser can take the right turn to make the text clickable. Researchers who are interested in the hyperlinks within news articles can exploit this information by tracking all text parts that are preceded by the respective sign. Another popular application is the recognition of *named entities*, i.e. the names of persons, organizations, and geographic locations, within texts. As rules are, in this case, based on the sentence structure within a given text, they are language-specific and not universally applicable.

To allow for more complicated variables that include multiple conditions, the retrieved information can also be used as an input for *decision trees*: given an arbitrary category that aims to identify documents that include both a hyperlink to an official US government website and the name "Obama", a decision tree with four possible outcomes can be constructed. The classification is then executed based on a combination of the above-mentioned text extraction tasks and the specified decision tree, and expressed as a dichotomous variable (for more information on decision trees, see Manning and Schütze 1999, 578).

In practice, the key to specify rules are *regular expressions*: as a part of many everyday applications (e.g. search engines, database queries) and programming languages (e.g. Python, Java), regular expressions are the basis to efficiently specify relevant text parts with a general pattern notation (Friedl 2006). Due to the universal nature of regular expressions, this approach is suitable for many categories that require text extraction of some sort. Depending on the level of standardization within the documents and the specifics of the task, applicability and preparation time can vary immensely.

Dictionaries

While *rule-based approaches* create a machine-readable map to the desired information within a text collection, *dictionaries* explicitly state which keywords to look for. For the automated classification, categories are described by lists of indicators that are then searched within the documents. When a text contains the terms "Merkel", "Obama", and "Jinping", for example, it is reasonable to assume that it is about politics. *Sentiment analyses* are a prominent example for this case (Pang and Lee 2008): based on a dictionary, the sentiment within a given document is evaluated by calculating the ratio of terms that are listed to indicate a positive versus a negative tone within the text.

Ready-made lists are available in some cases, such as for sentiment analyses. It is important to consider, however, that lists are often domain-specific and might not be applicable to the document collection at hand: Loughran and McDonald (2011) show that the prominent Harvard sentiment dictionary yields incorrect results when applied to another domain, such as financial texts. Almost three-quarters of the terms automatically classified as negative do not have this connotation in the financial context, but refer to company operations ("tax", "loss", "expense") or industry segments ("mine", "cancer", "tire"). For this reason, researchers have to be careful with external dictionaries or need extensive domain-specific knowledge to either adapt the dictionary or set up a new one by hand. The time and effort it takes to craft a reliable dictionary must not be underestimated. When the task is suitable, however, it is a computationally simple and conceptually straightforward solution to automate both formal and content-related categories.

Supervised Machine Learning

Supervised machine learning is a way to teach computers how to build a dictionary themselves. In this approach, documents are assigned to pre-defined categories based on labeled training data. In contrast to *rule-based approaches* and *dictionaries*, researchers do not have to specify the classification task themselves, but "teach" the computer by manually assigning some of the documents to the categories. The idea behind this is simple: in a first step, human coders conduct a manual content analysis by categorizing a random sample of the document collection based on a pre-defined codebook. In a second step, a learning classifier uses the category assignments (*classes*) in the training data to "learn" about the classification by deriving rules about the relationship between text features and categories. Finally, these rules are applied to label the remaining test set.

Of course, the underlying model is more complex and depends on the classifier that is used. Intensive research on classifier effectiveness has produced a large body of literature and a fair number of classifiers to choose from, such as Naïve Bayes, Support Vector Machines, Neural Networks, and Random Forests—each with different qualities and assumptions about the dataset (see Sebastiani 2002). They can also be combined in an *ensemble learning* approach (Dieterich 2000) to improve the classification outcome.

In recent years, supervised machine learning techniques have been successfully applied to several domains of journalism research. In order to study issue attention and legislative trends, Hillard, Purpura, and Wilkerson (2008) conducted a supervised topic analysis of bill titles introduced in the US Congress, concluding that the combination of several algorithms increases both analysis accuracy and researchers' confidence. Also using an *ensemble learning* approach, Burscher, Vliegenthart, and de Vreese (2015) conducted several experiments to evaluate the automated coding of frames in Dutch newspaper articles. With high levels of observed classification performance, the authors recommend supervised learning as a promising analysis strategy for framing research. In another empirical evaluation, Scharkow (2013) applied a learning classifier to a content analysis of news values in German news articles. The author concludes that supervised classification is a viable option for the social sciences, but does not work well for all categories.

A main advantage of *supervised machine learning* is that researchers only have to provide explicit examples, but do not have to specify the rules themselves. This is typically done by conducting a manual content analysis with a part of the original dataset, but training data can also come from an external dataset that has already been annotated by a third party: Flaounas et al. (2013) base their analysis of 2.5 million news articles on the Reuters and *New York Times* corpora, two well-known datasets in natural language processing that come, among others, with manual annotations for a topic category.

The success of this approach depends on the quality and quantity of the training set. First, the reliability of the manual content analysis has to be guaranteed to make sure the learning classifier is not applied to a flawed training set. Second, it is important to pass a sufficient number of examples to the learning classifier for every category. This number might vary, however, depending on the number of categories and specifics of the dataset.

Categorizing Automatically

In the previous section, we presented three approaches where categories are known before the analysis, but require some sort of translation into machine-readable tasks to be suitable for an automated analysis. When categories are unknown and there is little knowledge about the document collection, fully automated methods are a way to systematically explore its content or assist in defining the categories.

Document Clustering

While the methods outlined above allow researchers to automate the classification of a broad range of possible categories, the purpose of document clustering is more narrow: based on a cluster analysis, this approach is designed to reveal groups of documents with similar topics. Grimmer and King (2011), for example, perform a document clustering on US Senator Frank Lautenbach's press releases and find that they fulfill four basic functions: credit claiming, position taking, advertising, and partisan taunting. The authors apply the same method to George W. Bush's 2002 State of the Union Address to thematically group the then President's statements. As a bag-of-words approach, a term's syntactic properties and position within the article are not considered; the procedure is solely based on similarities between the documents' vocabularies, leaving out word order and syntax. Topics are then, in their most basic sense, simply defined as groups of documents with a similar term structure (Wartena and Brussee 2008).

The foundation for this procedure is the *Vector Space Model*: each document is represented as a vector in an n-dimensional space, where n is the total number of unique terms in all documents. As each dimension corresponds to one of the unique terms, a vector component's magnitude is defined by the number of times the respective term occurs within the given document. The basis for this is the so-called document–term matrix, which reports the frequencies of all n terms for each document. The Vector Space Model allows calculation of the semantic similarity between two documents based on their spatial proximity within the high-dimensional space (for more information, see Manning et al. 2009, 110).

To find groups of documents with a similar theme, several clustering algorithms can be used. Which one is best depends on the size of the document collection and researchers' interest: standard *k-means* is very popular due to its scalability, but requires researchers to define the desired number of clusters before the analysis. Hierarchical agglomerative clustering techniques, on the other hand, allow researchers to flexibly choose the best cluster solution after the analysis, but the respective algorithms are not efficient for large datasets. Combining the "best of both worlds", Steinbach, Karypis, and Kumar (2000) recommend the *bisecting k-means* algorithm, a divisive clustering algorithm with high performance efficiency, in a systematic evaluation of clustering techniques.

Even more than in a manual content analysis, a main part of the work begins after the analysis: while documents in the same clusters share a common ground based on their similar use of vocabulary, it is up to the researcher to make meaning of the results. To make the interpretation of the topic clusters easier, the most relevant words within each cluster are typically presented as cluster labels in the analysis output.

Topic Models

In recent years, *topic models* such as LDA have emerged as powerful tools to thematically organize content in large archives of digital texts (Blei and Lafferty 2009). Following the same logic as *document clustering*, they aim to uncover thematic patterns in document collections: in a fully automated classification, categories are estimated within the process, with documents simultaneously being assigned to these categories (Grimmer and Stewart 2013). The potential of *topic models* to work quickly through otherwise unstructured document collections offers new possibilities for social scientists: Quinn et al. (2010), for example, automatically examine the agenda of the US senate between 1997 and 2004 by fitting a topic model to more than 100,000 speeches. This way, they show how political attention towards the inferred topics such as defense or abortion changes over time. Roberts et al. (2014) present a way to apply *structural topic models* to open-ended survey responses, making an otherwise time-consuming task both easier and more revealing.

Introduced by Blei, Ng, and Jordan in 2003, topic models infer the hidden semantic structure in a collection of documents based on a hierarchical Bayesian analysis (Blei and Lafferty 2009). As latent variables, topics only become apparent in similar patterns of words used across documents. *Topic models* all refer to the idea of an imaginary generative process, in which the distribution of topics in a document and the distribution of words in a topic are drawn from a probability distribution. By reversing this stochastic procedure, they infer the hidden structure based on the resulting high co-occurrence of groups of words. In this process, every word in every document of the collection is allocated to one of the topics, so that a document is represented as a mix of topics (or, algebraically, a topic weight vector). Accordingly, topics are formally defined as "distribution[s] over a fixed vocabulary" (Blei 2012, 78) that report the probability of each word within that topic.

In contrast to *document clustering*, LDA realistically models multiple topics per document and provides a topic model that can also be generalized to new documents. Some of the assumptions, however, such as not taking account of word and document order, are unrealistic and have been relaxed and extended in several new approaches: Rosen-Zvi et al. (2004) extend LDA to also include authorship information, so that personal writing style is considered as a feature in the analysis. To be able to account for word order, Wallach (2006) developed a *topic model* that incorporates the assumption that, in the generative process, words are drawn conditionally on the previous word. *Hidden topic Markov models* also consider word order by assuming that words in the same sentence have the same topic. In addition, consecutive sentences are more likely to have the same topic (Gruber, Rosen-Zvi, and Weiss 2007). With the introduction of *dynamic topic models*, Blei and Lafferty (2006) furthermore account for the fact that topics change over time and enable researchers to study the evolution of topics within a document collection. Finally, the *Bayesian nonparametric topic model* estimates the number of topics within the analysis (in LDA, this has to be specified *a priori*) and is able to identify new topics when applied to additional documents (Blei 2012). As it is (so far) not possible to include all extensions into one comprehensive topic model, researchers have to decide which feature is most important for their analysis when choosing the appropriate approach.

Recommendations and Discussion

In this article, we have presented a roadmap of text analysis methods that assist researchers to document collections that are too large to read. The approaches come with different assumptions, costs, and benefits: the main difference obviously lies in the fact that categories are known for *rule-based* approaches, *dictionaries*, and *supervised learning*, while *document clustering* and *topic models* are designed for exploration without prior knowledge. This translates into varying analysis costs: the first three are defined by high pre-analysis costs, as categories have to be conceptualized in hours of tedious work. While the latter have low costs at the first stage of the research process, the amount of time it takes to interpret the results is disproportionately higher: post-analysis costs make up a substantial part of the research process for *document clustering* and *topic models*, due to the fact that the output is mostly not self-explaining and requires careful interpretation by a knowledgeable researcher. The choice of approach depends on the specifics of the document collection and, most importantly, the research interest. Benefits are often highest when approaches are combined: fully automated methods can also be used to get to know the dataset when preparing for a (manual) task that works with known categories. Before running a dictionary-based approach on a dataset, a simple co-occurrence analysis might also help to improve the dictionary by revealing search terms that researchers might have missed, and search terms that have to be excluded because they produce too many false-positives.

All methods that we presented are characterized by low costs for the analysis of large datasets: both by automating pre-existing categories as well as by categorizing automatically, researchers can save enormous amounts of time and effort when working with large datasets. The benefits of increased efficiency, reliability, and transparency, that are assets of the automated analysis, however, must not delude us that there are not also clear limitations: computers do not understand texts the way human coders can, and are only as good as the algorithms they perform. Furthermore, the application of methods and tools outlined in this article is not a trivial task. Implementing methods that originated in disciplines with significant differences to the social sciences therefore requires careful preparation. A solid understanding of the underlying statistical processes is needed to be able to assess how they will work on a given dataset and how their results can be interpreted. We need to be careful not to rely blindly on the power of algorithms to achieve large sample sizes—welcoming their benefits, but keeping their limitations in mind (for a discussion of limitations, see Mahrt and Scharkow 2013; Zamith and Louis 2015).

However, with open-source toolsets like Voyant Tools (voyant-tools.org) and vivid user communities for R and Python, there are many resources available for social scientists who aim to include automated text analysis methods into their projects. Using sophisticated tools and resources from disciplines such as computer science and computational linguistics, journalism scholars can gain insight into the constant information flow and make big data a regular feature in the scientific debate. As this innovative research area is constantly evolving, interdisciplinary collaborations are another great way to combine respective strengths and realize ambitious projects.

DISCLOSURE STATEMENT

No potential conflict of interest was reported by the authors.

REFERENCES

Abbasi, Ahmed, and Hsinchun Chen. 2005. "Applying Authorship Analysis to Extremist Group Web Forum Messages." *Intelligent Systems* 20 (5): 67–75.

Blei, David, and John Lafferty. 2006. "Dynamic Topic Models." In *Proceedings of the 23rd International Conference on Machine Learning*, edited by William Cohen and Andrew Moore, 113–120. New York, NY: ACM.

Blei, David, and John Lafferty. 2009. "Topic Models." In *Text Mining: Classification, Clustering, and Applications*, edited by A. N. Srivastava and M. Sahami, 71–92. London: Chapman & Hall/CRC Press.

Blei, David M., Andrew Y. Ng and Jordan Michael I.. 2003. "Latent Dirichlet Allocation." *Journal of Machine Learning Research* 3: 993–1022.

Blei, David M.. 2012. "Probabilistic Topic Models." *Communications of the ACM* 55 (4): 77–84.

Burscher, Björn, Vliegenthart Rens, and de Vreese Claes H. 2015. "Using Supervised Machine Learning to Code Policy Issues: Can Classifiers Generalize across Contexts?" *The Annals of the American Academy of Political and Social Science* 659 (1): 122–131.

Dietterich, Thomas G. 2000. "Ensemble Methods in Machine Learning." In *Lecture Notes in Computer Science 1857: Multiple Classifier Systems*, edited by Josef Kittler and Fabio Roll, 1–15. Berlin: Springer.

DuBay, William H. 2004. *The Principles of Readability*. Costa Mesa, CA: Impact Information.

Friedl, Jeffrey E. F. 2006. *Mastering Regular Expressions*. Sebastopol, CA: O'Reilly.

Flaounas, Ilias, Omar Ali, Thomas Lansdall-Welfare, Tijl De Bie, Nick Mosdell, Justin Lewis, and Nello Cristianini. 2013. "Research Methods in the Age of Digital Journalism: Massive-Scale Automated Analysis of News-Content—Topics, Style and Gender." *Digital Journalism* 1 (1): 102–116.

Greer, Jennifer D., and Yan Yan. 2011. "Newspapers Connect with Readers through Multiple Digital Tools." *Newspaper Research Journal* 32 (4): 83–97.

Grimmer, Justin, and Gary King. 2011. "General Purpose Computer-Assisted Clustering and Conceptualization." *Proceedings of the National Academy of Sciences of the United States of America* 108 (7): 2643–2650.

Grimmer, Justin, and Brandon M. Stewart. 2013. "Text as Data: The Promise and Pitfalls of Automatic Content Analysis Methods for Political Texts." *Political Analysis* 21 (3): 267–297.

Gruber, Amit, Michal Rosen-Zvi, and Yair Weiss. 2007. "Hidden Topic Markov Models." *Proceedings of the 11th International Conference on Artificial Intelligence and Statistics* 163–170.

Hillard, Dustin, Stephen Purpura, and John Wilkerson. 2008. "Computer-Assisted Topic Classification for Mixed-Methods Social Science Research." *Journal of Information Technology & Politics* 4 (4): 31–46.

Kilgarriff, Adam. 2012. "'Getting to Know Your Corpus'. in Text, Speech and Dialogue." *Lecture Notes in Computer Science* 7499: 3–15.

Kohlschütter, Christian, Nejdl Wolfgang, and Fankhauser Peter. 2010. "Boilerplate Detection using Shallow Text Features." In *Proceedings of the third ACM international conference on Web Search and Data Mining*, 441–450. New York, NY: ACM.

LaBerge, David, and S. Jay Samuels. 1974. "Toward a Theory of Automatic Information Processing in Reading." *Cognitive Psychology* 6 (2): 293–323.

Loughran, Tim, and Bill McDonald. 2011. "When is a Liability Not a Liability? Textual Analysis, Dictionaries, and 10-Ks." *The Journal of Finance* 66: 35–65

Mahrt, Merja, and Michael Scharkow. 2013. "The Value of Big Data in Digital Media Research." *Journal of Broadcasting & Electronic Media* 57 (1): 20–33.

Manning, Christopher D., Raghavan, Prabhakar, and Schütze, Hinrich. 2009. *Introduction to information retrieval*. Cambridge: Cambridge University Press.

Quinn, Kevin M., Monrow, Burt L., Colaresi, Michael, Crespin, Michael H., and Radev Dragomir R. 2010. "How to Analyze Political Attention with Minimal Assumptions and Costs." *American Journal of Political Science* 54 (1): 209–228.

Pang, Bo, and Lillian Lee. 2008. "Opinion Mining and Sentiment Analysis." *Foundations and Trends in Information Retrieval* 2 (1–2): 91–231.

Roberts, Margaret E., M. Brandon, Dustin Tingley, Christopher Lucas, Jetson Leder-Luis, Shana Kushner Gadarian, Bethany Albertson, and David G. Rand. 2014. "Structural Topic Models for Open-Ended Survey Responses." *American Journal of Political Science* 58 (4): 1064–1082.

Rosen-Zvi, Michal, Thomas Griffiths, Mark Steyvers, and Padhraic Smyth. 2004. "The Authorship-Topic Model for Authors and Documents." In *Proceedings of the 20th Conference on Uncertainty in Artificial Intelligence*, edited by Max Chickeringand Joseph Halpern, 487–494. Arlington: AUAI Press.

Scharkow, Michael. 2013. "Thematic Content Analysis Using Supervised Machine Learning: An Empirical Evaluation Using German Online News." *Quality and Quantity* 47 (2): 761–773.

Sebastiani, Fabrizio. 2002. "Machine Learning in Automated Text Categorization." *ACM Computing Surveys* 34 (1): 1–47.

Sjøvaag, Helle, & Stavelin, Eirik. 2012. "Web media and the quantitative content analysis: Methodological challenges in measuring online news content." *Convergence: The International Journal of Research into New Media Technologies* 18 (2): 215–229.

Michael, Steinbach, Karypis George, and Vipin Kumar. 2000. "A Comparison of Document Clustering Techniques." *KDD Workshop on Text Mining* 400 (1): 525–526.

Wallach, Hanna. 2006. "Topic Models: Beyond Bag-of-Words." In *Proceedings of the 23rd International Conference on Machine Learning*, edited by William Cohen, and Andrew Moore, 977–984. New York, NY: ACM.

Wartena, Christian, and Rogier Brussee. 2008. "Topic Detection by Clustering Keywords." In *Nineteenth International Workshop on Database and Expert Systems Application*, edited by A. Min, Tjoa , and Richard R. Wagner, 54–58. Los Alamitos, CA: IEEE.

Witten, Ian H., Frank Eibe, and Mark A. Hall. 2011. *Data Mining: Practical Machine Learning Tools and Techniques*. Burlington, MA: Morgan Kaufmann Publishers.

Zamith, Rodrigo, and Seth Louis. 2015. "Content Analysis and the Algorithmic Coder: What Computational Social Science Means for Traditional Modes of Media Analysis." *The ANNALS of the American Academy of Political and Social Science* 659 (1): 307–318.

QUANTITATIVE ANALYSIS OF LARGE AMOUNTS OF JOURNALISTIC TEXTS USING TOPIC MODELLING

Carina Jacobi, Wouter van Atteveldt and Kasper Welbers

The huge collections of news content which have become available through digital technologies both enable and warrant scientific inquiry, challenging journalism scholars to analyse unprecedented amounts of texts. We propose Latent Dirichlet Allocation (LDA) topic modelling as a tool to face this challenge. LDA is a cutting edge technique for content analysis, designed to automatically organize large archives of documents based on latent topics, measured as patterns of word (co-)occurrence. We explain how this technique works, how different choices by the researcher affect the results and how the results can be meaningfully interpreted. To demonstrate its usefulness for journalism research, we conducted a case study of the New York Times *coverage of nuclear technology from 1945 to the present, partially replicating a study by Gamson and Modigliani. This shows that LDA is a useful tool for analysing trends and patterns in news content in large digital news archives relatively quickly.*

Introduction: Latent Dirichlet Allocation, Topics and Issues

The shift of news media towards online publication and archiving provides journalism scholars with new opportunities for studying journalism. At the same time, understanding the complicated dynamics of this contemporary media landscape requires an ever-larger scale of analysis, with more outlets and more content per outlet. In this article, we show how topic modelling, a relatively new method developed in the computational linguistics field, can help analyse large amounts of text without requiring manual coding, thus reducing the time and costs of such projects. For a general overview of the available methods and pitfalls for topic models, see Grimmer and Stewart (2013). In this paper, we focus on one type of topic model, Latent Dirichlet Allocation (LDA; Blei, Ng, and Jordan 2003), and demonstrate its use for journalism research. Even though topic modelling is a promising method for text analysis, with the seminal paper in computational linguistics (Blei, Ng, and Jordan 2003) published around a decade ago, it is just starting to be used in the social sciences. Political scientists, who, like journalism researchers, have both the challenge and the opportunity of newly available online archives of textual data (such as political speeches, legislative documents and social media) have started to use topic models to automatically classify these documents.

Notably, Quinn et al. (2010) classify speeches in the US Senate into topics using topic modelling. Lucas et al. (2015) apply topic modelling to different types of documents such as fatwas and social media posts in order to facilitate comparison between countries. Following such studies, we explore whether topic modelling can be used to classify journalistic documents into categories that are meaningful to journalism researchers.

LDA, like other topic modelling algorithms, is an unsupervised technique that automatically creates topics based on patterns of (co-)occurrence of words in the documents that are analysed. Journalistic texts are thus "coded automatically" for topics, although it is up to the researcher to interpret the results of the model and to set up the analysis in such a way that the results are useful for the study at hand. Thus, the usefulness of the technique for studying journalism crucially depends on the correspondence between topics and the constructs of theoretical interest. The goal of this article is to introduce LDA to journalism scholars and to provide a practical guide in applying the technique to their own research. Concretely, we will deal with three broad topics:

- *What is topic modelling?* The first part of this article will give a brief and mostly non-technical description of LDA.
- *How to set up an LDA topic model*: Secondly, we will describe the different parameters of the LDA topic model, and discuss issues of validity.
- *Theoretical interpretation*: The last and most important part of the article discusses how LDA topic models relate to theoretical constructs of interest to journalism researchers, especially issues and frames. Using the example of the news discourse on nuclear technology from 1945 to now, we show how LDA topics mostly correspond to the important issues in this discourse, comparing our results to the earlier study by Gamson and Modigliani (1989).

What is Topic Modelling?

Topic models are computer algorithms that identify latent patterns of word occurrence using the distribution of words in a collection of documents. The output is a set of *topics* consisting of clusters of words that co-occur in these documents according to certain patterns. In an LDA model, each document may contain multiple topics. Each of the topics has an internal consistency—the words in that topic often occur together in the documents, and/or do not appear much outside that topic. The researcher determines what this consistency refers to, and thus how the topic can be interpreted (Chang et al. 2009). It is this interpretability that determines whether topic models in general, and LDA specifically, are of use to social scientists.

In the case of journalism research, the collection of topics inferred by the model would ideally resemble a categorization of issues or frames based on substantive theory, for example the issue list used by the Comparative Agendas Project that uses categories such as Macro-economics, Foreign Affairs and Crime to categorize legislative and journalistic texts (Jones and Baumgartner 2005). However, topics are created by the LDA algorithm based on patterns of word co-occurrence in documents, which do not necessarily match theoretical concepts. It seems plausible to equate a topic with the theoretical concept "issue" or "theme", but topics could potentially also represent writing or speaking styles (e.g. words referring to emotions), events (e.g. a natural disaster) or frames (e.g. immigrants framed as criminals), which, at least theoretically, are also formed through co-occurrence patterns of specific words. For example, in the study of Quinn et al. (2010) of topics in Congressional Record speeches, words such as violence, drug trafficking, police and prison were interpreted as being the topic *Law and Crime I: Violence/Drugs*. Another topic, *Abortion*, contained words such as baby, abortion, procedure and life (Quinn et al. 2010, 217). This study thus interprets topics as issues, whereas DiMaggio, Nag, and Blei (2013, 590–591) refer to "voices" or "frames" when interpreting different topics. However, what exactly topics represent, and if they represent different concepts given different input parameters in the model, is ultimately an empirical question.

To illustrate what topics look like and the interpretation challenges they present, consider the example newspaper article in Figure 1. This article, which appeared after the Chernobyl disaster, criticized the Soviet Union for suppressing news about the event. In the text, each word is highlighted to indicate which topic it was drawn from. These topics were found automatically by the algorithm, but we interpreted and named the topics in a way similar to how one would interpret a factor analysis outcome.[1]

As would be expected given the content of the article, many words are drawn from a topic that we interpret as the *Nuclear Accidents* topic, indicated in dark grey with white letters. This topic includes words such as "Chernobyl", "disaster" and "radiation", but interestingly also contains the words "last Friday", probably due to the episodic nature of accident reporting. The other main topic, *Cold War*, is indicated in medium grey and contains words such as "Soviet Union" and "Gorbachev" but also "confidence" and "pledge". Finally, a number of terms such as "secrecy" and "peaceful use" of "energy" are drawn from the Nuclear Research topic, and two words are drawn from other topics.

This example highlights a number of interesting points about LDA. First, this document is split between two main topics, *Cold War* and *Nuclear Accidents*. In a coding scheme forced to have a single topic per document, it would be very difficult to choose the "dominant" topic for this article, so in our opinion this accurately reflects the nature of the article. Second, you can see that not all words are included in the analysis: most of the words in the article are not used by the algorithm (the text without highlighting), either because they are non-substantive words such as determiners or prepositions ("the" or "it"), which we excluded, or because they are too rare ("Elbe", "perish") or too common ("have" but in this context also "nuclear", since that was used

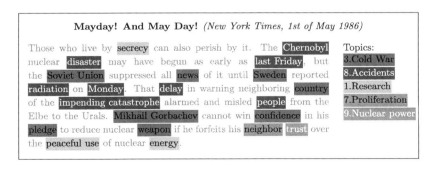

FIGURE 1
Example article with words from different topics highlighted in the text

to select the articles). Finally, it should be remembered that no *a priori* coding scheme was used by the computer, so the topics in this document were found completely automatically. The fact that the resulting topics (such as *Cold War* and *Nuclear Accidents*) make sense substantively and match the way we would define the subject or topic of articles—such as the example here—shows that to some extent our notion of "topic" matches the latent classes or co-occurrence patterns identified by the LDA algorithm.

Topics such as *Cold War* and *Proliferation* can be interpreted as issues, but also as ways of framing nuclear weapons. In such cases, a particular perspective on an issue can be signified by specific keywords, which can be seen as framing devices (Matthes and Kohring 2008). In general, if framing devices correspond to specific (latent) patterns of vocabulary use, LDA can capture these classes in specific topics, and as such LDA results can also include the frames used in a corpus of texts.

How to Set Up an LDA Topic Model

Before exploring a case study where we interpret LDA topics, we will explain how to perform an analysis using this technique. As previously mentioned, LDA processes a collection of documents and clusters the words in these documents into topics in an unsupervised way. As such, it is important to start by considering which documents should be included, and to make sure these documents consist only of the content of newspaper articles—other textual information such as author name or reader comments should be removed.

We will discuss the steps we took when conducting the analysis for our case study below. Our data consisted of 51,528 news stories (headline and lead) from the *New York Times* that mentioned nuclear power, published between 1945 and 2013. We retrieved all news stories from the *New York Times* online archive (http://developer.nytimes.com) that contained the search terms "nuclear", "atom" or "atomic" in the headline or lead.

Preprocessing: Tokenization and Lemmatization

A topic model does not analyse documents directly, but uses a so-called document–term matrix based on these documents. This matrix lists the frequency for each term (word) in each document. The first step in creating this matrix is tokenization, which means splitting the text into a list of words. Although this can be done by splitting on white space and punctuation, there are good word boundary detection tools that recognize acronyms, contractions, etc.

It is often better to begin by reducing the size of the matrix by preprocessing and feature selection, reducing computing time and improving results. An important step in preprocessing is stemming or lemmatizing. Stemming is a simple technique where the ending of words is "chopped off", leaving the stem. For example, using the frequently used Porter stemming algorithm, "weaknesses" becomes "weak", and both "failures" and "failure" become "failur". This technique does not handle irregular conjugations, for example "are" and "were" have different stems. A more powerful (and computationally demanding) technique is lemmatizing. Lemmatizing reduces all words to their "lemma" using a lexicon in combination with regular conjugation rules. Thus, lemmatization reduces both "is" and "were" to their lemma (to) "be". For English, stemming is often sufficient, but for more richly inflected languages such as German or Dutch, lemmatization tends to give better results (Haselmayer and Jenny 2014).

Feature Selection

The next step is feature selection. A moderately large corpus can typically contain more than 100,000 unique words, with most of these words occurring in only a few documents. Applying an LDA model on all words in a corpus is both computationally expensive and not very useful, as most words have distribution patterns that do not contribute to meaningful topics. For example, some words are too frequent to be informative—words like "the" and "have" generally occur in every document regardless of topic. A useful technique to filter out words that are too rare or too common is to use *tf-idf* (term frequency–inverse document frequency), which assigns a low score to words that are either very rare or very frequent. Another option is to have a minimal frequency cut-off to filter out the rare words and use a list of common stop words (and/or cap the inverse document frequency) to filter out overly common words.

Lemmatization software is often combined with POS-tagging. POS (part of speech) tags indicate the type of word, e.g. verb, noun or preposition. For topic modelling, it is often best to only use specific parts of speech, especially nouns, proper nouns and, depending on the task and corpus, adjectives and verbs. This automatically filters out the most common stop words, which tend to be determiners or prepositions (with the exception of common verbs like "to be" and "to have").

For the analysis presented here, we used the lemmatizer and POS-tagger from Stanford's corenlp suite (De Marneffe, MacCartney, and Manning 2006), and selected all nouns, verbs, adjectives and proper nouns. We filtered out all terms with a frequency of less than 20 and which occurred in more than 25 per cent of documents, and we removed all terms that contained a number or non-alphanumeric characters, yielding a total vocabulary of 8493 terms.

Choosing Parameters

After creating a sufficiently small and relevant document–term matrix on which to run the model, there are some more choices the researcher needs to make before running the model. Although one of the main advantages of a topic model is that no *a priori* coding schemes need to be supplied, there are certain parameters that need to be set. In particular, the number of topics (K) needs to be specified, which indicates into how many topics the LDA model should classify the words in the documents. There is no default or simple rule of thumb for this parameter. The trade-off is comparable to factor analysis: the goal is to describe the data with fewer dimensions (topics) than are actually present, but with enough dimensions so that as little relevant information as possible is lost. We first discuss and use the perplexity measure, which is a commonly used computational indication for the correct amount of topics (Blei, Ng, and Jordan 2003). However, we stress that this should be only used to make an initial selection of models with an acceptable amount of information loss, and that interpretability of topics is a more important criterion for social science purposes.

A second parameter is the *alpha* hyperparameter, which affects how many topics a document can contain.[2] A common default value for the alpha is 50 divided by the number of topics. Substantively, a lower alpha leads to a higher concentration of topic distributions within documents, meaning that documents score high on a few topics rather than low on many. Accordingly, if the goal is to assign one or a few topics per document then it makes sense to use a low alpha (Haselmayer and Marcelo 2014).

Perplexity

From a computational perspective, a good indication of the right number of topics is that number with which the model best predicts the data. This is comparable to goodness-of-fit measures for statistical models.[3] For topic models such as LDA, a commonly used indicator is perplexity, where a lower perplexity indicates a better prediction (Blei, Ng, and Jordan 2003). To calculate the perplexity, we first train an LDA model on a portion of the data. Then, the model is evaluated using the held-out data. This routine is repeated for models with different numbers of topics, so that it becomes clear which amount leads to the lowest perplexity.

Figure 2 shows the perplexity of different models for our data. We trained the LDA models using 30,000 of the 48,604 documents, and then calculated the perplexity of each model over the remaining 18,604 documents. We varied the number of topics

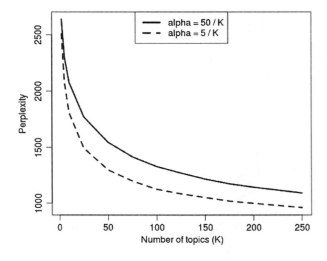

FIGURE 2
Perplexity of LDA models with different numbers of topics and alpha
Notes: The line graph shows how perplexity decreases (and model fit thus increases) as the number of topics increases. The number of topics that corresponds to a great change in the direction of the line graph is a good number to use for fitting a first model. For example, $K = 25$ for our model with alpha = 50/K.

used: 2, 5, 10, 25, and then on to 250 in steps of 25. The results show that perplexity decreases as the number of topics increases, implying that a model with more topics is better at predicting the held-out data. At around 25 and 50 topics, the decrease in perplexity for additional topics becomes notably less. This is one way to interpret the right number of topics, similar to the interpretation of the elbow in the scree plot of a factor analysis. The other way is to look at the number of topics with the lowest perplexity. We can see that this point will be somewhere beyond 250.

However, having the "right" number of topics in a mathematical sense does not say anything about the interpretability of the topics produced. In fact, mathematical goodness-of-fit measures and human interpretation may lead to contradicting conclusions on the best number of topics, given that especially with a high number of topics, the computer algorithm may find nuances that are not semantically meaningful to humans (Chang et al. 2009). Also, as we use topics to answer substantive questions about the documents we study, it is important that the topics that result from the analysis contribute towards answering these questions, instead of providing the best prediction of the data. For the analysis presented in this article, we thus looked both at perplexity and interpretability when deciding on the number of topics to use. Judging from the perplexity, a good choice is probably between 25 and 50 topics. However, to facilitate comparing our results with Gamson and Modigliani (1989), we will first use a simpler model with $K = 10$ topics, and then show the differences between this model and a model with $K = 25$ topics.

Alpha

Regarding the alpha hyper-parameter, since the data used for our analysis cover a long history of textual data concerning an issue that involves various events and viewpoints, it makes sense to define several clearly distinguishable topics. In addition to better scores for the lower alpha, this is a substantive argument for us to use the lower alpha of five divided by K instead of the default.

Tool Support for LDA

The easiest way to get started with LDA is through the open-source statistical package R.[4] Although specialized software for topic models is available, such as MALLET (McCallum 2002) or the Stanford Topic Modeling Toolbox (Ramage et al. 2009), an advantage of using R is that it is a statistical package that many social scientists already use for other analyses. However, LDA works the same no matter the software used to run the model. The tm package in R can automatically generate the document–term matrix from texts and includes options for stemming and feature selection (Meyer, Hornik, and Feinerer 2008). The topicmodels package can directly fit an LDA model from the document–term matrix object created by tm. For more sophisticated preprocessing, we use the Stanford corenlp suite (De Marneffe, MacCartney, and Manning 2006), which contains a collection of modules for grammatical analysis. For our case study, we uploaded our documents in the Web-based content analysis toolkit AmCAT.[5] For the preprocessing and the analysis itself, we used the statistical computing environment R, that can connect to AmCAT directly to retrieve the documents there.[6] AmCAT uses the xtas extensible text annotation suite to automatically perform the preprocessing in a scalable manner (De Rooij, Vishneuski, and De Rijke 2012).[7]

Nuclear Topics: 1945 to Now

In order to demonstrate the use of LDA to explore the topics in a given set of documents, and show the change in these topics over time, we have performed LDA on *New York Times* articles dealing with nuclear technology. The famous study by Gamson and Modigliani (1989) shows how the framing of the issue "nuclear power" in the news changed over time since 1945. We were interested to see whether the topics found by performing an LDA over newspaper articles from this period show similar changes over time. Additionally, we extended the research period to 2013, to include more recent coverage of nuclear technology.

The question is thus whether the change in culture surrounding nuclear issues found by Gamson and Modigliani is expressed in a change in word use over time that is captured by LDA. Gamson and Modigliani (1989) identified seven "packages" or frames in newspaper and television coverage of nuclear energy between 1945 and 1989: *Progress*, *Energy Independence*, *Devil's Bargain*, *Runaway*, *Public Accountability*, *Not Cost Effective* and *Soft Paths* (Gamson and Modigliani 1989, 24–25). If we compare the outcome of an LDA analysis with the results of Gamson and Modigliani's study, to what extent do we find similar results? Note that for a number of reasons we do not expect perfect correspondence between the LDA topics and Gamson and Modigliani's packages, even if we disregard the difference between manual and automatic analysis. First, these packages were identified by examining not only the text of news stories, but also images and cartoons, with a focus on editorial content, whereas our analysis is performed on the lead paragraphs of news stories only. Second, whereas Gamson and Modigliani only analyse nuclear power, our investigation deals with the whole coverage of nuclear technology, including nuclear weapons. Finally, our investigation covers the post-Cold War period as well, while Gamson and Modigliani of course only analyse the discourse until the 1980s. Nonetheless, it is interesting to compare our findings to theirs since it shows to what extent the results of an automatic topic modelling approach compare to those of a well-known and very thorough manual analysis.

As discussed above, for reasons of comparability to Gamson and Modigliani's seven packages, we will first focus on an analysis using 10 topics. Table 1 shows the topics that resulted from this analysis, including our interpretation and the 10 words that represent a topic most strongly. To facilitate interpretation we also made a topic browser,[8] which is a tool to interactively explore the results of a topic model (Gardner et al. 2010). Our topic browser features two extra pieces of information in addition to top words. One is the top documents assigned to a topic in which the topic words are highlighted. The other is a semantic network, or semantic map, which visualizes the co-occurrence of top words, thus showing topic coherence and facilitating interpretation. For our discussion, we categorized the topics into: (1) topics that show a pattern in their use over time; (2) topics that are more or less continuously present; and (3) three topics that turned out to be irrelevant for our case study.

TABLE 1
LDA results on US nuclear discourse, 10 topics

Topic	Interpretation	Most representative words
Topics with temporal patterns		
1	Research	atomic, Energy, WASHINGTON, scientist, energy, bomb, Commission, United, research, weapon
3	Cold War	United, States, Union, Soviet, soviet, weapon, arm, missile, President, treaty
7	Proliferation	Iran, United, North, Korea, program, weapon, States, official, country, China
8	Accidents/ Danger	plant, power, reactor, Island, Nuclear, accident, Commission, official, waste, safety
Continuous topics		
5	Weapons	test, submarine, Japan, first, Navy, year, explosion, missile, ship, bomb
9	Nuclear Power	power, plant, company, year, energy, percent, utility, cost, Company, reactor
10	US Politics	war, President, weapon, Mr., year, military, policy, world, Reagan, House
Irrelevant topics		
2	Summaries	New, new, year, government, official, York, people, business, President, state
4	Book Reviews	week, life, book, man, woman, John, year, New, family, University
6	Films & Music	Street, West, Theater, Mr., Sunday, East, show, New, tomorrow, p.m.

Topics That Show Some Pattern in Their Use Over Time

Firstly, we found a number of topics that have a strong temporal dimension, that is, they are strongly present in the news in some years or decades, but not in others. In that respect, these topics are most similar to the shifting packages found by Gamson and Modigliani. Figure 3 shows the change in occurrence over time for the four topics discussed below, which are discussed in chronological order.

News stories in which topic 1, which we labelled *Research*, deal with research on nuclear technology, including both energy research and nuclear weapons research. This topic is most strongly present in the early part of the data-set, and its usage sharply decreases over time, especially from the 1980s onwards. In terms of temporal focus, and in the focus on possibilities created by nuclear research, this topic is comparable to Gamson and Modigliani's Progress package, although the latter did not include nuclear weapons research as their research was focused on nuclear energy.

In topic 3, *Cold War*, the words "United", "States", "Soviet", "Union" and "weapon" immediately suggest that this is a topic about the US–Soviet conflict. Lower-ranking words include variations on the "weapon" theme as well as more diplomatic terms such as "agreement" and "proposal". The topic occurs most frequently between the mid-1950s and the mid-1980s, with a peak in the early 1960s that can be easily identified as the Cuban missile crisis.

Finally, the last topic in this category is topic 8, *Nuclear Power– Accidents/Danger*. Although the top words in this cluster, "plant", "power" and "reactor", are not very informative, peripheral words like "accident", "safety" and "radioactive" show how to

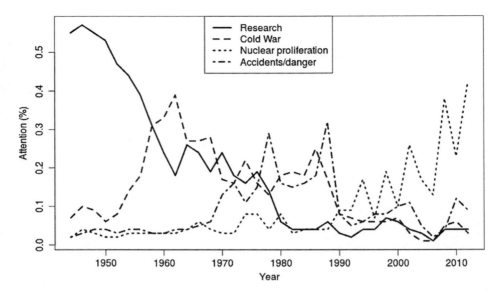

FIGURE 3
Occurrence of topics that have a strong temporal component

interpret it. Indeed, Chernobyl and Three Mile Island are both included in this topic, which shows peaks in news attention in both 1979 and 1986. Articles on smaller nuclear accidents or discussions on nuclear hazard in general also contain this topic. Interestingly, although this topic shows a small peak around the 2011 Fukushima reactor, most of the coverage of that event is classified in topic 5 (nuclear weapons), discussed below. This topic is most closely related to Gamson and Modigliani's *Runaway* and *Devil's Bargain* packages, as it focuses on the negative qualities of nuclear energy, and both the topic and the *Runaway* frame occur in roughly the same time period.

Finally, the articles in topic 7, *Nuclear Proliferation*, deal with nuclear weapons in countries such as North Korea, Iran and Pakistan, and US actions or policies against the possession of these weapons. Peaks of attention for these topics occur in the 1990s and especially the 2000s, with events in North Korea and later Iran as triggers. Although the topic occurs after the period covered by Gamson and Modigliani, semantically it resembles their *Runaway* package, in the sense that the technology is no longer under control and now poses a danger to its very inventors.

More or Less Continuously Present Topics

These topics do have some fluctuation in their occurrence over time, but this fluctuation shows no clear trend.

In topic 5, *Nuclear Weapons*, the words associated with the topic seem to be mostly related to the development and testing of nuclear bombs, especially nuclear submarines. This topic is most strongly present in the 1950s through the early 1970s, with a peak in 2011 after the Fukushima incident. This latter peak is possibly a confusion caused by the prevalence of ocean-related words in both the tsunami coverage and the discourse on nuclear submarines.

Topic 9, *Nuclear Power*, is a second cluster with words related to economics. Similar to topic 8, "power" and "plant" form the top words of a cluster. However, this time the peripheral words show a different focus: "company", "corporation", "year" and "percent" suggest that these articles are about nuclear energy as a business, and report on the earnings of companies that operate in this sector. Over time, we see a peak in the 1970s (the oil crisis) and in the 1980s.

The final relevant topic, topic 10, *US Politics*, concerns the policies of the United States on its own nuclear weapons and defence. The main peak for this topic is in the early 1980s, with the Rearming America programme.

Irrelevant Topics

These topics have nothing to do with nuclear power in terms of their content, but appear in our results anyway because we included all articles mentioning the word "nuclear", including book reviews and news summaries. In topic 2, news summaries and items from the section "Inside The Times" are clustered together as one topic. These tend to focus on New York and on politics (local, domestic or foreign). However, they do not deal with nuclear issues directly, so we discard this topic. Topic 4 consists of short book reviews, of which one or more use words related to the nuclear topic. Again, these do not deal with nuclear issues in the news directly. Lastly, topic 6 represents news stories on films or concerts, some of which have to do with nuclear power, others show up in articles that mention the nuclear issue elsewhere.

As this overview shows, not all topics contain useful results and the topics are not ordered in a way that makes it easy to distinguish the useful from the non-useful (as usefulness is of course something determined by the researcher, not the computer). However, the irrelevant topics were clearly distinguishable, which makes it easy to discard them altogether or ignore them in further analysis. Although it might seem annoying at first that such topics are also generated by the analysis, this is actually quite useful. Since most data-sets contain a degree of noise (such as book reviews or sports results), LDA can be used as an inexpensive way to locate those articles that are relevant for answering a particular research question from a larger sample.

Our purpose here, however, was to compare the topics we found using LDA with the outcome of the framing research by Gamson and Modigliani (1989). Compared to the frames or interpretive packages found in their analysis, the topics of our LDA analysis seem to be more concrete and specific. Similar to Gamson and Modigliani's study, we found that topics change over time, but not all of them increase or decrease in a linear way. Also, topics seem to either cluster a number of related events together (nuclear proliferation talks, nuclear accidents) or represent issues that are continuously present over a longer period of time (the economics of nuclear energy, nuclear weapons tests). It is not possible, however, to deduct a particular viewpoint or frame from a topic directly—for example, we found no clear "anti-nuclear" cluster, whereas Gamson and Modigliani found multiple frames that are critical of nuclear energy. It is quite likely that the coverage of nuclear accidents and danger is predominantly covered from an anti-nuclear perspective, but even in this case there is a clear difference between the "issue" or event being covered (nuclear accidents) and the frame with which it is covered. That said, for some of the topics, such as the *Research* and *Accidents* topics, we do see that the temporal pattern is similar to that identified for the *Progress* and *Runaway* packages, respectively.

To see whether increasing the number of clusters helps find word patterns that are more fine-grained and more frame-like than those representing issues, we will explore what happens if we increase the number of topics from 10 to 25.

Granularity: How Many Topics?

Changing the number of topics (K) changes what is called the granularity, or level of detail, of the model. The higher the granularity, the more detailed the analysis. Using a larger number of topics implies higher granularity: each topic then represents more specific content characteristics.

If a model with 25 topics is compared to a model with 10 topics, some of the topics in the model with 25 topics tend to blend together in the 10-topic model. The topics in the model with 50 topics can thus be considered to represent smaller grains of the 10 topics. As an example, consider the events in Chernobyl and Three Mile Island. Both events are clearly separated by time, space, the actors involved and various circumstances. Yet the two are related by the nature of the event, and thus in vocabulary used: a malfunction of a nuclear reactor, with awful consequences to health and the environment. In a model with many topics, these events can be distinguished in different topics, whereas in a model with fewer topics, these events are blended together, representing a broader theme. In our data, we saw this specific example in a comparison of models with 10 and 25 topics.

Table 2 gives an overview of the relevant topics from the 25-topic model. Each "detailed" ($K = 25$) topic is listed below the "broader" ($K = 10$) topic it resembles most. This similarity is computed by determining in which documents each $K = 10$ and $K = 25$ topic occurs, and then calculating the cosine similarity of these occurrence vectors. So, two topics with perfect similarity (1.0) would occur in exactly the same (relative) frequency in all documents. For instance, topic 24 which we labelled *3 Mile Island*, is most similar to topic 8 above it (with cosine similarity 0.70).

In the $K = 10$ model, coverage of Chernobyl is clustered together with coverage of the Three Mile Island incident, to form a cluster about nuclear accidents (topic 8), and coverage of Fukushima was split between this topic and the nuclear weapons topic (topic 5). However, in the $K = 25$ model, different connections between these events are found, and Chernobyl and Fukushima end up in the same cluster, while Three Mile Island gets its own cluster. Finally, topic 8 ($K = 10$) is highly similar to topic 15 ($K = 25$), which deals with power plant construction and especially the Shoreham nuclear power station. This power station was constructed on Long Island in the 1980s, but never actually used, as local residents objected in the wake of the Chernobyl disaster. As shown in Figure 4, these three constituent topics in the $K = 25$ model together trace the $K = 10$ *Accidents/Danger* topic (the per-year correlation between the $K = 10$ topic and the sum of the $K = 25$ topics is 0.95, $p < 0.001$), but each are focused around a specific time-point.

TABLE 2
Most similar $K = 25$ topics for each relevant $K = 10$ topic

Topic	Similarity
1: Research	
9: Research	0.68
8: Universities	0.39
17: Scientific Development	0.27
21: Nuclear Weapon Materials	
3: Cold War	
7: Rearming America	0.61
18: Cold War	0.61
20: NATO	0.50
8: Accidents/Danger	
24: 3 Mile Island	0.70
15: Power Plant Construction (Shoreham)	0.62
2: Chernobyl & Fukushima	0.32
7: Nuclear Proliferation	
6: Iran	0.63
4: North Korea	0.58
14: Iraq	0.42
3: India & Pakistan	0.25
21: Fissile Materials	0.25
5: Nuclear Weapons	
11: Nuclear Submarines	0.53
2: Chernobyl & Fukushima	0.39
19: Nuclear Weapons	0.31
23: Nuclear Power	0.52
10: US Politics	
1: Nuclear War Threat	0.68
5: US Politics	0.46
19: Nuclear Weapons	0.36
12: Protests	0.28

Topics from the 10-topic model ($K = 10$) are set in italics, with the most similar topics from the 25 topic model ($K = 25$) listed beneath each $K = 10$ topic. Some $K = 25$ topics occur twice when they were similar to more than one $K = 10$ topic. Similarity is based on whether topics occur in the same documents (calculated as cosine similarity). Example: Topic 3 from the $K = 10$ model, interpreted as the Cold War topic, is similar to three topics from the $K = 25$ model: topic 7 on Reagan and Rearming America (sparking the 1980s' arms race); topic 18 on the Cold War; and topic 20 on NATO.

Discussion: Best Practices

This article showcased a relatively recent tool, Latent Dirichlet Analysis, or LDA. LDA is an unsupervised topic modelling technique that automatically creates "topics", that is, clusters of words, from a collection of documents. These topics may represent issues that recur over time, related events or other regularities in articles.

We think LDA can be a valuable tool in any large-scale content analysis project. For preliminary analysis, LDA can very quickly give a rough overview of what kind of topics are discussed in which media or time periods. However, the best way of proving the statistical, internal and external validity of LDA and of topic models in general is still under discussion (Chang et al. 2009; DiMaggio, Nag, and Blei 2013; Ramirez et al. 2012). We would advise journalism scholars to start by making a perplexity plot for different numbers of topics, and then look at the models where the perplexity decrease drops

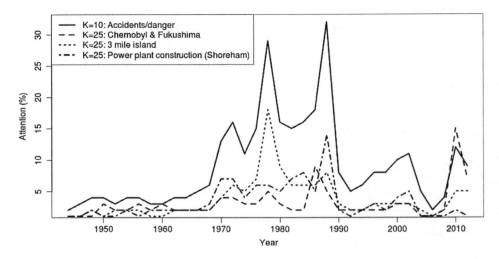

FIGURE 4
Occurrence over time of detailed ($K = 25$) topics that constitute the *Accidents/ Danger* topic from the $K = 10$ model

off. However, the researcher should also manually inspect these topic models, and for each topic decide on the correct interpretation by looking at the words in the topic, in which media and time frames it occurs, and also at the documents that are most indicative of a specific topic. For this purpose, we advise using a topic browser.[9] Manual interpretation reveals which topics are closely related to the theoretical quantities the researcher is interested in. Also, the researcher can decide to combine multiple topics that are semantically related and/or to remove irrelevant topics such as the book reviews identified in our case study. This should be followed by a formal internal validity evaluation of these topics by checking a sample of automatically coded articles or by comparing to a sample of manually coded articles (for a more elaborate discussion of validity checks of LDA topic models, see DiMaggio, Nag, and Blei (2013). Even though the validity may be insufficient for completely automatic analysis, it can be used as a form of semi-automatic coding by having the manual coder check whether the coding is correct, which is much quicker (and cheaper) than fully coding each document. Furthermore, even if the topics cannot be immediately used to answer the substantive research question, they can enhance the subsequent manual or automatic content analysis in numerous ways. First, by inductively showing which topics occur, it can help the researcher to create or improve the codebook by suggesting new codes and examples and by showing which codes might need to be combined or split up. Second, if the researcher is interested in doing automatic keyword analysis, the word lists per topic can offer inspiration for keywords and synonyms that might otherwise be left out. Third, LDA can be used to quickly find good example documents for infrequent topics or documents that use multiple topics, such as the example document in Figure 1. This can be used for manual coder training and evaluating the codebook, but also for creating the training data for subsequent machine learning, where rare topics usually give the worst performance because of the lack of training documents. Finally, as shown by the three "irrelevant" topics that were derived from our analysis, LDA can be used to filter out categories of texts that are not relevant from an overall sample.

The comparison in this paper also shows two limitations of LDA for analysing journalistic texts. First, not all topics represent substantive word clusters, but also other consistent patterns of co-occurrence such as genre and writing style. This is most dramatically shown by "irrelevant" topics such as book reviews, but can be considered beneficial by allowing the researcher to quickly discard such clusters of documents. However, it is also possible that shifts in word use, such as from "atomic" to "nuclear", caused documents to belong to different topics in the 1950s as compared to the 2000s even though they are substantively similar. The same would hold for writing style differences between different media and especially different formats (e.g. print media versus television or online). Dynamic Topic Models (Blei and Lafferty 2006) and Structural Topic Models (Roberts et al. 2014) are two extensions of LDA that explicitly deal with shifts over time and between groups of documents, respectively.

Second, the topics identified in this study did not approach what we could call a "frame" in the sense that Gamson and Modigliani (1989) or Entman (1993) would use this concept—as coherent interpretative packages. Similarly, the topics did not represent explicit valence or sentiment—there were no clear pro- or anti-nuclear topics. Although attempts to combine LDA and sentiment analysis in one model have been made (Lin and Yulan 2009), since news coverage is difficult for automatic sentiment analysis in general (Balahur et al. 2013), such methods will likely not yield sufficiently valid results for journalism studies in the near future. Following DiMaggio, Nag, and Blei (2013, 603), we suggest further research can combine LDA as described here with frame and sentiment analysis using other methods, e.g. using machine learning (e.g. Burscher et al. 2014).

By showcasing LDA and by showing some best practices for running and interpreting model results, this article contributes to the adoption of topic modelling in the practice of journalism research, which is a useful technique for every digital journalism scholar to have in their toolbox to deal with the very large data-sets that are becoming available. Although the burden of making sense of the results is still on the researcher, LDA offers a quick and cheap way to get a good overview of a collection of documents so that substantive questions can be answered immediately, especially about broad patterns in topic use over time or between media. Additionally, it is very helpful for performing preliminary analysis before venturing on a more traditional (and expensive) automatic or manual content analysis project.

DISCLOSURE STATEMENT

No potential conflict of interest was reported by the authors.

NOTES

1. Factor analysis is a dimensionality reduction technique: given a set of observed variables, a smaller set of factors is calculated that preserve as much information as possible in a lower-dimensional space. This is often used in the field of psychology as a measurement of latent, unobserved causes for certain observations. For instance, if a single factor largely explains the results for a set of questions

2. Technically, the alpha hyper-parameter controls the concentration of the Dirichlet distribution regarding the distribution of topics over documents. In Bayesian statistics, a hyper-parameter is a parameter that controls distributions such as the Dirichlet distribution. The term hyper-parameter is used to distinguish them from the parameters of the topic model that is the result of the analysis. For a good explanation of the role of hyper-parameters, we suggest the introduction to the Dirichlet distribution by Frigyik, Kapila, and Gupta (2010).
3. A goodness-of-fit measure describes how similar the predicted or expected values of a model are to the actual observed values. An example is the R^2 measure in linear regression, which indicates what proportion of variance of the dependent variable is explained by the independent variables.
4. See http://www.r-project.org.
5. See http://amcat.nl.
6. See http://github.com/amcat/amcat-r for the relevant R code. The R scripts that were used for our analysis can be downloaded from http://github.com/AUTHOR/corpus-tools.
7. See http://github.com/AUTHOR/xtas for the xtas modules for corenlp and other lemmatizers.
8. The topic browser can be found at http://rpubs.com/Anonymous/78,706.
9. Our R script for creating a topic browser is available at http://github.com/vanatteveldt/topicbrowser.

REFERENCES

Balahur, Alexandra, Ralf Steinberger, Mijail Kabadjov, Vanni Zavarella, Erik Van Der Goot, Matina Halkia, Bruno Pouliquen, and Jenya Belyaeva. 2013. "Sentiment Analysis in the News."*Proceedings of the 7th International Conference on Language Resources and Evaluation (LREC'2010)*: 2216-2220. Valletta, 19–21 May 2010.

Blei, David. M., and John D. Lafferty. 2006. "Dynamic Topic Models." In *Proceedings of the 23rd International Conference on Machine Learning*, 113–120. Pittsburgh, 2006. doi: 10.1145/1143844.1143859.

Blei, David M., Andrew Y. Ng, and Michael I. Jordan. 2003. "Latent Dirichlet Allocation." *The Journal of Machine Learning Research* 3: 993–1022.

Burscher, Björn, Daan Odijk, Rens Vliegenthart, Maarten de Rijke, and Claes H. de Vreese. 2014. "Teaching the Computer to Code Frames in News: Comparing Two Supervised Machine Learning Approaches to Frame Analysis." *Communication Methods and Measures* 8 (3): 190–206. doi: 10.1080/19312458.2014.937527.

Chang, Jonathan, Sean Gerrish, Chong Wang, Jordan Boyd-Graber, and David M. Blei. 2009. "Reading Tea Leaves: How Humans Interpret Topic Models." In *Advances in Neural Information Processing Systems*, 288–296.

De Marneffe, Marie-Catherine, Bill MacCartney, and Christopher D. Manning. 2006. "Generating Typed Dependency Parses from Phrase Structure Parses." In *Proceedings of Lrec* 6: 449–454.

De Rooij, Ork, Andrei Vishneuski, and Maarten De Rijke. 2012. "Xtas: Text Analysis in a Timely Manner." Paper presented at *Dir 2012: 12th Dutch-Belgian Information Retrieval Workshop*. Ghent, 23–24 February 2012.

DiMaggio, Paul, Manish Nag, and David Blei. 2013. "Exploiting Affinities between Topic Modelling and the Sociological Perspective on Culture: Application to Newspaper Coverage of U.S. Government Arts Funding." *Poetics* 41:570–606.

Entman, Robert M. 1993. "Framing: Toward Clarification of a Fractured Paradigm." *Journal of Communication* 43 (4): 51–58.

Frigyik, Bela A., Amol Kapila, and Maya R. Gupta. 2010. "Introduction to the Dirichlet Distribution and Related Processes". Technical Report UWEETR-2010-0006. Seattle: University of Washington Department of Electrical Engineering.

Gamson, William A., and Andre Modigliani. 1989. "Media Discourse and Public Opinion on Nuclear Power: A Constructionist Approach." *American Journal of Sociology* 95: 1–37.

Gardner, Matthew J., Joshua Lutes, Jeff Lund, Josh Hansen, Dan Walker, Eric Ringger, and Kevin Seppi. 2010. "The Topic Browser: An Interactive Tool for Browsing Topic Models." In *Proceedings of the Neural Information Processing Systems (NIPS) Workshop on Challenges of Data Visualization*: 5528–5235. Whistler, December 11, 2010.

Grimmer, Justin, and Brandon M. Stewart. 2013. "Text as Data: The Promise and Pitfalls of Automatic Content Analysis Methods for Political Texts." *Political Analysis* 21 (3): 267–297. doi:10.1093/pan/mps028.

Haselmayer, Martin, and Marcelo Jenny. 2014. "Measuring the Tonality of Negative Campaigning: Combining a Dictionary Approach with Crowd-Coding." Paper presented at *Political Context Matters: Content Analysis in the Social Sciences*. University of Mannheim.

Jones, Bryan D., and Frank R. Baumgartner. 2005. *The Politics of Attention: How Government Prioritizes Problems*. Chicago, IL: University of Chicago Press.

Lin, Chenghua, and Yulan He. 2009. "Joint Sentiment/Topic Model for Sentiment Analysis." In *Proceedings of the 18th ACM conference on information and knowledge management* (5), 375–384. Hong Kong, November 2–6, 2009.

Lucas, Christopher, Richard A. Nielsen, Margaret E. Roberts, Brandon M. Stewart, Alex Storer, and Dustin Tingley. 2015. "Computer-Assisted Text Analysis for Comparative Politics." *Political Analysis* 23: 254–277.

Matthes, Jörg, and Matthias Kohring. 2008. "The Content Analysis of Media Frames: Toward Improving Reliability and Validity." *Journal of Communication* 58 (2): 258–279. doi:10.1111/j.1460-2466.2008.00384.x.

McCallum, Andrew K. 2002. *Mallet: A Machine Learning for Language Toolkit*. Retrieved from http://mallet.cs.umass.edu

Meyer, David, Kurt Hornik, and Ingo Feinerer. 2008. "Text Mining Infrastructure in R." *Journal of Statistical Software* 25 (5): 1–54.

Quinn, Kevin M., Burt L. Monroe, Michael Colaresi, Michael H. Crespin, and Dragomir R. Radev. 2010. "How to Analyze Political Attention with Minimal Assumptions and Costs." *American Journal of Political Science* 54 (1): 209–228. doi:10.1111/j.1540-5907.2009.00427.x.

Ramage, Daniel, Evan Rosen, Jason Chuang, Christopher D. Manning, and Daniel A. McFarland. 2009. "Topic Modeling for the Social Sciences." *In Nips Workshop on Applications for Topic Models: Text and beyond* 5: 1–4.

Ramirez, Eduardo H., Ramon Brena, Davide Magatti, and Fabio Stella. 2012. "Topic Model Validation." *Neurocomputing* 76 (1): 125–133.

Roberts, Margaret E., Brandon M. Stewart, Dustin Tingley, Christopher Lucas, Jetson Leder-Luis, Shana K. Gadarian, B. Albertson, and David G. Rand. 2014. "Structural Topic Models for Open-Ended Survey Responses." *American Journal of Political Science* 58(4): 1064–1082. doi: 10.1111/ajps.12103.

GOOGLING THE NEWS[1]
Opportunities and challenges in studying news events through Google Search

Jacob Ørmen

Search engines provide a window into the changing association between websites and keywords across cultures and countries and over time. As such, they offer journalism and news researchers an opportunity to study how search engines, in this case Google, mediate news events and stories online. However, search results are not straightforward to study. Since search results are made in the act of searching and will have to be retrieved from Google Search in real-time, there is a range of different ontological and methodological issues related to this data source. This paper addresses these issues by discussing how factors in the search algorithm can be used proactively to study variations across searchers and in time. The paper identifies various endogenous and exogenous factors in the search algorithm one has to pay attention to and discusses ways to archive search results accordingly. Through a small case study, ways to work with the influence of endogenous factors (keywords, language settings, geo-location, Web history and clicking behaviour) and mitigate the effects of the exogenous factors (experimentation and randomisation) are suggested. Then, a new approach to studying search results is put forward, which builds on purposeful sampling of real-world participants or constructed research profiles. Finally, perspectives for news and journalism scholars in studying algorithmically generated content in a broader context are offered.

Introduction

Search engines in general and Google Search in particular remain important entry points to the Web for the majority of people in the Western world—approximately 65 per cent use Google regularly in the United States and probably more than 95 per cent in Europe (Hillis, Petit, and Jarrett 2013). Accordingly, search engines function as important gatekeepers (Bozdag 2013) for people to find information about topics, major events, news stories, disasters, etc.; and this provides us with a "unique empirical window into the study of culture" (Sanz and Stancik 2013, 2). Since most people only click on results at the top of the search page (Pan et al. 2007), the constellation of search results (commonly referred to as the search rankings) are of great importance in determining which perspectives, angles and topics on a given event or story are most salient for the public eye. During big news events, such as political elections, the importance of search engines increases as people turn to the Web to find more information about what is going on. For instance, during the 2015 UK General Election, search interest on Google for the leading candidates David Cameron (Conservative) and Ed Miliband (Labour) were greater than ever before—more than in previous elections and 5–10 times the number compared to non-election months.[2] For news organisations, search engines remain a key traffic source to stories online—on a par with or, in some cases, surpassing social media (Mitchell, Jurkowitz, and Olmstead 2014). Thus, it is important to document and study how search results appear across time and space to understand how Google functions as a gatekeeper or mediator of news and information to the public as well as online traffic to news organisations.

However, studying search results is anything but straightforward. First of all, search engines generally do not come with ready-made ways to retrieve data. Whereas social network sites such as Facebook and Twitter have become a popular way to study the online distribution of news stories and events (see Bro and Wallberg 2014; Bruns et al. 2012; Vis 2013) because of the relatively easy access they provide to data through Application Programming Interfaces (API), Google does not permit retrieval of the rankings for specific keywords. Secondly, in contrast to offline documents, online articles, posts or tweets, search results do not simply exist "out there" waiting to be found and analysed but have to be created in the act of searching. They exist as a particular type of document online (algorithmically generated content), based on the one hand, in the index of retrievable documents on the Web that the search engine compiles, and on the other hand, guided by a range of factors in the search algorithm that is informed by the person searching—*intentionally* (e.g., through search keywords) as well as *unintentionally* (e.g., through personalisation). In that sense, the particular results are a co-creation of the person searching (through signals) and the search engine (by providing an index to search). They are, so to speak, not "data found" by the researcher but "data made" in the research interaction (Jensen 2010). They exist as the unique coming-together of an individual searcher and the index as it existed at that particular moment. This entails that they cannot be retroactively retrieved or reproduced. Therefore, we need systematic approaches to the documentation of search results in real-time that can deal with these ontological and methodological challenges.

In this article, I present a first step in establishing a methodology for search engine analysis by discussing the opportunities and challenges in studying news events through Google Search. I use *events* here instead of just *stories* or *coverage* to emphasise the pre-planned, recurring or, at least, expected manner of occurrence. This understanding of events draws on the familiar concept of "media events" (Dayan and Katz 1992) but without the stringent semantic, syntactic and pragmatic genre requirements discussed in the original studies, and with a narrower focus on events covered by the news—rather than all—media. The reason for limiting the study to pre-planned events is that they are much easier to deal with when setting up a research design for documenting search results. Since these events comprise only a subset of news stories that it could be of interest to document through Google Search, I will address the difficulties of studying search results in relation to unexpected and disruptive events such as natural disasters and terrorism.

The article begins with a discussion of how factors in the search algorithm seem to influence search results and how this affects the way we can reasonably study search engines. Then, it turns to a discussion of feasible ways to archive these results and how research projects can actively work with some factors and seek to mitigate others. In this process, it provides examples from a small case study of a particular news event—Felix Baumgartner's skydive from the stratosphere in 2012, called the Red Bull Stratos. Finally, strategies for how to work with—instead of against—the algorithms with real-world participants or programmed research profiles are assessed.

Factors in the Algorithm: Opening the Black Box of Uncertainty

The greatest challenge facing research into search results is that the logics of search rankings are very difficult to uncover. The number of factors, all the signals the search algorithm takes into account when compiling the rankings for the individual search query, informing the search rankings, and the individual weight of each factor are impossible for outsiders not affiliated with Google to uncover fully. A number of studies have tried to "second-guess" Google's search algorithm(s) through systematic, large-scale mapping of search rankings across queries (see e.g. Edelman 2010; Edelman and Lockwood 2011; Jiang 2012), but in recent years, it has become increasingly clear that the multitude of factors that inform the exact constellation of search results for any given query (Granka 2010) as well as the increasing adaptation of results to individual users—personalisation—have made this task very difficult (Feuz, Fuller, and Stalder 2011). Because of the "black-boxed" (Marres and Weltevrede 2013) functions of these search algorithms, there simply exists no vantage point from which researchers can analyse search results objectively. Reverse-engineering the search algorithm seems neither technically feasible nor scientifically desirable. This does not mean, however, that it is not interesting or relevant to consider the workings of the search algorithm when studying search results.

Traditionally, search engines have operated on *query-dependent* factors—comprising the position and order of search queries, the amount and types of relevant keywords in the Web documents, as well as language settings and the geo-location of the user—and *query-independent* factors—including, among other things, the popularity of websites—determined, for instance, by the PageRank algorithm (Brin and Page 1998), the freshness of the documents and click popularity (Lewandowski 2005). Recently, Google has announced that it will start to display mobile-ready sites more prominently in searches conducted through mobile devices (Makino, Jung, and Phan 2015). These factors can also be supplemented with more general maintenance tasks done by the search operator (e.g., Google). This includes randomisation and experimentation (Zuckerman 2011). When Google receives a number of queries from the same Internet Protocol (IP) address, it might deliberately try to randomise search results a bit in order to mask the workings of the algorithm (Zuckerman 2011). At the same time, Google is constantly conducting experiments (e.g., A/B tests) to detect the kind of search results (and design elements) users are most likely to interact with (Zuckerman 2011). Thus, randomisation and experimentation can easily introduce random error into the search result study on top of the query-dependent and independent factors.

In recent years, a third type has increasingly come to inform search results: *personalisation* factors. There is no clear-cut definition of what personalisation encompasses, but it includes all those signals search engines might use to adapt the search results to the individual user—for example, prior search history, browsing behaviour, and whether the user is logged into services (e.g., Google Accounts). Even though the knowledge and criticism of personalisation measures have been around for many years (Spink et al. 2003; Zimmer 2008), only recently has personalisation been empirically tested by research. One study used artificial research profiles with designed browser histories to compare personalisation across a number of queries (Feuz, Fuller, and Stalder 2011). These researchers find personalisation to be extensive but did not attribute it to specific factors, and they held geo-location as a constant. A recent study of real-world search participants finds that, on average, about 11.7 per cent of Google Search results are personalised (Hannak et al. 2013), which would suggest that personalisation is not as influential as previously assumed (*pace* Pariser 2012). The authors do note, however, that there is considerable variation across topics—"politics" and "news" showcase greater levels of personalisation and tend to fluctuate more (Hannak et al. 2013). Hannak and colleagues find geo-location based on users' IP addresses and Google Accounts logins to be the sole significant causes of personalisation. A different study using a similar design finds variation across about 98 per cent of the results (Xing et al. 2014) but also identifies geo-location to have the greatest influence. Thus, personalisation can be considered as the great "known unknown" of search engines—we know it is there but not exactly how it works—that seems to exercise lesser or greater influence on the rankings, depending on the type of search and the steps taken by users to avoid personalisation.

In short, the number and type of factors that go into the search algorithm are very difficult to assess. The factors discussed here are merely those commonly identified in the literature, which is an ever-open list that remains largely unknown. Nonetheless, I find it helpful to divide the range of factors discussed above into two analytical categories: one comprised of all the factors that the individual searcher and, thus, researchers have some control of, and another consisting of all the factors that are beyond our reach when using the search engine. I call the first category *endogenous factors*, since these factors are, so to speak, endogenous to the particular act of searching. It includes the search queries, language settings and geo-location, as well as the known list of personalisation factors (search history, browsing behaviour, whether one is logged into services). The second category, *exogenous factors*, includes all those factors that are beyond the direct control of the user and affect the search results on a more general level. This involves experimentation and randomisation done by Google as well as all the factors that go into deciding the PageRank and other measures of importance for websites.

The primary research interest is in the relationship between the endogenous factors, on the one hand, and the exogenous factors, on the other. It is foremost the exogenous factors dealing with rankings of websites based on importance that is of primary interest, since we would assume experimentation and randomisation to be affecting the search results more by chance, or at least not purposefully. The latter can be considered akin to random error that one has to watch out for in the study. To study this relationship between endogenous and exogenous factors we need archiving methods that can take the workings of search algorithms into account.

Retrieving and Archiving Rankings for Search Results

The practical question of how to archive search results has only become more complicated in recent years. Whereas the popularity of individual keywords across time can be accessed through Google's own tool Google Trends, there is currently no interface that can retrieve the exact constellation of websites (the search results) for these keywords. The official API to search through the whole index of Google Search has been discontinued by Google as of November 2010 and replaced by a Custom Search API that offers very limited search options.[3] It also appears that the results produced by the search APIs (both the present one and the discontinued one) produce quite different search results from manual searches (Hannak et al. 2013). This again reiterates the lack of a baseline search result ranking to which to compare individual searches. This entails that results will have to be scraped or retrieved in other ways directly from the search page (e.g., google.com or affiliated subdomains) by individual searchers themselves or through software.

The first issue with this is how to produce and archive the search results for later analysis. One commonly applied method for retrieving search results is to use programs that can query Google automatically and repeatedly. These programs can be designed from the bottom up through various programming languages, or one can use ready-made programs, e.g., Google Search Scraper by Amit Agarwal (2015). The upside of this approach is that it is possible to set up "lobster traps" that sit passively and collect data, waiting for interesting changes to happen (Karpf 2012). However, this solution is problematic for four reasons. First, Google bans this option in the Terms of Service[4] and it is generally seen as a "dirty research method" (Rogers 2013a). Second, since the organic search results are at the core of Google's business model, it is considered proprietary and guarded with great care. Therefore, Google is particularly aware of attempts to scrape search results repeatedly, so there is a high risk of facing restrictions on access (e.g., through CAPTCHAs) or getting the IP banned for a shorter or longer amount of time. Figure 1 shows an example of the latter. Third, ironically, these programs easily introduce a layer of complexity on top of the search algorithm. When

FIGURE 1
Google Search error message

using a piece of software that retrieves the search results automatically, it can be hard to tell or adjust the signals provided to the search engine by the program (e.g., the language settings, IP address and Web history). Fourth, the scraped data usually only include the organic search results and, thus, excludes the paid-for search content (usually, on top of and to the right of the organic content) as well as other information displayed in the search window (such as fact boxes and other information displayed by Google on the search result page).

To retain the visual information in the search results, one can use research tools that can make automated screen dumps of search results at regular intervals. This approach has the benefit of retaining all the visual information from the browser window (Karlsson and Strömbäck 2010) that might work well in research projects that are more interested in the constellation of search results (e.g., the size of each result in the query list, the placement of links, images, videos and other contextual data). It has its obvious drawbacks if the goal is to conduct statistical analysis, since the information is "flattened" in one image instead of being nicely ordered in a structured database. Manual recoding of features in the image into quantifiable variables is, of course, possible (Kautsky and Widholm 2008) but will quickly become quite laborious. Therefore, screen dumping functions work best in small-N studies that integrate the visual elements in the analysis.

A second option would be to let the archiving be done by real-world searchers (participants in the study), e.g., as manual screen dumping. This form of micro-archiving (Brügger 2011) has the great advantage that it stays closest to real acts of searching without the risk of being too artificial like the programmed scraping. The real-world searchers would be instructed to search for specific keywords and take a screenshot every time they make searches. The downside of this approach is that one relies on people actually completing the tasks assigned to them and that the researcher has no direct influence on how people do the search (for instance, whether they choose to be logged in, clean their browser cache, etc.). In short, there is no superior method for archiving search results. One is technically difficult to set up and manage properly (programmed archiving) and the other is costly and relies on compliance by others (human archiving). It depends on the type of archiving one wishes to conduct.

A second issue is how much to archive. Since the search results will have to be generated and saved in real-time, this depends on the scale of the research project. Niels Brügger has outlined three different strategies for archiving websites more generally: *snapshot* (a large range of websites at one point in time), *selective* (a narrow list of important sites for prolonged periods) and *event* (archiving websites particularly relevant for a specific event) strategies (Brügger 2011). I introduce three models for search result archiving here that correspond closely to Brügger's strategies:

1. *The cross-sectional model*: The most basic form of search result archiving would be to have multiple real-world searchers or computer programs conduct searches for specified keywords *at one point in time*. Then, variations could be assessed according to the sampling of real-world searchers (variations across geographic location, languages, gender, age, etc.) or the settings for the computer programs, that is, the construction of search profiles according to criteria mimicking real-world searchers. This model is suitable for suddenly occurring stories (breaking news, memes, etc.) where there is no time to plan ahead. This model would make a strong case for

establishing similarity in search results, given different searchers and profiles, e.g. the same major news outlets on top of the search results across all or most searches. The drawback with a cross-sectional model would be that it would be hard to assess whether large variations are due to the characteristics of the searchers or profiles or due to randomness, experimentation or a range of undisclosed factors in the algorithm. This would require multiple points of observation to assess.

2. *The longitudinal model*: Another approach would be to archive search results for specific queries *at multiple points in* time, e.g., on a regular pre-planned basis such as once per week for several years in a row. The point here would be to document certain keywords that retain salience in the popular mind (politicians, societal institutions, etc.). This approach, first of all, makes it possible to engage with how search results of specific terms appear in various stages over time (Borra and König 2013) and in various geographic locations. In that way, we can conduct "studies at the micro-level" (Granka 2010) as a supplement to general search trends at the macro-level (as offered, for instance, by Google Trends).

3. *The short burst model*: Another approach would be to collect more material in shorter, yet more intensive waves of documentation. This model is especially relevant for documenting the developments of news events, since high publication frequency by news outlets around spectacular stories tends to cause fluctuations in the search rankings (Hannak et al. 2013) and search activity increases around big events (as mentioned in the Introduction). Here, the objective could be to investigate the various news sources that attain the highest rankings in various geographical regions and over time. By relating the results to online and offline news media coverage and social network sites' activity, it is possible to compare the relative importance and prevalence given to certain angles, perspectives, news organisations, etc. Furthermore, by archiving search results before, during and after certain influential events have occurred (e.g., major pre-planned spectacles such as elections), we could assess how these events influence the relative ranking of search results. The short burst can still provide an interesting insight into the shifting constellations of search results during important news events.

Naturally, it is possible to combine these models in a hybrid (for an example in a different context, see the Danish Web archive,[5]) and the models outlined above should be seen more as archetypical approaches to the archiving of search results than precise recipes. All three models require us to attend to the ways the search algorithms work and possibly affect the searches. As mentioned earlier, news events (short burst model) offer us a particularly good case for studying how search results vary across searchers. Below, I explore various ways to work with the endogenous and exogenous factors in relation to a specific case, the Red Bull Stratos.

Working with the Algorithm: The Case of the Red Bull Stratos

On 14 October 2012 at about 12:08 MDT, some 38 kilometres above the face of the earth, Felix Baumgartner (an Austrian skydiver) stepped out of a capsule and jumped into the stratosphere, beginning his four-minute-long record-breaking freefall towards the ground. Millions followed the event (named the "Red Bull Stratos" after its main sponsor) through simultaneous live streams on the Web (YouTube alone reported more than 7 million viewers at its peak moments) and on Discovery Channel (which obtained the highest ratings for a non-prime-time programme ever) (Heitner 2012). Most importantly in this context, it was a pre-planned event that could be documented using the short burst model introduced above. The goal was to document how dominant news organisations would be in the search rankings before, during and after the event. The project was also interested in seeing whether there would be any variations in search rankings in three countries: Denmark (where the researcher is based), the United States (where the jump took place) and Austria (where the jumper is from). Here, I only use the event to illustrate how the factors can be worked with, not to try to answer these questions directly.

A screen dumping method was chosen to archive the search results. This was largely because the initial research design required the full content of the search result page as it appeared to human searchers, that is, with organic and paid searches, as well as video and images shown. The tool Siteshoter (only for PC) was chosen, because of its reliability and the ability to make automated screen dumps of websites at specified intervals. Google Results could be retrieved by posting the full URL to the specific query, e.g., https://www.google.com/search?q=felix+baumgartner. Siteshoter can only capture the first page of search results with the predefined setting in Google of 10 search results per page. Since it was not clear how fast the rankings would change, a decision was made to document the event every hour from four days before until two days after the jump was scheduled to take place. In total, about 600 screen dumps were made of queries on Google.com, Google.dk (Danish sub-domain) and Google.at (Austrian sub-domain).

Obviously, when one tries to document an event like this through Google Search, the exact keywords used as search queries are of the greatest importance, since they determine the exact angle taken on the subject.

Endogenous Factors: Keywords

Finding the right keywords poses similar problems to identifying hashtags for Twitter studies. It is very difficult to know in advance which search queries (keywords or phrases) will resonate with a broader population. Like hashtags, one has to pay attention to what is hot and what is not among real-life searchers. Luckily, Google provides a tool to do exactly that, Google Trends. This tool allows for comparisons of search intensity for various search queries over time and across geographical space. Thus, it is possible to find out which of several keywords have been used most intensively by searches at various points in time and in different regions of the world. The past is, of course, only indicative of future behaviour to a certain extent; memes, political slogans, sudden events, etc., will attain sudden and often unexpected attention from a large number of searchers. On those occasions, one would have to rely on keywords popular in news or social media and, then, make qualified guesses. Therefore, Google Trends is most helpful if one seeks to document predictable or recurring events such as the Red Bull Stratos.

The decision to archive searches in relation to the Red Bull Stratos was made about a week before the event took place. At that point, both the event itself and the main character, Felix Baumgartner, the jumper, had already received lot of attention from established news media. To find the exact queries for the study, a number of different words were tested on Google Search in the days leading up to the jump. After comparing queries affiliated with the event with the queries affiliated with the jumper, it was quite obvious that they captured very different aspects of the event. The event queries associated the event much more with the official sources (including Red Bull itself), whereas a search for the jumper yielded more person-focused results (among other things, his Facebook page). Eventually, two queries were chosen for the study: one capturing the event itself, "Red Bull Stratos", and one for the jumper, "Felix Baumgartner". More general queries such as "jump", "stratos", "felix" and "baumgartner" were tested but proved to include many search results not specifically relevant for the purpose of mapping this particular event. The decision was made to stick with the more precise queries rather than a catch-all approach (obviously, many people looking for information about the event would use different search terms). Faced with this issue, I decided that false negatives (excluding relevant results) were a better option than false positives (including too many irrelevant results). Making decisions like this depends on the context of the study, naturally.

Google Trends also came in handy in the selection process. After comparing the search volume on Google Trends for the two queries, it was clear that "Felix Baumgartner" had a greater resonance than "Red Bull Stratos" in the total population of searchers.[6] It was also apparent that the popularity of the search queries was greatest in the Central European countries—particularly Austria, even though the event took place in air space above Nevada in the United States. Since Felix Baumgartner is Austrian, the fact that Austrians were interested in this event was not that surprising, but these numbers suggested that there would be a point in looking at various country-specific Google domains in Europe as well.

Endogenous Factors: Language Settings and IP Address

As noted earlier, the geographic location appears to be one of—if not the most—influential cause of fluctuations in search rankings (Xing et al. 2014). These factors are probably some of the easiest to control for or, at least, influence to a large extent through the search settings and third-party software. Unfortunately, the case study did not take enough caution in managing the settings or changing the IP address. The assumption was that using the specific Google subdomains, google.at and google.dk, would be sufficient to get geo-specific results for Austria and Denmark, respectively. This did not turn out to be the case. Figure 2 shows the outcome of an attempt to query "Felix Baumgartner" on google.at (the Austrian version of Google Search) to see the event from an Austrian perspective. Even though I specifically tried to avoid the particular Danish search results by using a different country-specific search domain (.at instead of .dk), Google overrides this. In the search results, you find a video from the Danish-language version of Red Bull's website (redbull.dk) as well as a news story from the largest Danish TV channel (nyhederne.tv2.dk). Furthermore, the language settings in the panel on the left side remain Danish. Since I did not change my IP address to a server in Austria and had Danish as my default language setting, it was quite likely these factors informed the search engine's decision to provide me with

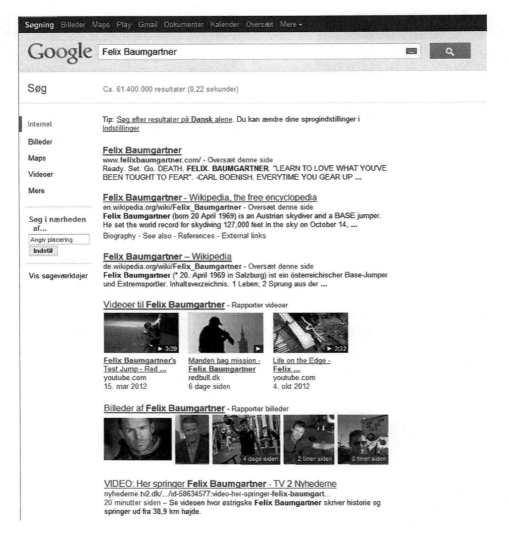

FIGURE 2
Search query "Felix Baumgartner" on google.at

Danish search results on Google.at. Language settings could be fixed manually on the computer; but, as indicated in earlier studies of personalisation, the IP address also matters to a great extent for the geo-location factors.

One obvious method to manipulate geo-location is to use some kind of IP scrambler that changes the IP address to an alternative IP address, e.g., through virtual private network (VPN) servers, or disguises the IP address altogether, e.g., through The Onion Router (TOR) (Fernando, Tina Du, and Ashman 2014). Many VPN providers allow users to specify from which country or region within a country they would like the IP address to be based. Thus, the geographic location can be directly manipulated and, thus, treated in a similar way to an independent variable in experimental designs. One can, for instance, alternate between IP addresses to influence the geo-location signals on which the search algorithm relies. Thus, it is theoretically possible for the same computer to appear as if it is based in different countries and, thus, retrieve search results that mimic what people in these countries would see. Another approach would, of course, be to recruit human participants physically based in the countries or regions under study. This is probably more desirable in many cases, since the whole project would not have to rely on a specific VPN provider, but it is resource demanding and has a risk that people will not comply or drop out.

To get a clearer idea of whether the language settings or IP addresses influence the constellation of search results, I conducted a small test (see Figure 3) some weeks after the study was concluded. Here, I queried "Felix Baumgartner" on Google.de (German domain) with four different settings: one with the language set to Danish with an IP address in Copenhagen, Denmark (Figure 3a); one with the language set to German with an IP address in Denmark (Figure 3b); one with the language set to German and with a German IP address (Figure 3c); and one with the language set to

FIGURE 3

Search on Google.de with varying settings for language and IP address

Danish and with a German IP address (Figure 3d). The greatest changes in the organic search results seem to come from the language settings. Notice, for example, how the country domains on Wikipedia follow the language settings and not the IP address. Meanwhile, the IP address informs the type of advertisements that are shown to the user in the top banners. It is simply not sufficient to change the IP address to direct Google towards the desired geo-location. Accordingly, the IP address seems, in fact, less important than language settings in influencing the ranking of organic search results.

Endogenous Factors: Web History, Click Behaviour, Account Logins

The personalisation of search results based on prior behaviour and other account signals (true personalisation, one could say) is very difficult to operate with and control for. Therefore, some have proposed various attempts to exclude these factors from influencing search rankings altogether. Richard Rogers, among others, has suggested operating with a "research browser", that is, a browser cleansed of any history of prior usage that boots directly from scratch each time it is opened (Rogers 2013b). This browser would only be influenced by factors such as the keywords used, geo-location and exogenous factors. This is probably a viable way to deal with personalisation issues if used in the stringent manner outlined by Rogers (2013b). However, this method also introduces one major downside as I see it: it runs the risk of being too artificial and detached from real-world search situations. Even though people in general might be opposed to personalisation and targeted advertisement (Purcell, Brenner, and Rainie 2012), many people are either logged into Google when they search (knowingly or unknowingly), do not clear their search history and cookies, or do not think more generally about how their Web behaviour influences the search engine. Accordingly, even though it might be possible to strip the search engine of some of the factors, it also comes with the cost of operating within an artificial environment. It might be a reliable way to mitigate some personalisation, but it is not necessarily valid.

In the case of the Red Bull Stratos, click behaviour was the only clear-cut indicator of a change in the rankings. At one point, I interacted with one of the links in the rankings, the Wikipedia page for Felix Baumgartner, and that resulted in a particular page attaining a much better ranking (from the bottom three sites to the top four sites) one hour later. Investigating Web history and account logins was not directly part of the design (the computers changed IP addresses and none of them logged into any accounts during the study). However, it would be possible to work with those factors as well. For account logins, one can alternate between being logged in and not (at least, with real-life participants) and compare differences. Web history would be more difficult to manipulate directly (for an attempt to do so with research profiles, consult Feuz, Fuller, and Stalder 2011). However, it is possible to assess the influence of individual browsing history (both Web visits, previous searches, and so on) if all other factors are sought to be held constant. This would be a passive way of estimating influence. If there were no variations across participants with otherwise similar search profiles, then there would be a case for a limited influence of browsing history. This is a slightly problematic approach, since we cannot hold all other factors constant, because we do not know all the other factors, as discussed earlier. Nonetheless, it is not impossible to work with these factors in the design, either.

Exogenous Factors: Randomisation and Experimentation

Common among the endogenous factors is—as mentioned earlier—that the researcher can have a large degree of control on how they interfere with the project. The exogenous factors, on the other hand, pose a more imminent threat to consistent and reliable results both over time and with respect to participants. This is primarily because these factors are very difficult to control for. Experimentation and randomisation cannot be directly observed; but, in studies over periods of time, it is possible to observe their influence or lack thereof. If odd results cannot be reproduced across searchers or for the same searcher over time, then it should warrant caution in the interpretation of the results. It could be a sign that randomisation, experimentation or other exogenous factors are at work in the search algorithm. As long as we assume that randomisation and experimentation are randomly distributed across our searchers (research profiles or real-world participants) or, at least, not correlated with the endogenous factors we are interested in studying (e.g., geo-location), then it is actually a lesser problem for the validity of the study. Primarily, they serve as a caution for how many other factors can be involved in the engine and a reminder that we should always interpret search rankings very carefully due to their specific ontology as algorithmically generated content on the Web.

Ways Forward: Experimental Design or Careful Sampling

Instead of trying to explain all the factors that go into the algorithm or ignoring them altogether, researchers are advised to use the factors actively in the research design. This can be done by turning the focus to how search results for specific queries vary for individual searchers across space and over time. This means paying attention to variability in three dimensions: *what* is searched for (variations across search queries), *who* does the searching (variations across searchers) and *when* is the search conducted (variations over time). Thus, instead of treating these factors as a problem, we should seek to work with the variability they provide as an opportunity. To explore variations across search results the endogenous factors can be used actively as experimental variables (trying to hold some factors constant in the design of search profiles while letting others vary) or as criteria for sampling in the research design (e.g., by employing a "maximum variation sampling strategy" [Kuzel 1992] in which participants most different on one or more endogenous factors are selected for the study). Here, differences across searchers would indicate that the particular endogenous factors under study make a difference for the search rankings (e.g., the geo-location of participants), whereas similarity would indicate the opposite. Thus, such a design would be able to document and assess the variations in the sources to which people are exposed through Google Search in relation to news events and stories. This type of design lends itself to questions such as: Which genre of Web content (Helles 2013) is typically associated with different search queries? Which types of news brands are prominently displayed in the search results? Do rankings of genre and news brands change across individual searchers or over time—for instance, in relation to a major news event?

Depending on the emphasis, such a design can either be cross-sectional (variation across searchers *at one point in time*) or longitudinal (variation across *multiple points in time*) in some form or another. The short burst model discussed here is actually a variation of the two (it should ideally go across searchers and with multiple points within a short time-frame). The short burst model documenting a pre-programmed news event is advantageous for research, because it allows for planning, setting up and possible recruiting participants in advance. However, this is, of course, not how most news stories play out. They are rather more sudden, disruptive and either not scheduled in advance, such as natural disasters, or not made public before the act, such as terrorism (Katz and Liebes 2007). On these occasions, the cross-sectional model with research profiles seems most feasible initially to capture developments in real-time. Shortly thereafter, the design can be adapted to suit real-world participants or more carefully designed research profiles.

The decision concerning whether to use research profiles programmed by the researcher or real-world participants depends on the study design. In general, the strength of using real-world participants is, first and foremost, that their search result would reflect more realistic search behaviour (in the best of all worlds, neither over- nor underestimating the amount of privacy protection people use themselves). Research profiles, on the other hand, offer the researcher better control of the study design. Profiles could be set up with alternating characteristics (for instance, based on the design in Hannak et al. [2013] or Xing et al. [2014]), which is easier to control experimentally but also risks becoming too detached from real-world users and thereby detrimental to the validity of the study. To achieve geographical variation in research profiles, which the literature so far has identified as the most important factor causing personalisation, one would have to take great caution in selecting proper ways of masking IP addresses and change language settings accordingly.

A final issue that has not been treated directly so far is how to report the search results in research. As should be clear from the discussion so far, it is very important how the data have been generated (e.g., as screen dumps) for what one can conclude from the data. At a minimum, time stamps should be supplied for the exact moment the query was posted on Google; the language setting and geo-location (e.g., as IP address) should be included, and it should be clearly specified on which device (computer, tablet, mobile) the search was conducted. It should also be noted whether factors were specifically manipulated (e.g., whether one was logged into Google services). Lastly, it should be clear from the context whether the data were generated by a human searcher or through a program. If the latter is the case, it should be made clear how this program might distort the factors (e.g., personalisation factors generally). In short, all the information that could theoretically be thought to make a difference should be included either on the individual screen dumps or generally for the context of the study.

On a final note, Google Search is not the only important algorithmically generated material to document. The algorithmic curation of content plays a growing importance online. Not only are search engines and social media, such as Facebook (Bucher 2012) and YouTube (Dijck 2013), using algorithms to display and rank content to the users but, to an increasing extent, so are websites more generally (Mayer-Schönberger and Cukier 2013) and news sites in particular (Thurman and Schifferes 2012). Personalisation of content and segmentation of Web traffic into targetable user groups is a valuable business for Web companies and, very likely, a practice we will see spread to even more websites and mobile apps in the coming years (Couldry and Turow 2014). The methodological challenges discussed here are relevant to broader studies of personalisation on the internet.

Conclusion

Search engines provide a window into the changing association between websites and keywords across cultures and countries and over time. As such, they offer journalism and news researchers an opportunity to study how search engines, in this case Google, mediate news events and stories online. Here, I have discussed how the ontological nature of search results as peculiar documents on the Web condition the way we are able to archive them as sources for further research. The most prominent factors informing the search engine algorithms have been identified and assessed. Through a small case study, ways in which researchers can operate with the influence of endogenous factors (keywords, language settings, geo-location, Web history, click behaviour) and consider the effects of the exogenous factors (experimentation, randomisation) have been proposed. In the last part, a new approach to studying search results has been suggested, which builds on purposeful sampling of real-world participants or constructed profiles suited for more qualitative studies. This is both an analytically fruitful approach, which offers new perspectives on search engine research, and one that actively works with—instead of against—the algorithm. Finally, perspectives on studying algorithms in a broader context than search have been offered.

FUNDING

This work was supported by The Danish Council for Independent Research and Humanities (FKK), June 2012.

DISCLOSURE STATEMENT

No potential conflict of interest was reported by the author.

NOTES

1. An earlier version of this article appeared as Ørmen, Jacob. 2014. "Historicizing Google Search: A Discussion of the Challenges Related to Archiving Search Results". In *Society of the Query Reader #9: Reflections on Web Search*, edited by René König and Miriam Rasch, 188–203. Amsterdam: Institute of Network Cultures
2. According to a search for "david cameron" on Google Trends: https://www.google.com/trends/explore#q=david%20cameron%2C%20%2Fm%2F04qdjv&cmpt=q&tz= (accessed 12 May 2015).
3. See, for instance, the official remarks from Google on https://developers.google.com/custom-search/ (accessed 16 January 2015).
4. See http://www.google.com/intl/en/policies/terms/ (accessed 20 August 2015).
5. The Danish Web archive (netarkivet.dk) archives certain culturally and politically important websites on a routine basis and then archives an extensive number of websites determined on an *ad hoc* basis for specific pre-planned or suddenly occurring events. In that way, they combine the models presented here.

6. Comparison made with the free tool Google Trends (available at www.google.com/trends/).

REFERENCES

Agarwal, Amit. 2015. "How to Scrape Google Search Results inside a Google Sheet." *Digital Inspiration*, June 4. http://www.labnol.org/internet/google-web-scraping/28450/.

Borra, Erik, and René König. 2013. "Googling 9/11: The Perspectives of a Search Engine on a Global Event." Paper presented at the Society of the Query Reader #2 conference, Amsterdam, Institute of Network Cultures, November 7–8.

Bozdag, Engin. 2013. "Bias in Algorithmic Filtering and Personalization." *Ethics and Information Technology* 15: 209–227.

Brin, Sergey, and Lawrence Page. 1998. "The Anatomy of a Large-scale Hypertextual Web Search Engine." *Computer Networks and ISDN Systems* 30 (1–7): 107–117.

Bro, Peter, and Filip Wallberg. 2014. "Digital Gatekeeping." *Digital Journalism* 2 (3): 446–454.

Brügger, Niels. 2011. "Web Archiving—Between past, Present, and Future." In *The Handbook of Internet Studies*, edited by Mia Consalvo and Charles Ess, 24–42. Chichester: Wiley-Blackwell.

Bruns, Axel, Jean E. Burgess, Kate Crawford, and Frances Shaw. 2012. "#Qldfloods and @QPSMedia: Crisis Communication on Twitter in the 2011 South East Queensland Floods." *ARC Centre of Excellence for Creative Industries and Innovation*. http://eprints.qut.edu.au/48241/1/floodsreport.pdf.

Bucher, Taina. 2012. "Want to Be on the Top? Algorithmic Power and the Threat of Invisibility on Facebook." *New Media & Society* 14 (7): 1164–1180.

Couldry, Nick, and Joseph Turow. 2014. "Big Data, Big Questions. Advertising, Big Data and the Clearance of the Public Realm: Marketers' New Approaches to the Content Subsidy." *International Journal of Communication* 8. http://ijoc.org/index.php/ijoc/article/view/2166.

Dayan, Dayan, and Elihu Katz. 1992. *Media Events: The Live Broadcasting of History*. Cambridge, MA: Harvard University Press.

Dijck, José van. 2013. *The Culture of Connectivity: A Critical History of Social Media*. Oxford & New York: Oxford University Press.

Edelman, Benjamin. 2010. "Hard-coding Bias in Google 'Algorithmic' Search Results." *Benjamin Edelman*, November 15. http://www.benedelman.org/hardcoding/.

Edelman, Benjamin, and Benjamin Lockwood. 2011. "Measuring Bias in 'Organic' Web Search." *Benjamin Edelman*, January 19. http://www.benedelman.org, http://www.benedelman.org/searchbias/.

Fernando, Anisha T. J., Jia Tina Du, and Helen Ashman. 2014. "Personalisation of Web Search: Exploring Search Query Parameters and User Information Privacy Implications—the Case of Google." In *Proceeding of the 1st International Workshop on Privacy-preserving IR: When Information Retrieval Meets Privacy and Security* (PIR 2014), edited by Luo Si, Grace Hui Yang, Sicong Zhang, and Lei Cen, 31–36. Gold Coast, Australia.

Feuz, Martin, Matthew Fuller, and Felix Stalder. 2011. "Personal Web Searching in the Age of Semantic Capitalism: Diagnosing the Mechanisms of Personalisation." *First Monday* 16 (2). http://firstmonday.org/ojs/index.php/fm/article/view/3344/2766.

Granka, Laura A. 2010. "The Politics of Search: A Decade Retrospective." *The Information Society* 26 (5): 364–374.

Hannak, Aniko, Piotr Sapiezynski, Arash Molavi Kakhki, Balachander Krishnamurthy, David Lazer, Alan Mislove, and Christo Wilson. 2013. "Measuring Personalization of Web Search." In *Proceedings of the 22nd International Conference on World Wide Web* (WWW '13), edited by Daniel Schwabe, Virgilio Almeida, Hartmut Glaser, Ricardo Baeza-Yates, and Sue Moon, 527–538, Rio de Janeiro, Brazil.

Heitner, Darren. 2012. "Red Bull Stratos worth Tens of Millions of Dollars in Global Exposure for the Red Bull Brand." *Forbes*, October 15. http://www.forbes.com/sites/darrenheitner/2012/10/15/red-bull-stratos-worth-tens-of-millions-of-dollars-in-global-exposure-for-the-red-bull-brand/.

Helles, Rasmus. 2013. "The Big Head and the Long Tail: An Illustration of Explanatory Strategies for Big Data Internet Studies." *First Monday* 18 (10). http://firstmonday.org/ojs/index.php/fm/article/view/4874/3753.

Hillis, Ken, Michael Petit, and Kylie Jarrett. 2013. *Google and the Culture of Search*. New York: Routledge.

Jensen, Klaus Bruhn. 2010. "New Media, Old Methods-internet Methodologies and the Online/Offline Divide." In *The Handbook of Internet Studies*, edited by Mia Consalvo and Charles Ess, 43–58. Chichester: Wiley-Blackwell.

Jiang, Min. 2012. "The Business and Politics of Search Engines: A Comparative Study of Baidu and Google's Search Results of Internet Events in China." *New Media & Society* 16 (2): 212–233.

Karlsson, Michael, and Jesper Strömbäck. 2010. "Freezing the Flow of Online News." *Journalism Studies* 11 (1): 2–19.

Karpf, David. 2012. "Social Science Research Methods in Internet Time." *Information, Communication & Society* 15 (5): 639–661.

Katz, Elihu, and Tamar Liebes. 2007. "'No More Peace!': How Disaster, Terror and War Have Upstaged Media Events." *International Journal of Communication* 1: 157–166. http://ijoc.org/index.php/ijoc/article/view/44.

Kautsky, Robert, and Andreas Widholm. 2008. "Online Methodology: Analysing News Flows of Online Journalism." *Westminster Papers in Communication and Culture* 5 (2): 81–97.

Kuzel, Anton J. 1992. "Sampling in Qualitative Inquiry." In *Doing Qualitative Research*, edited by B. F. Crabtree and W. L. Miller, 31–44. Thousand Oaks, CA: Sage Publications.

Lewandowski, Dirk. 2005. "Web Searching, Search Engines and Information Retrieval." *Information Services & Use* 25: 137–147.

Makino, Takaki, Chaesang Jung, and Doantam Phan. 2015. "Finding More Mobile-friendly Search Results." *Google - Webmaster Central Blog*, February 26. http://googlewebmastercentral.blogspot.dk/2015/02/finding-more-mobile-friendly-search.html.

Marres, Noortje, and Esther Weltevrede. 2013. "Scraping the Social? Issues in Real-time Social Research." *Journal of Cultural Economy* 6 (3): 313–335.

Mayer-Schönberger, Viktor, and Kenneth Cukier. 2013. *Big Data: A Revolution That Will Transform How We Live, Work, and Think*. New York: Houghton Mifflin Harcourt.

Mitchell, Amy, Mark Jurkowitz, and Kenneth Olmstead. 2014. "How Readers Get to News Sites: Social, Search and Direct - Pathways to Digital News." *Pew Research Center - Journalism & Media*, March 13. http://www.journalism.org/2014/03/13/social-search-direct/.

Pan, Bing, Helene Hembrooke, Thorsten Joachims, Lori Lorigo, Geri Gay, and Laura Granka. 2007. "In Google We Trust: Users' Decisions on Rank, Position, and Relevance." *Journal of Computer-Mediated Communication* 12 (3): 801–823.

Pariser, Eli. 2012. *The Filter Bubble: How the New Personalized Web is Changing What We Read and How We Think*. New York: Penguin Books.

Purcell, Kristen, Joanna Brenner, and Lee Rainie. 2012. "Search Engine Use 2012". *Pew Research Center—Internet, Science & Tech*, March 9. http://www.pewinternet.org/2012/03/09/main-findings-11/.

Rogers, Richard. 2013a. "Plenary Session: 'The Network Tradition in Communication Research and Scholarship.'" In International Communication Association (ICA) Conference, London, June 17-22, 2013.

Rogers, Richard. 2013b. *Digital Methods*. Cambrdige, Mass.: MIT Press.

Sanz, E., and J. Stancik. 2013. "Your Search - 'Ontological Security' - Matched 111,000 Documents: An Empirical Substantiation of the Cultural Dimension of Online Search." *New Media & Society* 16 (2): 252–270.

Spink, Amanda, Yashmeet Khopkar, Prital Shah, and Sandip Debnath. 2003. "Search Engine Personalization: An Exploratory Study." *First Monday* 8 (7). http://firstmonday.org/ojs/index.php/fm/article/view/1063.

Thurman, Neil, and Steve Schifferes. 2012. "The Future of Personalization at News Websites." *Journalism Studies* 13 (5–6): 775–790.

Vis, Farida. 2013. "Twitter as a Reporting Tool for Breaking News." *Digital Journalism* 1 (1): 27–47.

Xing, Xinyu, Wei Meng, Dan Doozan, Nick Feamster, Wenke Lee, and Alex C. Snoeren. 2014. "Exposing Inconsistent Web Search Results with Bobble." In *Passive and Active Measurement SE – 13*, edited by Michalis Faloutsos and Aleksandar Kuzmanovic, 8362:131–140.

Zimmer, Michael. 2008. "The Externalities of Search 2.0: The Emerging Privacy Threats When the Drive for the Perfect Search Engine Meets Web 2.0." *First Monday* 13 (3). http://firstmonday.org/ojs/index.php/fm/article/view/2136

Zuckerman, Ethan. 2011. "In Soviet Russia, Google Researches You! | … My Heart's in Accra." …My Heart's in Accra. http://www.ethanzuckerman.com/blog/2011/03/24/in-soviet-russia-google-researches-you/.

GRASPING THE DIGITAL NEWS USER
Conceptual and methodological advances in news use studies

Ike Picone

In recent years, people's news consumption has become increasingly fragmented over different devices, news sources and, especially with the advent of mobile technologies, different situational contexts. This renders a growing part of our (news) media consumption very volatile, even transparent. Journalism scholars are compelled to expand the existing methodological toolset at their disposal if they hope to grasp news audiences' changing practices. This article investigates the lines along which such a toolset should be conceived. As the digitisation of media and journalism challenges our understanding of news audiences, the article opens by paying considerable attention to the conceptual underpinning of news audiences by revisiting the notion of audience activity in the light of evolving news use practices. This reflection results in an integrated conceptualisation of the term "audience activity", which in turn makes out a case for adopting "news users" as a more versatile concept to denote people engaging with news. Subsequently, this article addresses how such a more encompassing notion of news users can shape new topical and methodological directions in news audience studies. The article concludes by exploring the current advancements in modular online time use surveys as an illustration of a data-gathering method combining traditional techniques with digital tools to study news users as they cross different devices, platforms, sources and contexts.

Introduction: What Happened to the News Audience?

When we take a moment to look at how news can be consulted today, we can figuratively wonder what happened to the news audience as we once knew it. More precisely, the question is how we have come to conceive of those people consulting the news through media in a different way, reflecting the technological advancements profoundly altering the way news is mediated. Academic thinking about audiences has long been framed by theories of mass communication (Livingstone 2003). The mass audience was a way to describe the cultural formation of groups of people around mainly televised content. Today's societies are characterised by a different form of mediation that allows a more active, multidirectional role for the audience in the communication process (Castells 2007). This role is difficult to grasp through the lens of mass communication theory. The question of how to conceptualise the audiences of new, digital and mobile media has been addressed at various occasions in audience studies over the past decades (Livingstone 2003, 2004). Also in digital journalism studies "the user in control" has been incorporated in various descriptions of the journalistic audience. Jay Rosen's (2006) description of "the people formerly known as the audience" probably best illustrates the need to part from mass-media thinking. But the many different descriptions share the common assumption that people have more control in the process of collecting, reporting, filtering, analysing and distributing news, something that previously was considered the almost exclusive domain of news producers (Lasica 2003; Singer et al. 2011).

As such, we witness both journalists and journalism researchers adopting the lens of digital, connected or distributed media through which to view today's news audience. However, this "exchange of lenses" has also been addressed critically by scholars like Carpentier (2011) and Couldry (2011), who stress that we should not throw out the baby with the bathwater when it comes to complement existing but still applicable insights with new ones. As elaborated below, such conceptual vagueness affects our theoretical understanding of evolutions in the way people relate with media. Consequently, they also steer the direction in which scholars look for new methods to empirically validate theoretical assumptions. In other words, investigating methods in the age of digital journalism requires us to explicate through which conceptual lens we look at new phenomena, because it shapes the questions we want to find an answer to and, in turn, the methods that will allow us to find those answers.

Hence, this article will pay considerable attention to the changing conceptualisation of the media audience. I do so in the spirit of continuity, seeking to marry still applicable existing concepts with much needed emerging ones. The active audience serves as a starting point, as this notion might be the one most in need of conceptual clarification in the light of current trends in news consumption. More precisely, the affordances of digital media are often heralded as rendering media users more active compared to the "passive" mass-media audience. But within audience studies, mass-media audiences are long since believed to be active audiences (see below). So, would that mean media users now are *more* active than previous generations of audiences?

The article seeks to elucidate this conceptual vagueness by revisiting the notion of audience activity in reception studies. This will lead us to question "news audience" as an adequate denominator for people engaging with news and instead put forward "news users" as a more appropriate term. Before we start, we would like to stress that we consider audience activity to be a theoretical concept aimed at refining our understanding of media use, not at surfacing the ideological or structural inequalities in power that might shape it. The political dimension, although more than relevant, lies beyond the scope of this article.

Expanding the Notion of Audience Activity

As discussed, media audiences are ascribed more control over content production processes than was the case in the pre-internet era. However, when focusing specifically on the possibility of sharing, distribution and production of content afforded by current digital media, we might overlook aspects that have become constitutive of our understanding of the "active audience" within audience studies. So, when expanding our notion of audience activity in order to incorporate the affordances of digital media, we should simultaneously reaffirm existing interpretations of audience activity when still applicable. This continuity is important, as networked audiences on many occasions still act as broadcast audiences merely consuming broadcasted content (Couldry 2011, 213).

Within audience studies, two main interpretations of audience activity can broadly be discerned. First to speak of an active audience were scholars within the Uses and Gratifications (U&G) tradition, who conceived the audience as conscious individuals able to identify their own needs and interest and select media sources and messages accordingly (Rubin 2002, 528). I would argue that this same kind of "selective activity" underlies many ideas of interactivity as developed within the broad domain of New Media studies and Human Computer Interaction studies. Authors such as Lievrouw and Livingstone (2006, 7) see interactivity as "the selectivity and reach that media technologies afford users in their 'choices of information sources and interactions with other people'. The immediacy, responsiveness, and social presence of interaction via new media channels constitute a qualitatively and substantively different experience than what was possible via mass media channels". Through the notion of interactivity, the idea of "selective activity" has been adapted to suit the more lean-forward environment enabled by new media.

A second interpretation of an active audience emerged within the field of reception studies, where the idea of an active audience is closely linked to the text-reader or encoding–decoding metaphor of Stuart Hall (1980), which addressed people's ability to interpret media messages in different and opposing ways than intended by the sender. Like U&G, this theoretical perspective has also been developed to address how audiences act in relation to mass media. Still, as Livingstone (2004, 78–79) suggests, we should not only apply this to television audiences, but also to audiences and users of new media, as they "are increasingly active—selective, self-directed, producers as well as receivers of texts". Livingstone here already speaks of both audience and users, and also refers to their role as producers. Still, the "reader" as "producer of text" implies the reader as actor of meaning making, not as an actor of content production. As such, the "interpretative activity" put forward here does not comprise the actual production of content by media users central in the use of digital media.

Exactly the possibility of using digital, distributed technologies not merely to consume but also to produce content is what many authors have seen as an important affordance. When new technologies link people together in online social networks, "productive energy" (Hartley 2009, 234) can come from anywhere in the system, rather than from centralised media companies. This "productive activity" (Picone 2011) comes in different gradations. People can create an original piece of information and put it online, but can also comment or share existing content with others. In any of these instances, content is (re)produced by the media user. Professional and amateur media users alike can use the technology to produce content in similar ways—yet not necessarily equal ways.

In summary, the various attempts to rethink the "audience" in order to grasp better how people engage with media have revealed a new form of audience activity, i.e. the productive activity. Productive activity can be positioned next to selective activity and interpretative activity as the three main ways audience activity has been conceived in audience and reception studies. While one could question whether these three dimensions do fully encompass the range of audience activity, I would argue that other notions such as interactivity, co-creation and participation can be reduced to a gradation of interpretative, selective or productive activity. Deconstructing the widely accepted notion of audience activity in this manner delineates the "room to manoeuvre" people have when using media, without implying that everyone takes advantage of it to the same extent. More appropriate then would be to consider the selective, interpretative and productive dimension of activity as continuums on which a user can be active to varying degrees.

This conceptualisation now allows us to address more concretely the direction of methodological advancements to study news audiences in a digital media system. If we want to grasp the full scope of how audiences are "active", we need methodologies that enable us to incorporate all three forms of audience activity in order to obtain a more holistic view of audience activity. This does not alter the fact that specific data-gathering methods will still be needed to separately study each form of activity in depth. Still, could we conceive of methods that allow incorporation of these forms of activity, even measure them one against the other and see relations between them emerge? This would imply taking into consideration the many different, almost individual constellations of media use that can be found within audiences (see below). This leads us to another conceptual issue to clarify, namely the notion of "audience".

Why Turn to the Media User?

The term "audience" as such also seems to be trapped between the need for conceptual continuity and new concepts to capture changes in media consumption adequately. The adequacy of the term has been debated extensively within the broad field of audience research, especially in relation to other terms like "consumers", "publics" and "citizens" (Couldry, Livingstone, and Markham, 2007; Livingstone 2005). In respect to new media, the notion of "users" has already been suggested before. Opposed to "audience", Livingstone (2003, 348) sees "users" as "allowing for a greater variety of modes of engagement". For one, it does indeed cover the productive dimension of activity better. "News users" has also been widely adopted by journalists, media professionals and academics alike. It forms a more natural fit for describing people that comment on articles, share stories with their social networks, upload pictures, etc.

However, various media scholars have critically addressed the adoption of "user" and "use" as terms to describe people in relation to media for different reasons. One recurring argument, reflected in the work of Carpentier (2011) and Couldry (2011), is that new conceptualisations of media audiences too easily overlook the applicability of existing insights and concepts from the long-lasting tradition of audience studies. Couldry (2011, 213), for example, explicitly pleads for the continuation of "audience research" as a domain in reaction to the "Web 2.0" ideal of audience members all interacting with and producing content. He rightly points out that even in today's converged media environment, a large majority of people are still just consuming content and, as such, are acting like an audience. At the same time still, he acknowledges the need for "a more accurate register of what people are doing with media" (213).

This said, "media user" and subsequently "media use" still might do a better job at describing people in relation to media. First, because the notion of the user settles the score with "the linear relationship among production, text and audience" (Lievrouw and Livingstone 2006, 3) that has been haunting media studies for decades. The signifier "audience" both etymologically and historically implies an endpoint in the media infrastructure, the moment where the message is "heard" and interpreted. This makes it difficult to conceptually incorporate the productive activity enabling audience members to distribute existing or generate new content. "Media user" does not have this connotation.

Second, "media user" does not require defining people in relation to a specific media device or media practice. If we take news use for example, data from the 2015 *Reuters Institute Digital News Report* shows that a key global trend is that ever-more people are using two or three devices to access the news, with specifically smartphones and tablets "extending our access points [and] making us more connected to the news at home and on the move" (Newman and Levy 2015, 8). "Media user"—and not "medium" user for that matter—allows this increase in cross-device consumption to be taken into account. Similarly, "media use" accommodates under a single moniker the whole range of media practices that a person can undertake via his or her media repertoire, from watching, reading and listening to sharing, commenting and posting. Employing "media user" can hence be considered medium-agnostic.

Third, in contrast to, for example, "the audience", "the user" has a singular and plural form, as such encompassing both the very individual as the collective nature of media practices. Livingstone (2003, 348) argues that the notion of user "tends to be overly individualistic and instrumental, losing the sense of a collectivity which is central to 'the audience'". Still, more than a decade later, users seem ever-more likely to spread their media consumption over multiple platforms, hence creating their own "personal information space" (Deuze 2007, 30–33). Speaking about "media users" does not have to imply that people can no longer act as an audience in certain circumstances. Ironically, Livingstone (2014) herself gives an impetus for a more relational approach to audiences in a recent essay when she takes the "user" as a starting point and moves on to address him/her in his/her different capacities: the user as proletariat, the user as public, the user as audience, the user as consumer and even the user as worker.

In sum, turning to news users instead of news audiences offers media and journalism scholars more conceptual flexibility to address persons in relation to various media and exercise various forms of media activity. As I have sought to illustrate, this does not stand in the way of conceptual continuity. By coupling the notion of media users to the notion of audience activity, we can still address media users in their capacity as audiences of mass-distributed content. What adopting "media users" does allow us to do is to acknowledge the more individual, cross-media and productive ways in which media can be consumed.

How to Conceptualise News Use?

Having expanded the notion of activity in the context of media use and reaffirmed the conceptual adequateness of the term "media users", we can now address media users in their capacity as people engaging with the specific kind of content that is news:

news users. News use can then be conceptualised as an emanation of selective, interpretative and productive activity (see Table 1), enabling us to identify specific domains around which research about news users in an age of digital journalism can develop. I now give an indication of what these research domains could be in order to end up with a clear view of the methodological implications of researching news users in today's digital media system. In this overview, media are conceived both as content and as devices via which this content is accessed. At the same time, the notion of device can be limiting when studying media in a digital, multimedia context. A tablet, for example, combines so many possibilities, from audio-visual to written and even playable news, all with their own dynamics and logics, that it becomes difficult to see it as one device. Therefore, I speak of platforms, following Opgenhaffen's (2011) distinction between a meta-medium, a platform and a format. A meta-medium, like a tablet, includes different sub-media or platforms, such as news sites, Twitter or Reddit, each with their specific combination of formats and features, e.g. an article, news video, tweet or "like".

News users can actively select, give meaning and produce news media. When selecting news, they constitute a news repertoire, where certain sources or devices are preferred over others to follow what happens in the world. *What* is happening can vary according to how news users interpret the news, which in turn will depend on their socio-cultural background in general, but more specifically also on their levels of news literacy. At the same time, they can consult the news on an increasingly varied and continuously expanding set of devices, which are, or are not, appropriated in different ways in their daily lives. Finally, sharing, commenting, remixing, etc., all are forms of productive activity that media users can apply to news. But news users also contribute to the development of new news platforms. Let us elaborate on these topics to give an impression of what a future agenda for user-oriented news research could look like.

News Repertoires

More than ever, audiences are confronted with a broad pallet of choices in composing a media diet or media repertoire (Hasebrink and Popp 2006). Relating this to media users' selective activity brings up the question "how media users combine different media contacts into a comprehensive pattern of exposure …, how they integrate the increasing number of options into their everyday lives" (Hasebrink and Popp 2006, 369–370). As noted by Couldry, Livingstone, and Markham (2007, 190–191), "the particular constellation of media on which one individual draws may be quite different than another's". This illustrates that next to the study of individual modes of media

TABLE 1
Levels of user activity in relation to news content and device

	News content	News platforms
Level of selective activity	Repertoire of news sources	Repertoire of news platforms
Level of interpretative activity	News literacy	Domestication of news platforms
Level of productive activity	Production of news content	Creation of news platforms

consumption, looking at the cross-media combinations people select, and why they do so, becomes equally important (Picone, Courtois, and Paulussen 2015; Schrøder 2011).

Adopting a repertoire approach offers the opportunity to gain new insights about audiences specifically by studying what combinations of media people choose over others (Edgerly 2015, 4; for a theoretical and methodological underpinning of this approach, see also Hasebrink and Popp 2006). Applied to news repertoires, this means investigating the combination of different news sources, rather than looking at which single source or medium is potentially eclipsing another one (Van Damme et al. 2015, 3). Van Damme et al. (2015) take this approach in their study on mobile news consumption to find that the choice of one device over another is mainly based on the spatial context of news defining the available devices. As such, the smartphone becomes the preferred device when no other devices are at hand. Therefore, the question of which sources and devices people choose to use over others should be complemented by the questions "when", "where" and "with whom", i.e. the socio-spatial context of use.

Recent qualitative and quantitative studies like the one of Hasebrink and Domeyer (2012) or Van Damme et al. (2015) have applied this "repertoire-oriented" approach to the study of news, identifying different types of news users based on their news repertoires. Remarkably, as Edgerly (2015, 5) also notes, these studies have scrutinised news repertoires mainly in terms of selection of devices, leaving a white space as regards repertoires that function at the content level. In her own research, Edgerly therefore takes into account more content-related aspects of news like its ideological perspective or the level of infotainment. She shows how some news users develop repertoires based on preference for a set of devices, while others constitute their repertoires in order to consume specific types of ideological news or, on the contrary, look for a variety of styles and voices.

In further developing this approach on news use, differentiating between platform and content should be put forward, also in order to account for the ways in which choice of content and choice of platform will mutually affect each other. Somebody constituting a repertoire based on, for example, mobile media might be more prone to use news sources that offer updates or short summaries like Yahoo News Digest or news via Instagram. Vice versa, somebody looking for investigative reporting might constitute a repertoire comprising platforms that favour comfortable reading like long-form articles on e-readers and newspapers. As such, the effort of Edgerly to incorporate attributes of news content in investigating news repertoires is not only necessary, but should be further expanded to include factors such as topics and brands (updates, breaking news, long-form, etc.).

News Literacy and Domestication

On the level of interpretative activity and news content, the critical interpretation of news is a theme that is gaining attention as a specific form of media literacy (see the edited collection by Mihailidis 2012a). News literacy has been paid little academic attention to so far (Mihailidis 2012b; Ashley, Maksl, and Craft 2013). It requires applying to news the common notion of media literacy as the ability to access, analyse, evaluate and communicate messages in a wide variety of forms (Aufderheide and Firestone 1993).

Methodological tools to probe people's news literacy are limited. Developing such instruments requires adapting existing media literacy scales to news content (Ashley, Maksl, and Craft 2013). Within the current measuring systems for internet skills, news literacy closely coincides with content-related internet skills, more precisely information skills (Van Deursen and van Dijk 2014). Information skills include people's way of selecting and evaluating information sources, but do not really include more specific forms of critical attitudes towards news content. Ashley, Maksl, and Craft (2013, 9) suggest that news literacy requires media users "to have some specific knowledge of the normative goals of journalism and the forces that influence news media content", referring to dynamics of framing, gate keeping, agenda setting and media bias (Stroud 2011).

Within journalism studies, news literacy should be both a matter of concern and an object of study. It obviously links to journalism education, but also implies a broader scope not limited to journalism students. In fact, students of all ages should learn to comprehend, evaluate, analyse and produce news, skills that serve as "strategies for more empowered, tolerant, aware, active participants in twenty-first century civic society" (Mihailidis 2012b, 3).

When applying the interpretative activity to news platforms, the domestication theory explored by Roger Silverstone and Leslie Haddon during the 1980s (Silverstone and Haddon 1996; see also Haddon 2006; Livingstone 2007) offers a valuable starting point. Domestication theory attributes to users of technology the possibility to give their own congruent or oppositional meaning to technological artefacts. The added value of a technology lies not merely in the way it is produced, but also in the way users experience it (Punie 1997, 251). By actually using technological artefacts, users value specific characteristics over others and define which characteristics are most relevant (Hyysalo 2007, 230).

The same is true for news platforms. The qualitative study of Humphreys, Von Pape, and Karnowski (2013), for example, takes domestication as one of its starting points to look at people's smartphone use for information purposes. It reveals a difference in using information in a more extractive (outcome-oriented, focused on getting specific information) or immersive way (process-oriented, getting "in the flow"), and links this to specific devices (smartphone versus laptop) and temporal, spatial and social contexts (see below).

News Production and Creation

Finally, many people's media repertoires are very likely to include media that allow them to be "productive" in their news use. In studies of citizen or participatory journalism (see e.g. Singer et al. 2011), "productive" processes have been mainly focused on the way that journalists deal with the user in his or her capacity as content provider. From a user perspective, the productive activity can apply to far more forms of engagement with news than the co-creation of content. Think of the production of original content created by news users, sharing or liking existing content and even the mere liking of news. The internet has rendered user-generated news production intrinsically public—compared to, for example, sharing clipped newspaper stories or discussing the news face to face. I have previously argued that the dynamics underlying various forms of productive media use are the ones of self-publication (Picone 2011)—in line with other studies such as Papacharissi's (2011) work on social network use.

This productive activity can also be applied to news platforms. This is by no means an obvious activity for media users to undertake. However, the history of media shows how amateurs have played an active role in the production of different media forms like radio, cable television, video production and personal computers (Fish 2013). Douglas (1988, 44), in an historical analysis of radio adoption in the United States, shows how at the beginning of the previous century amateurs driven by fascination for electronic communication used available household appliances to build home radios when Marconi's technology was expensive and focused on shipping. This "productive" role of "ordinary" people in the creation of technology has received a lot of attention within disciplines like participatory design studies or (user) innovation studies (Löwgren and Reimer 2013). Of course, when applied to a meta-medium like the internet, the substructure of technology remains fairly inaccessible to media users. On the other hand, setting up a platform, like a website or blog, on which to publish news content that can potentially reach a large audience has never been easier.

What I hope to have demonstrated by now is how the notions of interpretative, selective and productive activity not only allow for a deeper theoretical understanding of evolution in people's news use, but can also form the basis of a thematic agenda for news user research. As such, while on a theoretical perspective all three levels of activity form an integral part of the notion of news use, specific research areas can focus on a specific level of activity. This brings us to the final topic of this article, namely what these conceptualisations imply for the empirical study of news users.

How to Grasp the Digital News User? An Agenda for Methodological Innovation in News Use Studies

Journalists and journalism scholars alike are in need of ways to probe and understand how media users "are making their presence felt by *actively* shaping media flows" (Jenkins, Ford, and Green 2013, 2, emphasis added). This article proposes to conceive active news use in terms of selective, interpretative and productive activity, but also touched briefly upon the increased importance of socio-spatial context in which news is used. News flows are more intricate than ever, intertwining professional and collaborative information production, journalistic, social and individual news selection, private and public, sedentary and nomadic news use. As such, grasping the digital news user as he or she "flows" through different news "settings" grows more complex, especially from a methodological point of view. Hence, rethinking our methodological toolkit— evaluating existing and exploring new methods—should start from an understanding of news users both as individuals as well as social groups, *actively* engaging with news media through a variety of socio-spatial contexts of news use (see also Picone 2013). How then can this conceptual base inform the way in which we seek new methods in news use studies?

As I will propose in this final section, we can consider a set of guiding principles for methodological innovation in news use studies, taking these insights as a starting point. In line with the idea of conceptual continuity, not all application domains identified above are in equal need of methodological innovation. News literacy, for example, while relatively new, can build on the vast research in ICT skills and media literacy, while domestication research still offers a sound methodological framework to tackle the use of news platform repertoires. A big challenge lies in how to take into account news users' repertoires as well as the socio-spatial contexts of news use. Therefore, by way of example, time use research is now presented as a source of inspiration in methodological innovation that takes into account both of these issues.

Guiding Principles for Methodological Innovation in News Use Studies

First, if we want to study people's news experience, we need to take the whole media repertoire into account. The specific constellation of people's news diet is constituted by what people perceive to be worthwhile to pay attention to in a specific situation (Schrøder and Kobbernagel 2010, 116). Here, news competes with various other possible occupations, ranging from skimming through social media to playing games. But also within one's news repertoire various types of news content and platforms compete for a news user's attention. News use should then be studied in relation to people's other media activities. This implies a more holistic approach, where the study of news use is more strongly embedded into the study of media repertoires as a whole.

Second, this variation in the constellation of media repertoires is amplified even further as media content can be consumed "anywhere, anytime", increasing the importance of situational factors in shaping people's media experience. Our research should take into account the socio-spatial context of news use, in order to answer the question when and where specific news channels are given a more prominent role within news repertoires. This requires methodologies that take into account where and when news is used, and how it is embedded in people's daily lives.

Adopting these principles offers the advantage of studying news in a way closer to how media users actually access news. News reaches us through various platforms throughout the day. Every platform will, of course, have intrinsic affordances that appeal to people. Still, the more news content and platforms will truly "live" next to each other, the more news becomes a cross-platform experience, the more these affordances will become relative to the affordances of other news media. Previous research on channel repertoires has shown that the availability and access of media can be more significant predictors of media repertoires than individual demographics or content preferences (Taneja et al. 2012). But what about when a lot of choices are available at the same time? Second-screen activities illustrate this well. When watching the news on television one can easily consult news sites, check Twitter for updates or watch news videos on Snapchat, simultaneously; what are the factors that will affect news users' preference at that specific moment? The same holds throughout the day, when news users continuously have an array of news content and platforms at their disposal. Exactly the interplay between these various options becomes key in understanding how news users experience the news.

RETHINKING RESEARCH METHODS IN AN AGE OF DIGITAL JOURNALISM

Time Use Research as Inspiration for Innovation in News Use Studies

By way of an example, I turn to time use research and how it has become an important source for methodological inspiration in our own research. Our research group has been collaborating with sociologists and mobility experts to set up a large-scale diary study in Flanders, Belgium using MOTUS, a digital survey tool.[1] I will outline the research design of the project to illustrate the methodological advancements made.

At its core, time use research "describes the allocation of time among various circumstances and subjective states … It can provide measures of the extent, durations and purposes of access to leisure activities, or of information technology use" (Gershuny 2011, 4). Activities form the basic unit of analysis indicating "an event or episode, with a finite duration, that has an explicit (readily understandable) meaning or purpose" (Gershuny 2003, 1). Time use surveys aim to register the sequence of activities people perform during the day, usually complementing the time and duration of the activity by also asking people where they did it, with whom, what they were doing to accompany these activities (primary and secondary activities) and less often also how they felt about it (Robinson and Godbey 1999, 5).

Our study comprises 3412 respondents who completed an intake survey probing for general socio-demographic information as well as information on the media devices they have at their disposal. They were then asked to fill in an online diary for a period of seven days. We used responsive design to make the diary module easily accessible on any digital device. A subset of the sample ($N = 981$) received a specific media module, including more media-related questions in the intake survey as well as two complementary options in the diary: when selecting a media activity, they were subsequently asked to specify which kind of content and which kind of platform they used (see below). The respondents could fill in the diary on a 10-minute basis—although the software now allows a minute per minute registration. The diary comprised a large set of time-spending activities, all divided in subcategories, in a closed template. Only at specific occasions were respondents asked open questions, e.g. when using a media device that was not listed. They were asked to do this as regularly as possible, but not prompted further through mails or text messages.

Media use is one of the categories of activities. Echoing the approach on media time by the Dutch Social and Cultural Planning Bureau (SCP) in their most recent time use survey (Sonck and Pennekamp 2014), we have defined media activities on the level of the sensory experience, i.e. listening, watching, reading, communicating, gaming and surfing. Each of these broad categories is subdivided into more specific ones, like listening to a radio programme or watching a television series, asking in more detail about the format of media use. At this point, our study adds an extra level of analysis compared to many existing ones. Every time a respondent registers a media activity, he or she is prompted to answer two consecutive questions: what device was used for the activity and what kind of content was consulted. As a result, an example of a possible registered activity would be reading (main activity), more specifically reading news, more precisely news headlines (content), via tablet (device).

Advantages and Limitations of Time Use Research

We definitely do not stand alone in our effort to explore methodological opportunities to grasp today's news users. Media researchers are trying to advance their research methods in order to find ways to follow media users over the different contexts in which they access (news) media throughout the day. Time use research has both advantages and limitations compared to other new methods.

An important plus of time use research is that it can be considered "non-media centric". This refers to the call of media scholars like David Morley and Shaun Moores to put the particularities of media less central in the study of media to the benefit of a stronger focus on everyday practices and experiences (Krajina, Moores, and Morley 2014). The more media are ubiquitous, the less they should be seen as standing outside of lived experience (Deuze 2011, 138). By looking at time spent as a whole, time use research does approach media use in relation to media users' other daily activities and routines. In that sense, it does not only allow positioning of news use in the larger perspective of media use, e.g. in relation to the use of social media, but media use in turn as part of people's daily activities and routines. This enables researchers to go beyond the relationship between users and media to find correlations between media or news use and other aspects of life like the availability of leisure time, commuting patterns, etc.

A related advantage is that time use research enables researchers to follow individual respondents across the various daily situations in which they turn to news media. News use is not bound to occur in a specific setting. The news can be accessed at home, at work, on the go, etc. Time use research takes this into consideration, as it does not only probe the time dimension, but also simultaneous activities, and where and with whom these occur. As such, this methodology considers an argument heard especially in recent ethnographic research, namely that users and the way they wander through various contexts should be the focus of observation (Picone 2013; Vittadini and Pasquali 2013). Admittedly, ethnographic research will offer more thick descriptions of user practices and the situations in which they take place, but at the same time it remains very invasive, especially for studying something rather individual like consulting news. Time use research, however, particularly as a quantitative methodology, still offers a rather substantial view on the context of use, while being less intrusive—without denying the burden it can be for respondents.

Also, adopting the activity as the object of analysis and probing for device and content on a secondary level has the crucial advantage of being media-agnostic. Decoupling activity, content and device, each of which is registered independently, but always in relation to time and place, allows us to shift our focus depending on the questions we want to tackle. When it comes to news, for example, we can get a picture of when and where people consult news, irrespective of the device they use to do so. Or we can focus on a specific news genre and look at the situations that genre is consumed in most of the time.

A first and obvious caveat then is the inevitable limitation of self-reporting. Media use research primarily uses data that are gathered, be it in a quantitative or qualitative way, by asking people to report what they do, think, feel or experience. The issues that have been associated with this form of data collection, like retention bias, socially desirable responding or flawed self-assessment, are regarded as a necessary evil. Researchers have traditionally turned to various forms of data triangulation to minimise these shortcomings. Still, when applied specifically to the measurement of news use in a world where "media are ubiquitous—they are everywhere—and pervasive—they cannot switch off" (Deuze 2012, xi), the issue of self-reporting becomes even more pressing.

More precisely, as we use media everywhere, anytime, it becomes difficult for people to consciously single out when they are engaging in a media activity. A lot of media moments do not consist of substantial segments devoted to necessary activities like working, sleeping and eating. Rather, mobile media, freeing users from the space–time constraints of traditional media, allow for news to be consulted in the interstices of people's schedules, those in-between moments of free time when we reach for our mobile devices in anticipation of our next activity (Dimmick, Feaster, and Hoplamazian 2011, 25). Also news use in the interstices is likely to increase. In a recent blogpost posted on NiemanLab on 11 September 2014, news entrepreneur Dan Shanoff reflects on what smart watches will mean for journalism and considers how the "glance" could be a "new subatomic unit of news". As such, it becomes virtually impossible to report all the moments when you have "got the news".

Here, a lot is expected from tracking or logging users, particularly through their mobile devices. This specific form of "big data" holds the promise of new insights about users' choices and behaviour. Newsrooms, in particular, might see more benefit in the real-life, "raw" data about their readers to inform their editorial decisions. But also academics will be looking into it. This should be encouraged, but this kind of data is not free of issues either. From the perspective of news user research, two issues are of particular relevance: openness and representativeness. Openness refers to the fact that large databases of user data are collected by private companies, be it hardware or service providers, which are often not very eager to share this sensitive information, neither with each other nor with academic institutions. As such, we are still in need of publicly accessible data on media consumption, which researchers will have to gather themselves. Representativeness might not seem an issue at first, as media companies get information on the absolute numbers of users. Still, many media companies are getting all the data of *their* users, but nobody is getting any data on *the* user. Time use research, in contrast, puts media users central and follows them as they individually move through different situations, over different devices and while accessing different kinds of content. The advantage of a digital, modular diary tool like MOTUS is the possibility of complementing the traditional self-reporting of activities with the automated logging of respondents' use of digital media—e.g. through smartphone apps and browsing history—as well as with various other available data-sets.

Finally, tying this back to conceptual work on the notion of audience, time use research also shows the advantage of adopting "media user" instead of "media audiences" as a common term for people engaging with media. When putting people central and following them across different contexts, devices and consulting various forms of content, it is difficult to hold on to "audience". "Media user" is more versatile, and allows people to be addressed in their different capacities as watchers, readers, listeners, communicators, commenters, posters, sharers, etc., simultaneously. As this article hopefully has shown, the successful new methods for studying active news use will be those which can grasp news users in as many of their various capacities.

DISCLOSURE STATEMENT

No potential conflict of interest was reported by the author.

NOTE

1. Within the MOTUS project (Modular Time Use Survey), three research groups within the Faculty of Social Sciences collaborate to develop a digital online and mobile diary tool that can be easily adjusted to the needs of specific research projects. The first on-going phase includes the development of the desktop tool and an accompanying large-scale study in Flanders. In a second phase, a mobile application will be developed and a panel will be set up. Finally, the architecture of the tool is open to allow for GPS coordinates, sensors or app use to be logged.

REFERENCES

Ashley, Seth, Adam Maksl, and Stephanie Craft. 2013. "Developing a News Media Literacy Scale." *Journalism & Mass Communication Educator* 68 (1): 7–21.

Aufderheide, Patricia, and Charles Firestone. 1993. *Media Literacy: A Report of the National Leadership Conference on Media Literacy*. Conference report. Queenstown, MD: The Aspen Institute.

Carpentier, Nico. 2011. "New Configurations of the Audience? The Challenges of User-Generated Content for Audience Theory and Media Participation." In *The Handbook of Media Audiences*, edited by Virginia Nightingale, 190–212. Malden: Blackwell Publishing.

Castells, Manuel. 2007. "Communication, Power and Counter-Power in the Network Society." *International Journal of Communication* 1 (December): 238–266.

Couldry, Nick. 2011. "The Necessary Future of the Audience… and How to Research It." In *The Handbook of Media Audiences*, edited by Virginia Nightingale, 213–229. Malden: Blackwell Publishing.

Couldry, Nick, Sonia Livingstone, and Tim Markham. 2007. *Media Consumption and Public Engagement. Beyond the Presumption of Attention*. Basingstoke: Palgrave Macmillan.

Damme, Van, Cédric Courtois Kristin, Karel Verbrugge, and Lieven De Marez. 2015. "What's APPening to News? A Mixed-Method Audience-Centred Study on Mobile News Consumption." *Mobile Media & Communication* 3 (2): 1–18.

Deuze, Mark. 2007. *Media Work*. Cambridge: Polity Press.

Deuze, Mark. 2011. "Media Life." *Media, Culture & Society* 33: 137–148.

Deuze, Mark. 2012. *Media Life*. Cambridge: Wiley.

Dimmick, John, John Christian Feaster, and Gregory J. Hoplamazian. 2011. "News in the Interstices: The Niches of Mobile Media in Space and Time." *New Media & Society* 13 (1): 23–39.

Douglas, S. J. 1988. "Amateur Operators and American Broadcasting: Shaping the Future of Radio." In *Imagining Tomorrow*, edited by Joseph J. Corn, 35–57. Cambridge: MIT Press.

Edgerly, Stephanie. 2015. "Red Media, Blue Media, and Purple Media: News Repertoires in the Colorful Media Landscape." *Journal of Broadcasting & Electronic Media* 59 (1): 1–21.

Fish, Adam. 2013. "Participatory Television: Convergence, Crowdsourcing, and Neoliberalism." *Communication, Culture & Critique* 6 (3): 372–395.

Gershuny, Jonathan. 2003. *Time and the Socioeconomic Atom: The Thirty-Second Geary Lecture*. Geary Lecture. Economic and Social Research Institute

Gershuny, Jonathan. 2011. *Time-Use Surveys and the Measurement of National Well-Being*. Research report. Oxford: Centre for Time Use Research, University of Oxford. http://www.ons.gov.uk/ons/rel/environmental/time-use-surveys-and-the-measurement-of-national-well-being/article-by-jonathan-gershuny/index.html.

Haddon, Leslie. 2006. "The Contribution of Domestication Research to in-Home Computing and Media Consumption." *The Information Society: An International Journal* 22: 195–203.

Hall, Stuart. 1980. "Encoding/Decoding." In *Culture, Media, Language*, edited by S. Hall, D. Hobson, A. Lowe and P. Willis, 128–138. London: Hutchinson.

Hartley, John. 2009. "From the Consciousness Industry to the Creative Industries: Consumer-Created Content, Social Network Markets, & the Growth of Knowledge." In *Media Industries: History, Theory & Method*, edited by Jennifer Holt and Alisa Perren, 231–244. Malden: Wiley-Blackwell.

Hasebrink, Uwe, and Hanna Domeyer. 2012. "Media Repertoires as Patterns of Behaviour and as Meaningful Practices: A Multimethod Approach to Media Use in Converging Media Environments." *Participations. Journal of Audience and Reception Studies* 9 (2).

Hasebrink, Uwe, and Jutta Popp. 2006. "Media Repertoires as a Result of Selective Media Use. a Conceptual Approach to the Analysis of Patterns of Exposure." *Communications* 31: 369–387.

Humphreys, Lee, Thilo Von Pape, and Veronika Karnowski. 2013. "Evolving Mobile Media: Uses and Conceptualizations of the Mobile Internet." *Journal of Computer-Mediated Communication* 18 (4): 491–507.

Hyysalo, Sampsa. 2007. "Versions of Care Technology." *Human Technology* 3: 228–247.

Jenkins, Henry, Sam Ford, and Joshua Green. 2013. *Spreadable Media: Creating Value and Meaning in a Networked Culture*. New York: NYU Press.

Krajina, Zlatan, Shaun Moores, and David Morley. 2014. "Non-Media-Centric Media Studies: A Cross-Generational Conversation." *European Journal of Cultural Studies* 17 (6): 682–700.

Lasica, Joseph D. 2003. "Participatory Journalism Puts the Reader in the Driver's Seat." *Online Journalism Review*. August 7. http://www.ojr.org/ojr/workplace/1060218311.php.

Lievrouw, Leah, and Sonia Livingstone. 2006. "Introduction to the Updated Student Edition." In *The Handbook of New Media. Social Shaping and Consequences of ICTs*, edited by L. A. Lievrouw and S. Livingstone, Updated Student, 1–14. London: SAGE.

Livingstone, Sonia. 2003. "The Changing Nature of Audiences : from the Mass Audience to the Interactive Media User." In *Companion to Media Studies*, 337–359. Oxford: Blackwell Publishing.

Livingstone, Sonia. 2004. "The Challenge of Changing Audiences: Or, What is the Audience Researcher to Do in the Age of the Internet?" *European Journal of Communication* 19 (1): 75–86.

Livingstone, Sonia. 2005. "On the Relation between Audiences and Publics." In *Audiences and Publics: When Cultural Engagement Matters for the Public Sphere*, edited by Sonia Livingstone, 17–41. Bristol: Intellect Books.

Livingstone, Sonia. 2007. "On the Material and the Symbolic: Silverstone's Double Articulation of Research Traditions in New Media Studies." *New Media & Society* 9: 16–24.

Livingstone, Sonia. 2014. "Identifying the Interests of Digital Users as Audiences, Consumers, Workers, and Publics." In *Media Technologies: Essays on Communication, Materiality, and Society*, edited by T. Gillespie, P. J. Boczkowski and K. A. Foot, 241–250. Inside Technology. MIT Press.

Löwgren, Jonas, and Bo Reimer. 2013. *Collaborative Media: Production, Consumption, and Design Interventions*. Cambridge: MIT Press.

Mihailidis, Paul, ed. 2012a. *News Literacy. Global Perspectives for the Newsroom and the Classroom*: Peter Lang Publishing.

Mihailidis, Paul. 2012b. "News Literacy in the Dawn of a Hypermedia Age." In *News Literacy. Global Perspectives for the Newsroom and the Classroom*, edited by Mihailidis, Paul, 1–20. New York: Peter Lang Publishing.

Newman, Nic, and David A. L. Levy. 2015. *Reuters Institute Digital News Report 2015. Tracking the Future of News*. Survey Report. Reuters Institute Digital News Report. Oxford: Reuters Institute for the Study of Journalism. http://bit.ly/digitalnews2015.

Opgenhaffen, Michael. 2011. "Multimedia, Interactive and Hypertextual Features in Divergent Online News Platforms: An Exploratory Study of Flemish Online News." *First Monday* 16 (3).

Papacharissi, Zizi, ed. 2011. *A Networked Self: Identity, Community, and Culture on Social Network Sites*. New York: Routledge.

Picone, Ike. 2011. "Produsage as a Form of Self-Publication. a Qualitative Study of Casual News Produsage." *New Review of Hypermedia and Multimedia* 17 (1): 99–120.

Picone, Ike. 2013. "Situating Liquid Media Use: Challenges for Media Ethnography." *Westminster Papers in Communication and Culture* 9 (3): 49–70.

Picone, Ike, Cédric Courtois, and Steve Paulussen. 2015. "When News is Everywhere." *Journalism Practice* 9 (1): 35–49.

Punie, Yves. 1997. "Gebruik Van Media En Informatie- En Communicatietechnologie [Uses of Media and Information and Communication Technology]." In *De Interpretatieve Benadering in De Communicatiewetenschap. Theorie, Methodologie En Case-Studies* [The Interpretative Approach in Communication Science. Theory, Methodology and Case Studies], edited by Jan Servaes and Valerie Frissen, 251–272. Amersfoort: Acco.

Robinson, John, and Geoffrey Godbey. 1999. *Time for Life: The Surprising Ways Americans Use Their Time*. 2nd ed. Pennsylvania State University Press.

Rosen, Jay. 2006. "The People Formerly Know as the Audience." Blogpost. *Pressthink*. June 27. http://journalism.nyu.edu/pubzone/weblogs/pressthink/2006/06/27/ppl_frmr.html.

Rubin, Alan M. 2002. "The Uses-and-Gratifications Perspective of Media Effects." In *Media Effects. Advances in Theory and Research*, edited by Jennings Bryant and Dolf Zillmann, 2nd ed., 525–548. Mahwah: Lawrence Erlbaum Associates.

Schrøder, Kim Chrisian. 2011. "Audiences Are Inherently Cross-Media. Audience Studies and the Cross-Media Challenge." *Communication Management Quarterly* 18 (6): 5–27.

Schrøder, Kim Christian, and Christian Kobbernagel. 2010. "Towards a Typology of Cross-Media News Consumption: A Qualitative-Quantitative Synthesis." In *Northern Lights: Film & Media Studies Yearbook*, 8, 115–137. London: Intellect.

Silverstone, Roger, and Leslie Haddon. 1996. "Design and the Domestication of Information and Communication Technologies: Technical Change and Everyday Life." In *Communication by Design: The Politics of Information and Communication Technologies*, edited by Robin Mansell and Roger Silverstone, 44–74. New York: Oxford University Press.

Singer, Jane, Alfred Hermida, David Domingo, Ari Heinonen, Steve Paulussen, Thorsten Quandt, Zvi Reich, and Marina Vujnovic. 2011. *Participatory Journalism. Guarding Open Gates at Online Newspapers.*. Oxford: Wiley-Blackwell.

Sonck, Nathalie, and Sjoerd Pennekamp. 2014. *Media:Tijd 2014*. Research Report. Media:tijd. Den Haag: Sociaal Cultureel Planbureau. http://www.mediatijd.nl/images/pdf/MediaTijd_Brochure_WEB.pdf.

Stroud, Natalie. 2011. *Niche News: The Politics of News Choice*. USA: Oxford University Press.

Taneja, Harsh, James G. Webster, Edward C. Malthouse, and Thomas B. Ksiazek. 2012. "Media Consumption across Platforms: Identifying User-Defined Repertoires." *New Media & Society* 14 (6): 951–968.

Van Deursen, Alexander J. A. M., and Jan A. G. M. van Dijk 2014. "Modeling Traditional Literacy, Internet Skills and Internet Usage: An Empirical Study." *Interacting with Computers* (published electronically July 16). doi:10.1093/iwc/iwu027.

Vittadini, Nicoletta, and Francesca Pasquali. 2013. "Virtual Shadowing: Online Ethnographies and Social Networking Studies." In *Audience Research Methodologies: Between Innovation and Consolidation*, edited by Patriarche, Geoffrey, Helena Bilandzic, Jakob Lina Jensen, and Jelena Jurisic, 160–173.

SAME, SAME BUT DIFFERENT
Effects of mixing Web and mail modes in audience research

Annika Bergström

The audience plays an important role in the journalistic context. The audience implications of journalistic work and output, business matters and policy making requires knowledge of public preferences and whether and how they take part in the news. Mixed-mode survey designs including Web and mail are becoming increasingly common in audience research, but it is unclear how mixing the survey modes affects the results. With the possibility of increasing response rates, is the risk of degrading the quality of answers. As audience research constitutes an important cornerstone of journalism studies, and because survey design including the Web is becoming more and more attractive, it is relevant to study the implications of merging audience data from different collection modes. This large-N survey provides a unique opportunity to analyse representative data on the matter. Altogether, 6603 respondents completed the survey, of whom 7.5 per cent chose the Web mode. Both habitual questions and opinion questions on different media were included in the study. The largest differences were found for item non-responses, whereas response distribution among respondents only differed to a small extent due to mode. There is no urgent need for caution when combining mail and Web responses in one data-set. However, thorough analyses of item non-response are necessary to control measurement errors when surveying media audiences and habits of using digital and other media in mixed-mode designed surveys.

Introduction

The audience plays a significant role in journalistic practice and constitutes an important external influence (Loosen and Schmidt 2012; Napoli 2011). "Journalism exists because—and if—it is capable of attracting and maintaining public attention" (Heinonen 2011, 34). Users serve, for instance, as idea generators and observers of newsworthy events (Heinonen 2011). Images of the audience are also shaping journalistic routines and are embedded in the news-making process (DeWerth-Pallmeyer 1997; Vobic 2014). Further, audience data are perceived to help journalists to serve their readers in multiple roles both as consumers and citizens (Hujanen 2008).

Then there are the financial implications of the media audience. The audience pays for journalistic content and, aside from owners and advertisers, constitutes the base on which journalism relies financially (McQuail 2005; Picard 2002). Audience data also constitute a platform for cooperation and mutual understanding between the advertising, marketing and editorial departments (Hujaren 2008).

Media audiences and measurement of audience practices not only have implications for journalistic work and revenues, but also guide regulation and policy making related to media and communication industries (Napoli 2011). Further, news journalism is considered an important component in democratic societies because it keeps citizens informed about current affairs (Lauf 2001; McLeod, Scheufele, and Moy 1999; Ostertag 2010; Strömbäck 2005).

It is evident that audience research has implications for journalism in a wide sense, and audience knowledge has become far more extensive with digital journalism (Anderson 2011; Vobic 2014). It is essential to understand whether the public takes part in the news, how their channel and platform preferences look, and how their opinions about media and journalism are formed.

Images of the audience are usually not based on direct interactions, but on measurements (Loosen and Schmidt 2012). Audience studies have most often been designed as either telephone interviews or mail surveys, and lately, Web surveys have become increasingly common. Driving forces for including the Web mode in data collection are the pressure to reduce administration costs and attempts to reduce measurement errors. Mixing survey modes has the potential for extending the reach of a survey by encouraging participation across a broader mix of the population (De Leeuw 2005; Dillman, Smyth, and Christian 2009; Diment and Garrett-Jones 2007; Holmberg, Lorenc, and Werner 2010; Link and Mokdad 2006; Shih and Fan 2007; Vannieuwenhuyze, Loosveldt, and Molenberghs 2010; Voogt and Saris 2005). It is of great importance to understand how data gathering with mixed methods might affect the figures appearing in both news rooms and on policy makers' desks. In journalistic research, however, the use of such research methods has been a neglected area (Hujanen 2008; Vobic 2014).

Mixed-mode approaches can affect the comparability of the results (Link and Mokdad 2006; Voogt and Saris 2005). It is recognised that measurement errors compromise data comparability when mixing data collection modes (Buelens and van den Brakel 2014; De Leeuw 2005; Jäckle, Roberts, and Lynn 2010; Link and Mokdad 2006; Vannieuwenhuyze, Loosveldt, and Molenberghs 2010; Voogt and Saris 2005). Responding via the Web requires some degree of familiarity with computers and digital features (Shin, Johnson, and Rao 2012). If the demographic profile for internet respondents is unique from that of respondents to other modes, we might see substantive differences in survey answers by mode (Bates 2001). The response rate gains may then be offset by undesirable changes in measurement (Dillman et al. 2009; Revilla 2014). Analysts of data generated by different modes of data collection need to be sure that answers to the same questions asked under different modes are equivalent, and survey researchers designing mixed-mode surveys need to know which modes can safely be combined in analysis (Denscombe 2006; Klausch, Hox, and Schouten 2013; Revilla 2014). The present study analyses response distribution among Web and mail respondents in an audience survey including questions on media habits and attitudes.

There are several studies dealing with mode effects, mostly conducted in fields other than journalism and audience research. Further, there seems to be a lack of analysis on representative populations (Ansolabehere and Schaffner 2014; Diaz de Rada and

Dominguez-Álvarez 2013; Schonlau, Asch, and Can 2003; Shin, Johnson, and Rao 2012), and response distribution beyond non-response rates.

As audience research constitutes an important cornerstone of journalistic work and outcomes, and because mixed-mode survey design including Web questionnaires is becoming increasingly common, it is relevant to study the implications of merging audience data from different collection modes. This large-N survey provides a unique opportunity to analyse representative data on the matter. The present study was a full-scale survey based on a representative sample. The analysis focused on implications of mixing Web and mail responses in one data-set. Mode effects were analysed with control for respondent characteristics and include response distributions over the scales and potential differences between habit and opinion questions. The findings reveal potential risks with merging audience data collected with different modes by analysing response distribution of media habits and attitudes controlling for factors previously proven to affect mode choice among respondents.

Theoretical Views and Research Questions

It has been established that different survey modes could produce different answers to the same question. Measurement errors might originate from differences in presentation of items sequentially or simultaneously to the respondent, interviewer effects and social desirability, primacy and recency effects, recall bias and acquiescence (De Leeuw 2005; Dillman, Smyth, and Christian 2009; Vannieuwenhuyze, Loosveldt, and Molenberghs 2010). In addition, question topics and wordings, question order, question format and visual designs might influence data quality across modes (Shin, Johnson, and Rao 2012). It is evident that mail and Web survey modes resemble each other on several of the mentioned dimensions, but differ to some extent. Both modes are self-administered with a high level of respondent control, but mail surveys are restricted to a single visual channel, whereas Web surveys offer flexibility in terms of channels of communication.

Mode effects are defined as "the observed differences in outcomes between identical surveys administered through different modes and are the combined result of selection and measurement effects" (Buelens and van den Brakel 2014, 3). This study deals with dimensions of measurement effects while, for instance, psychological effects, such as cognitive processing (De Leeuw 2005) and mode stimuli of different survey instruments (Van Vaerenbergh and Thomas 2013), are not addressed. More specifically, the article concerns mode choice, item non-responses, and response distribution for habitual and attitudinal questions in Web and mail mode.

When offered a choice between mail and Web mode, it seems that the proportion choosing the Web option in a concurrent set-up has, in general, been low (Diment and Garrett-Jones 2007; Holmberg, Lorenc, and Werner 2010; Shih and Fan 2007; Shin, Johnson, and Rao 2012). Different modes attract different respondents. There is an inverse correlation between preference for Web-based responses and the age of the respondent (Börkan 2009; Carini et al. 2003; Diaz de Rada and Dominguez-Álvarez 2013; Diment and Garrett-Jones 2007; Kwak and Radler 2002; Link and Mokdad 2006). Internet response is found to be more attractive to male respondents than to females (Carini et al. 2003; Diment and Garrett-Jones 2007; Kwak and Radler 2002). The use of the mail survey is more likely to be the main choice of people with lower education levels, whereas the Web survey is more frequently used by respondents with medium to high education levels (Diaz de Rada and Dominguez-Álvarez 2013). After controlling for internet access and computer skills, some socio-demographic factors, such as age and race, still affect respondents' willingness to complete a Web survey (Fan and Yan 2010). Further, respondents who are more likely to be adaptive to new technologies tend to be overrepresented in Web surveys (Kwak and Radler 2002; Smyth, Olson, and Millar 2014).

Previous studies comparing data quality obtained in Web and mail surveys have produced mixed findings in the item non-response topic (Shin, Johnson, and Rao 2012). The item missing data rates for Web-based questionnaires have been found to be slightly higher than for the paper-based questionnaires, and e-questionnaires contained fewer missing responses (Barrios et al. 2011; Denscombe 2006; Diaz de Rada and Dominguez-Álvarez 2013; Dillman, Smyth, and Christian 2009; Evans and Mathur 2005; Fraze et al. 2003; Kwak and Radler 2002; Voogt and Saris 2005). But, other studies report few or no differences across modes or disappearing differences when controlling for background characteristics due to self-selection (Buelens and van den Brakel 2014; Carini et al. 2003; De Leeuw 2005).

Much research on Web-mail mixed-mode is about response rates and non-responses. Data quality is often defined as non-missing items and missing data (Barrios et al. 2011; Dillman, Smyth, and Christian 2009; Fricker and Schonlau 2002; Shin, Johnson, and Rao 2012). There are, however, few studies on the response distributions and to what extent they might differ due to administration mode (Jäckle, Roberts, and Lynn 2010). Similarly to non-responses, the few studies conducted are inconclusive regarding mode effects of response distribution. There is evidence that survey mode might affect respondents' answers to survey questions that are worded the same (Dillman and Christian 2005). Nevertheless, there are also studies reporting no significant difference in response distribution based on the mode of data collection (Fraze et al. 2003).

It turns out that mode effects might differ when comparing different question designs. The Web has, for instance, been found to decrease the likelihood of obtaining a "don't know" response to close-ended questions on a general level. However, the mode effect disappeared when socio-demographic characteristics of respondents were introduced (Shin, Johnson, and Rao 2012). Further, mode differences for identically worded questions are more likely to occur for some types of questions than others (Dillman and Christian 2005). Measurement effects seem to be strongest on socially desirable topics. Respondents act according to social norms and tend to give culturally acceptable answers (Couper 2011; Jäckle, Roberts, and Lynn 2010; Vannieuwenhuyze, Loosveldt, and Molenberghs 2010; Voogt and Saris 2005). Computer-mediated surveys may yield more honest responses on items of a sensitive nature (Carini et al. 2003). There is also evidence in previous research that information technology-related questions could be overestimated in Web surveys compared to mail surveys (Carini et al. 2003; Kwak and Radler 2002).

To understand fully if and how the internet differs from other modes, controlled comparisons with the internet are needed in different situations using a variety of topics to enhance the generalisability of findings (De Leeuw 2005). Many mode comparisons of Web with mail presented in the literature have been carried out in specific, internet-savvy populations, such as with college students or professionals. Further, much of the previous research was conducted in experimental settings, whereas analysis of mode effects in full-scale surveys are rare. There are few studies on general population samples and the implications of merging data from different collection modes into one data-set. Studies of variances of response distribution are also rarely found (Ansolabehere and Schaffner 2014; Diaz de Rada and Dominguez-Álvarez 2013; Jäckle, Roberts, and Lynn 2010; Schonlau, Asch, and Can 2003; Shin, Johnson, and Rao 2012).

The purpose of this study was to reveal whether merging data from mail and Web responses in the same survey would introduce bias to the final data. Three research questions were posed. The first one captures item non-responses and response distribution over the scale among respondents who have answered the questions:

RQ1: To what extent does response distribution differ depending on mail or Web mode?

Survey questions on media habits and attitudes are analysed in this respect. Broadcast media, print media and digital news media are included in the analysis. As outlined, mode choice differs, and the second research question deals with mode effects when controlling for factors related to mode choice:

RQ2: Could any mode effect be detected when controlling for factors previously known to affect mode choice?

Regression analyses are used to reveal mode effects on habitual and attitude questions under control for background characteristics. Previous research has reported on potential mode effects depending on type of question, and the third issue is whether such differences can be traced:

RQ3: Are there different mode effects when comparing questions of media habits and media attitudes?

Method and Data

Mode effects were captured in a quantitative mail survey with a representative probability sample of the Swedish population aged between 16 and 85 years. The study was based on data collected in the so-called national SOM survey (Society, Opinion, Media), which was conducted in the autumn and winter of 2013. The SOM survey has been conducted as an annual mail survey since 1986. Each year, between 3000 and 17,000 people living in Sweden receive the survey. The design of the survey, with regard to age groups and sample sizes, has changed somewhat over the years (for detailed method reports, see Bové, Hägglund, and Vernersdotter 2015; Vernersdotter 2014).

The 2013 survey was sent to 13,600 persons, and the net response rate was 53 per cent (6603 respondents). The respondents were divided in almost the same way as the Swedish population in terms of gender, social class and level of education. Older people were, however, overrepresented since the response rate in the youngest group was below average (64 per cent among those 80–85 years old and 40 per cent among those 16–19 years old). This means that there might be some underestimation of habits strongly related to younger people's, for instance, internet consumption practices (for an in-depth analysis on representativity, see Markstedt 2014).

From the 2012 surveys, a mixed-mode choice was offered as a service to the respondents with the aim of increasing the response rates. A key distinction was whether different modes were used for the contact phase, the response phase or the follow-up phase (Couper 2011). In the SOM survey, different modes were offered in the response phase, whereas the contact phase was identical for the whole sample. The SOM surveys had no random assignment of mode—mail and Web were used subsequently and offered to all respondents. This means that a mode choice was applied, opposite from mode preference, where respondents were asked which mode of data collection they may prefer (Couper 2011). Several studies have revealed positive effects of first offering a mail survey, then, in the reminder, offering a Web survey (Börkan 2009; Diment and Garrett-Jones 2007; Schonlau, Asch, and Can 2003): the SOM surveys were designed in accordance with this. When the Web survey option was offered in the first reminder, 23 per cent of the total respondents had already taken the mail survey. Altogether, the analyses were based on 6104 mail answers and 499 Web answers.

The SOM survey used a unified mode (Dillman, Smyth, and Christian 2009), which means that there was a maximum resemblance between the procedures of the two administration modes to get consistency. There were, however, some minor differences. In the Web survey, some follow-up questions were hidden until they became relevant for the respondent. The Web tool allowed forced-choice questions, but this facility was not used. The pages from the paper mode were not fully transferred to the Web mode. In the online version, the pages were shorter to avoid scrolling. On the Web, unlike on paper, the appearance of a survey might also vary from respondent to respondent because of different browser settings, and variations in hardware and platforms (Couper 2000). Such issues were out of the control in the analysed survey and will not be commented on further.

The average mail questionnaire consisted of approximately 20 pages and 80–90 questions, most of them with fixed-answer options. The dependent variables were chosen to give in-depth insight to response distribution (RQ1) and potential mode effects (RQ2) when studying exposure to journalistic content and attitudes to media issues (RQ3): national public service radio news, national public service television news, morning papers and evening tabloids in print and online, mobile news services, reading comments to online news articles, trust in television and daily press, and attitudes towards file sharing and press subsidies. The questions were posed:

- *How often do you usually make use of the following news programmes?* National radio news (public service), national television news (public service).
- *How often during the last 12 months have you used the internet/read reader comments? Do you read any of the following newspapers?* (Evening tabloids are named and print and digital platforms are separated in different items).
- *Do you read any printed morning papers?* There is an option to write up to two different morning papers. Below the scale, the option *I never read printed morning papers* is posed.
- *Do you read any online morning papers?* There is an option to write up to two different morning papers. Below the scale, the option *I never read printed morning*

papers is posed.
- *How much confidence do you have for the content in the following media?* The item *Sveriges Television* (the public service television company in Sweden) is analysed.
- *How much confidence do you have in how the following institutions are performing their work?* The item *daily press* is analysed.
- *What is your assessment of the following political suggestions? Decriminalise all file sharing* and *Increase press subsidies* were used in the analysis.

To control mode effects for respondent characteristics (RQ2), independent variables were chosen in accordance with previous research: gender, age, level of education and internet habits. Gender is captured in a question with fixed alternatives. Age was derived from an open question with year of birth, which has been completed with data from official registers. Education level was asked in a question with close-ended responses, and eight categories were suggested. Internet use was captured in a close-ended question with an ordinal scale with seven options: "Daily", "Several times a week", "At least once a week", "Once every month", "Once every six months", "Once in the last 12 months" and "Never".

Before taking a closer look at mode choice and response distribution in Web and mail mode, the Swedish context needs to be mentioned. About 80 per cent were frequent (several times a week) internet users before the survey, and access to Web devices were: personal computer 86 per cent, tablet computer 38 per cent, and smartphone 63 per cent (Bergström and Oscarsson 2014). The potential for taking the survey online was, at least theoretically, good.

Results

The aim of the study was to reveal whether merging data from mail and Web responses in the same survey would introduce bias to the final data. Before turning to the issue of mode effects on response distribution, one needs, however, to know who chose either mode. The results reveal differences in the respondents' choice of survey mode. A linear regression analysis showed the impact of each factor mentioned above (see Table 1). Age was the single most important factor when trying to explain the choice of mode in the settings of the conducted study. Younger persons were more likely to use the Web mode. There were also significant, but small, effects of gender

TABLE 1
Mode choice due to gender, age, level of education and internet use (ordinary least-squares regression, standard beta)

	Standard beta
Gender	0.05***
Age	−0.18***
Level of education	−0.00
Internet use	0.04**
Adjusted R^2	0.04
N	6382

**$P < 0.01$,
***$P < 0.001$.

and internet use. Men were more likely than women to use the Web mode, and the more frequent internet use, the higher shares of Web respondents. Educational level did not significantly contribute to the understanding of mode choice among the respondents. The findings were expected with references to previous research (Börkan 2009; Carini et al. 2003; Diaz de Rada and Dominguez-Álvarez 2013; Diment and Garrett-Jones 2007; Kwak and Radler 2002; Link and Mokdad 2006).

The conducted study offers a unique opportunity to analyse mode effects on a journalism audience in a representative sample of the Swedish adult population. Altogether, the findings provide guidance concerning how self-reported use of journalistic content and opinions towards media issues should be interpreted depending on survey mode, and problematises potential obstacles of treating data collected from different modes equally.

The issues of response distribution and types of questions were emphasised in the study. The first research question deals with response distribution over the whole scales including item non-response. As outlined in the Methods section, use of several news media and attitudes to media issues were analysed from the user's perspective. One should be cautious of different wording and scales, which are commented on in Table 2.

Significant differences in response distribution between mail and Web respondents were found for all the studied media habits, and for three of the four opinion questions. Most of the differences found could be directly related to the relationship between media habits and the composition of the two groups of respondents. Broadcast news has an older audience, which was reflected in the response differences between modes. Printed newspapers also have an older audience, whereas online newspapers and other Web sources have audiences characterised by lower average age. It is therefore expected that we would find significant differences in response distribution for media habits with a bivariate analysis. A multivariate analysis follows below.

As outlined above, mail and Web mode differed in non-responses to single items. An analysis of the non-response figures in Table 2 revealed that there are both smaller and larger effects, and that these were somewhat inconsistent. The non-response rate was higher for radio news than for television news in both modes. This might be a result of radio news being less frequently used, and a non-response could be interpreted as non-use, even though the scale option "Never" was offered. Secondly, the non-response rate for radio news was twice as low in the Web mode as compared to the mail mode, which most likely mirrored the composition of the respondent groups and their use of radio news (Westlund and Weibull 2013).

The non-response rate for printed tabloids was higher in Web mode, and the non-response rate for online tabloids was higher in mail mode. Also in this question, the scale option "Never" was offered. Again, a likely explanation is that non-response equals non-use, and that respondents who do not read evening tabloids simply skipped the item. The non-response rate for printed tabloids was, however, higher in mail mode than the non-response rate for online tabloids in Web mode, pointing to the possibility that Web mode produces lower non-response rates on a more general level (Barrios et al. 2011; Denscombe 2006; Diaz de Rada and Dominguez-Álvarez 2013; Dillman, Smyth, and Christian 2009; Evans and Mathur 2005; Fraze et al. 2003; Kwak and Radler 2002; Voogt and Saris 2005).

TABLE 2
Response distribution for media habits and media attitudes (% and χ^2)

National broadcast news	Radio*** Paper mode	Radio*** Web mode	Television*** Paper mode	Television*** Web mode	Evening tabloids	Print edition*** Paper mode	Print edition*** Web mode	Web edition*** Paper mode	Web edition*** Web mode	Mobile news***	Mobile news*** Paper mode	Mobile news*** Web mode	Read article comments***	Read article comments*** Paper mode	Read article comments*** Web mode
Daily	18.7	10.0	36.4	13.4	6–7 days a week	4.2	1.6	20.0	33.4	More than 20 times a day	0.6	2.3	Daily	3.8	7.8
5–6 days a week	6.8	4.6	13.9	11.8	3–5 days a week	5.6	2.5	13.3	14.5	11–20 times a day	0.9	3.0	Several times a week	5.2	8.2
3–4 days a week	8.7	7.2	14.1	16.2	1–2 days a week	11.1	8.5	10.3	12.1	4–10 times a day	5.9	14.3	Once a week	10.7	17.1
1–2 days a week	9.7	10.4	14.3	22.4	More seldom	36.5	28.5	18.3	18.4	1–3 times a day	14.6	20.3	Once a month	12.0	15.1
More seldom	23.2	26.9	11.9	19.4	Never	34.5	45.2	27.1	18.1	One or several times a week	14.9	12.8	Once the last 6 months	7.1	6.1
Never	22.9	35.5	5.6	13.4						A few times every month	10.4	13.5	Once the last 12 months	9.2	11.4
Item non-response	10.0	5.4	3.7	3.2	Item non-response	8.1	13.7	11.1	3.6	Never	49.5	21.1	Never	39.1	34.3
										Item non-response	3.2	12.8	Item non-response	12.8	0.0
N	6094	499	6086	499	N	4613	365	4613	365	N	1573	133	N	3063	245

(Continued)

TABLE 2
(Continued)

Morning papers	Print edition*** Paper mode	Print edition*** Web mode	Web edition *** Paper mode	Web edition *** Web mode	Confidence in media	Public service television*** Paper mode	Public service television*** Web mode	Daily press*** Paper mode	Daily press*** Web mode	Media attitudes	Decriminalise all file sharing Paper mode	Decriminalise all file sharing Web mode	Increase press subsidies*** Paper mode	Increase press subsidies*** Web mode
7 days a week	25.8	11.0	7.7	10.7	Very high	26.8	27.8	2.5	2.4	Very good proposal	11.6	14.3	3.2	1.5
6 days a week	20.8	9.3	2.0	2.7	Fairly high	47.0	29.3	23.9	19.8	Fairly good	15.3	14.3	13.3	7.5
5 days a week	8.2	6.0	3.7	5.5	Neither high nor low	14.1	12.0	42.2	43.9	Neither good nor bad	43.6	39.8	52.6	40.6
4 days a week	3.0	5.5	2.9	3.8	Fairly low	1.8	2.3	20.6	17.6	Fairly bad	14.6	15.8	17.1	32.3
3 days a week	6.4	4.1	3.0	3.8	Very low	1.5	3.0	7.4	10.0	Very bad	9.4	8.3	10.2	10.5
2 days a week	3.1	7.1	3.0	1.9	No opinion	6.0	12.8	–	–					
1 days a week	2.3	3.3	2.4	3.6										
More seldom	4.1	5.5	7.4	7.1										
Never	19.9	35.6	47.2	30.4										
Item non-response	6.5	12.6	20.7	30.4	Item non-response	2.7	12.8	3.3	6.2	Item non-response	5.5	7.5	3.5	7.5
N	4613	365	4613	365	N	1572	133	6090	499	N	1573	133	1573	133

*** $P < 0.001$.

The questions of morning paper reading in print and online provided relatively high item non-response. This was especially evident for Web mode and online newspaper reading. Morning paper readership was less frequent in groups that took the Web survey, and online morning papers were less used than printed on an aggregate level. Higher non-response rates for online news and among Web respondents together with considerably lower response rates for printed papers in mail mode clearly indicates that non-responses could be interpreted as non-use in the light of reading figures in the two respondent groups (Westlund and Weibull 2013), just as for broadcast news.

The use of mobile news was hard to interpret in this regard. The non-response level was significantly higher among Web respondents (12.8 per cent) than among mail respondents (3.2 per cent). This is opposite to what was expected from the Web group composition and from mobile news consumption habits (Westlund 2015). It is also opposite to previous research, where it was found that information technology-related questions could be overestimated in Web surveys (Carini et al. 2003; Kwak and Radler 2002). One plausible explanation of this variance was the low number of respondents on this particular item in Web mode ($N = 133$). The 12.8 per cent means only 17 persons. It is evident that larger groups are needed to capture response distribution on this matter.

There were no missing items for the habit of reading comments to news articles in the Web survey, whereas the non-response rate was 12.8 per cent in the mail mode. Also this could, most probably, be a reflection of the composition of the two respondent groups in relation to patterns of comment-reading habits (Bergström and Wadbring 2015; Karlsson et al. 2015). But the finding also strengthens the impression that the Web mode may lead to a higher willingness to respond to single items, especially those related to internet use as internet habits were more frequent among Web respondents.

Item non-responses in opinion questions slightly differed from the levels found for habitual ones. First, the non-response rates were consistently lower in mail mode than in Web mode. This is somewhat surprising. One explanation offered above is that use affects the willingness to take a standpoint. We would then expect more mail respondents to have an opinion on traditional media, and more Web respondents to have their say on internet-related issues. The findings do not support this, and the results are hard to interpret.

Several significant effects of mode were found in the bivariate analysis. As elaborated in the Methods section, the sample composition significantly differed between modes. The second research question concerns whether mode differences remain when controlling for factors related to the likeliness to choose the Web mode. A linear regression analysis could reveal whether the differences found in the previous analysis will remain when controlling for gender, age, level of education and internet habits.

In Table 3, it is evident that survey mode affected response distribution among respondents answering the question only to a small extent. Significant mode effects were found for national television news, evening tabloids in print and online, morning papers in print, trust in public service television and for attitudes towards press subsidies. The effects were weak in all cases.

Instead, other explanatory factors contributed to the understanding of response distribution. Age was the single most important factor explaining most of the habits measured in the presented study: broadcast news, printed newspapers, mobile news

TABLE 3

Effects of sex, age, education, internet use and survey mode on response distribution (ordinary least-squares regression, standard beta)

	National radio news	National television news	Evening tabloid, print	Evening tabloid, Web	Morning papers, print	Morning papers, Web	Mobile news	Reading news comments	Trust in public service television	Trust in daily press	Decriminalise all file sharing	Increase press subsidies
Sex	-0.08***	-0.03**	-0.04**	-0.05***	0.00	-0.11***	0.11***	0.19***	-0.04	0.07***	-0.01	0.10***
Age	-0.36***	-0.59***	-0.16***	0.15***	-0.46***	0.09***	-0.36***	-0.21***	-0.08**	-0.09***	0.15***	-0.09***
Education	-0.11***	-0.02*	0.15***	0.03*	-0.09*	-0.16***	0.14***	0.12***	-0.16***	-0.10***	0.06*	-0.02
Internet use	-0.06***	0.03*	0.01	-0.31***	-0.04*	-0.18***	0.07***	0.11**	-0.06*	0.00	0.04	0.03
Survey mode	0.03*	0.02*	0.04*	-0.01	0.06***	-0.02	0.04	-0.00	0.08**	-0.01	0.01	0.06*
Adjusted R^2	0.13	0.36	0.07	0.15	0.20	0.12	0.22	0.12	0.03	0.02	0.02	0.02
N	2840	3032	2167	2157	1592	794	791	1424	1620	6198	1578	1608

*$P < 0.05$,
**$P < 0.01$,
***$P < 0.001$.

and reader comments. Education was equally important for reading evening tabloids in print. Education, together with internet habits, was most important for morning papers online.

The explanatory power of the independent variables chosen for analysis was overall weaker for media attitudes. Education was significantly most important for trust in public service television. Trust in the daily press was best understood by education and age. Age also predicted attitudes to file sharing, and, together with gender, assessment of press subsidies.

Turning to the third research question—whether mode effects differ between questions of media habits and media attitudes—small, but significant effects were detected for the measured issues. Mail respondents expressed higher trust in public service television whereas Web respondents to a larger extent chose the "No opinion" option. Further, the support for increased press subsidies was stronger among mail respondents. It can be assumed that these opinions are influenced by the habits of using television news and news reading in a positive way.

It was shown in previous research that sensitive questions would gain from the Web mode (Couper 2011; Dillman and Christian 2005; Jäckle, Roberts, and Lynn 2010; Vannieuwenhuyze, Loosveldt, and Molenberghs 2010; Voogt and Saris 2005). One can conclude that there was a tendency of slightly larger mode effects on attitude questions compared to questions of use, but that differences were small. The study conducted cannot identify what answers would be more genuine, and it is not evident that the analysed attitude questions would be particularly sensitive compared to habitual questions.

Using a mixed-mode design does not seem to harm data quality in terms of response distribution among those responding to the questions. The non-response rates to single items differed, however, and lower non-response figures among Web respondents might lead to overestimates of habits related to the characteristics of this group (i.e. male, young, heavy internet users).

When given the mode choice, as in the conducted study, it is evident that most respondents prefer to take the mail survey. In that case, we would rather expect underestimated measures of internet-related questions. As in most other studies, the findings reported here do not provide a possibility to analyse habits and attitudes of non-respondents. This is a challenge for all survey work.

Conclusions

The present study analysed mode effects in a survey where the respondents within the same sample were given the choice of mail or Web mode. Among the 6603 who responded to the survey, in total 7.5 per cent chose the Web mode. Altogether, the analysed survey provides a representative sample, making in-depth analysis of smaller groups possible, and thereby contributing to the research field of mixed-mode design. The study also contributes to the field of audience research in the age of digital journalism by deepening the understanding of one of the challenges, but also the opportunity facing audience analysis: the increasingly popular Web survey.

It is evident from the presented findings that mail and Web surveys provide basically the same response distribution among those responding to single items. This applies to both media habits and attitudes to media issues. Mode effects can indeed be discerned, but are comparatively small. Other factors, first and foremost, age and education, have stronger explanatory power. The findings contribute to the understanding of mode effects on data quality by adding response distribution over the whole scale to previous research on non-responses (Barrios et al. 2011; Buelens and van den Brakel 2014; Carini et al. 2003; De Leeuw 2005; Denscombe 2006; Diaz de Rada and Dominguez-Álvarez 2013; Dillman, Smyth, and Christian 2009; Evans and Mathur 2005; Fraze et al. 2003; Kwak and Radler 2002; Shin, Johnson, and Rao 2012; Voogt and Saris 2005).

There are, however, differences in non-responses for single items which deserve attention when analysing mixed-mode data. The conducted study partly supports the findings from previous research showing higher completion rates for the Web mode (Barrios et al. 2011; Denscombe 2006; Diaz de Rada and Dominguez-Álvarez 2013; Dillman, Smyth, and Christian 2009; Evans and Mathur 2005; Fraze et al. 2003; Kwak and Radler 2002; Voogt and Saris 2005), but there are a few exceptions. Because the character of the respondents choosing to take the Web survey differed from those choosing mail, this might matter for the overall data quality. One needs to be cautious about what media is studied in what mode. A mail survey on digital media might well underestimate use whereas a Web survey on the same topic might give the opposite impression.

In previous research, measurement effects have been found when comparing socially desirable topics with less sensitive questions (Carini et al. 2003; Couper 2011; Dillman and Christian 2005; Jäckle, Roberts, and Lynn 2010). The presented analysis points to slightly lower non-response rates for attitude questions in Web mode, than for habits, but the findings are not conclusive on this matter. A non-response to news habits is most likely interpreted as non-use. The same cannot be stated in terms of attitudes. In-depth analysis of media attitudes in relation to attitudes on other matters is needed. It is also a topic for future research to widen the scope of mode effects by including other variables important for understanding opinion formation.

Web surveys, in particular, have led to large increases in the number of surveys available to the population. There is much competition for the attention of respondents. The widespread adoption of internet surveys could threaten to crowd out serious research approaches. There is an increased concern about "professional respondents" (Couper 2011, 902)—a small number of people who complete a large number of surveys. The conducted study has limitations in this sense. It gives clear indications about the overall representativeness for mail and Web, but cannot reveal what drives the respondents to take the survey in one mode or the other. Qualitative research is needed to get beyond general questionnaire completion.

The present study offered Web mode in the first reminder. It might be different if administrators started with Web mode and then offered mail mode later in the fieldwork. Future research needs to study this. Tests conducted at the SOM Institute in 2014 might shed some light on how design of the contact phase affects mode choice and mode effects.

Based on the findings presented here, there is no urgent need for caution when combining mail and Web modes in the same audience survey and merging data into one set. Mode effects on response distribution were small, and it seems that the Web mode option could have positive effects on data quality by providing fewer left-out items. Images of the audience—a vital part of journalism not least in the digital era—might well be drawn from data collected digitally or in mixed-mode surveys. However, one may need to make thorough analyses of item non-response in each conducted survey to control measurement errors.

One of the biggest challenges surveying online journalists and their audiences is to define the population. Most often you need to draw a random sample, but it has, thus, become common to rely on self-selection of respondents or to simply put a survey questionnaire on a Web page. By letting go of the control of sampling and random selection, you cannot control representativeness and thereby lose the possibility of predicting more general behaviours or opinions. Accessible Web tools have also led to an increase in the number of surveys, and there is much competition for the attention of the respondents. "There is a growing realization that willing and able respondents are becoming an increasingly scarce commodity" (Couper 2011, 902). Easily available responses might harm both representativeness and data quality, and there is reason to be cautious not only when merging data-sets, but also when designing surveys.

DISCLOSURE STATEMENT

No potential conflict of interest was reported by the author.

REFERENCES

Anderson, Christopher W. 2011. "Between Creative and Quantified Audiences: Web Metrics and Changing Patterns of Newswork in Local US Newsrooms." *Journalism* 12 (5): 550–566.

Ansolabehere, Stephen, and Brian F. Schaffner. 2014. "Does Survey Mode Still Matter? Findings from a 2010 Multi-Mode Comparison." *Political Analysis* 22 (3): 285–303.

Barrios, Maite, Anna Villarroya, Angel Borrego, and Candela Ollé. 2011. "Response Rates and Data Quality in Web and Mail Surveys Administered to PhD Holders." *Social Science Computer Review* 29 (2): 208–220.

Bates, Nancy. 2001. "Internet versus Mail as a Data Collection Methodology from a High Coverage Population." Proceedings of the Annual Meeting of the American Statistical Association, Atlanta, GA, August 5–9.

Bergström, Annika, and Henrik Oscarsson. 2014. "Mittfåra & Marginal." [Mainstream & Marginal]. In *Mittfåra & Marginal* [Mainstream & Marginal], edited by Annika Bergström and Henrik Oscarsson, 11–36. Gothenburg: The SOM Institute, University of Gothenburg.

Bergström, Annika, and Ingela Wadbring. 2015. "Beneficial Yet Crappy: Journalists and Audiences on Obstacles and Opportunities in Reader Comments." *European Journal of Communication* 30 (2): 137–151.

Börkan, Bengü. 2009. "The Mode Effect in Mixed-Mode Surveys: Mail and Web Surveys." *Social Science Computer Review* 28 (3): 371–380.

Bové, Josefine, Jonas Hägglund, Frida Vernersdotter. 2015. *Fördjupad Metodanalys—SOM-Undersökningen 2013.* [In-depth Method Analysis. The, 2013. SOM Survey]. Gothenburg: The SOM Institute, University of Gothenburg.

Buelens, Bart, and Jan A. van den Brakel. 2014. "Measurement Error Calibration in Mixed-Mode Sample Surveys." *Sociological Methods & Research*, 1–36. First published on May 12, 2014. Accessed November 17, 2014. doi: 10.1177/0049124114532444.

Carini, Roberg M., John C. Hayek, George D. Kuh, John M Kennedy, and Judith A. Ouimet. 2003. "College Student Responses to Web and Paper Surveys: Does Mode Matter?" *Research in Higher Education* 44 (1): 1–19.

Couper, Mick P. 2000. "Web Surveys. A Review of Issues and Approaches." *Public Opinion Quarterly* 64 (4): 464–494.

Couper, Mick P. 2011. "The Future of Modes of Data Collection." *Public Opinion Quarterly* 75 (5): 889–908.

Denscombe, Martyn. 2006. "Web-Based Questionnaires and the Mode Effect: An Evaluation Based on Completion Rates and Data Contents of near-Identical Questionnaires Delivered in Different Modes." *Social Science Computer Review* 24 (2): 246–254.

DeWerth-Pallmeyer, Dwight. 1997. *The Audience in the News.* Mahwah, NJ: Lawrence Erlbaum Associates, Publishers.

Diaz de Rada, Vidal, and Juan Antonio Dominguez-Álvarez. . 2013. "Response Quality of Self-Administered Questionnaires: A Comparison between Paper and Web Questionnaires." *Social Science Computer Review* 32 (2): 256–269.

Dillman, Don A., and Leah Melani Christian. 2005. "Survey Mode as a Source of Instability in Responses across Surveys." *Field Methods* 17 (1): 30–52.

Dillman, Don A., Glen Phelps, Robert Tortora, Karen Swift, Julie Kohrell, Jodi Berck, and Benjamin L. Messer. 2009. "Response Rate and Measurement Differences in Mixed-Mode Surveys Using Mail, Telephone, Interactive Voice Response (IVR) and the Internet." *Social Science Research* 38 (1): 1–18.

Dillman, Don A., Jolene D. Smyth, and Leah Melani Christian. 2009. *Internet, Mail, and Mixed-Mode Surveys. The Tailored Design Method.* Hoboken, NJ: John Wiley & Sons, Inc.

Diment, Kieren, and Sam Garrett-Jones. 2007. "How Demographic Characteristics Affect Mode Preference in a Postal/Web Mixed-Mode Survey of Australian Researchers." *Social Science Computer Review* 25 (3): 410–417.

Evans, Joel R., and Anil Mathur. 2005. "The Value of Online Surveys." *Internet Research* 15 (2): 195–219.

Fan, Weimiao, and Zheng Yan. 2010. "Factors Affecting Response Rates of the Web Survey: A Systematic Review." *Computers in Human Behavior* 26 (2): 132–139.

Fraze, Steve D., Kelly K. Hardin, M. Todd Brashears, Jacqui L. Haygood, and James H. Smith. 2003. "The Effects of Delivery Mode upon Survey Response Rate and Perceived Attitudes of Texas Agri-Science Teachers." *Journal of Agricultural Education* 44 (2): 27–37.

Fricker, Ronald D., and Matthias Schonlau. 2002. "Advantages and Disadvantages of Internet Research Surveys: Evidence from the Literature." *Field Methods* 14 (4): 347–367.

Heinonen, Ari. 2011. "The Journalist's Relationship with Users: New Dimensions to Conventional Roles." In *Participatory Journalism. Guarding Open Gates at Online Newspapers*, edited by Jane B. Singer, Alfred Hermida, David Domingo, Ari Heinonen, Steve Paulusen, Thorsten Quandt, Zvi Reich and Marina Vujnovic, 34–56. Malden, MA: Wiley-Blackwell.

Holmberg, Anders, Boris Lorenc, and Peter Werner. 2010. "Contact Strategies to Improve Participation via the Web in a Mixed-Mode Mail and Web Survey." *Journal of Official Statistics* 26 (3): 465–480.

Hujanen, Jaana. 2008. "RISC Monitor Audience Rating and Its Implications for Journalistic Practice." *Journalism* 9 (2): 182–199.

Jäckle, Annette, Caroline Roberts, and Peter Lynn. 2010. "Assessing the Effect of Data Collection Mode on Measurement." *International Statistical Review* 78 (1): 3–20.

Karlsson, Michael, Annika Bergström, Christer Clerwall, and Karin Fast. 2015. "Participatory Journalism—The (R)evolution that Wasn't. Content and User Behavior in Sweden 2007-2013." *Journal of Computer-Mediated Communication*, 295–311. doi: 10.1111/jcc4.12115.

Klausch, Thomas, Joop J. Hox, and Barry Schouten. 2013. "Measurement Effects of Survey Mode on the Equivalence of Attitudinal Rating Scale Questions." *Sociological Methods & Research* 42 (3): 227–263.

Kwak, Nojin, and Barry Radler. 2002. "A Comparison between Mail and Web Surveys: Response Pattern, Response Profile and Data Quality." *Journal of Official Statistics* 18 (2): 257–273.

Lauf, Edmund. 2001. "Research Note: The Vanishing Young Reader. Socio-Demographic Determinants of Newspaper Use as a Source of Political Information in Europe, 1980–98." *European Journal of Communication* 16 (2): 233–243.

De Leeuw, Edith D. 2005. "To Mix or Not to Mix Data Collection Modes in Surveys." *Journal of Official Statistics* 21 (2): 233–255.

Link, Michael W., and Ali Mokdad. 2006. "Can Web and Mail Survey Modes Improve Participation in an RDD-Based National Health Surveillance?" *Journal of Official Statistics* 22 (2): 293–312.

Loosen, Wiebke, and Jan-Hinrik Schmidt. 2012. "(Re-)Discovering the Audience." *Information, Communication & Society* 15 (6): 867–887.

Markstedt, Elias. 2014. *Representativitet Och Viktning*. [Representativity and Weighing]. Gothenburg: The SOM Institute, University of Gothenburg.

McLeod, Jack M., Dietram A. Scheufele, and Patricia Moy. 1999. "Community, Communication, and Participation: The Role of Mass Media and Interpersonal Discussion in Local Political Participation." *Political Communication* 16 (3): 4–87.

McQuail, Denis. 2005. *McQuail's Mass Communication Theory*. 5th ed. London: Sage.

Napoli, Philip M. 2011. *Audience Evolution. New Technologies and the Transformation of Media Audiences*. New York: Columbia University Press.

Ostertag, Stephen. 2010. "Establishing News Confidence: A Qualitative Study of How People Use the News Media to Know the News-World." *Media, Culture and Society* 32 (4): 597–614.

Picard, Robert G. 2002. *The Economics and Financing of Media Companies*. New York: Fordham University Press.

Revilla, Melanie. 2014. "Comparison of the Quality Estimates in a Mixed-Mode and Unimode Design: An Experiment from the European Social Survey." *Quality & Quantity* 2014: 97–114. First published on June 13 2014. Accessed November 17, 2014. doi: 10.1007/s11135-014-0044-5.

Schonlau, Matthias, Beth J. Asch, and Can X. Du. 2003. "Web Surveys as Part of a Mixed-Mode Strategy for Populations That Cannot Be Contacted by E-Mail." *Social Science Computer Review* 21 (2): 218–222.

Shih, Tse-Hua, and Xitao Fan. 2007. "Response Rates and Mode Preferences in Web-Mail Mixed Mode Surveys: A Meta-Analysis." *International Journal of Internet Science* 2 (1): 59–82.

Shin, Eunjung, Timothy P. Johnson, and Kumar Rao. 2012. "Survey Mode Effects on Data Quality: Comparison of Web and Mail Modes in a U.S. National Panel Survey." *Social Science Computer Review* 30 (2): 212–228.

Smyth, Jolene D., Kristen Olson, and Morgon M. Millar. 2014. "Identifying Predictors of Survey Mode Preference." *Social Science Research* 48: 135–144.

Strömbäck, Jesper. 2005. "In Search of a Standard: Four Models of Democracy and Their Normative Implications for Journalism." *Journalism Studies* 6 (3): 331–345.

Van Vaerenbergh, Yves, and Troy D. Thomas. 2013. "Response Styles in Survey Research: A Literature Review of Antecedents, Consequences, and Remedies." *International Journal of Public Opinion Research* 25 (2): 195–217.

Vannieuwenhuyze, Jorre, Geert Loosveldt, and Geert Molenberghs. 2010. "A Method for Evaluating Mode Effects in Mixed-Mode Surveys." *Public Opinion Quarterly* 74 (5): 1027–1045.

Vernersdotter, Frida. 2014. "Den Nationella SOM-Undersökningen 2013 [The National SOM Survey, 2013]." In *Mittfåra & Mariginal* [Mainstream & Marginal], edited by Annika Bergström and Henrik Oscarsson, 531–559. Gothenburg: The SOM Institute, University of Gothenburg.

Vobic, Igor. 2014. "Audience Conceiving among Journalists: Integrating Social-Organizational Analysis and Cultural Analysis through Ethnography." In *Audience Research Methodologies. between Innovation and Consolidation*, edited by Geoffroy Patriarche, Helena Bilanzic, Jakob Linaa Jensenand Jelena Jurisic, 19–36. New York and London: Routledge.

Voogt, Robert J. J., and Willem E. Saris. 2005. "Mixed Mode Designs: Finding the Balance between Non-Response Bias and Mode Effects." *Journal of Official Statistics* 21 (3): 367–387.

Westlund, Oscar. 2015. "News Consumption in an Age of Mobile Media: Patterns, People, Place, and Participation." *Mobile Media & Communication* 3 (2): 151–159.

Westlund, Oscar, and Lennart Weibull. 2013. "Generation, Life Course and News Media Use in Sweden 1986–2011." *Northern Lights* 11: 147–173.

ACTION RESEARCH
Collaborative research for the improvement of digital journalism practice

Stephanie Grubenmann

The combination of technological, organizational, and societal change constitutes a highly dynamic and complex research setting for Digital Journalism Studies, calling for process-oriented and inclusive research perspectives. At the same time, journalistic organizations have to generate sustainable innovativeness and creativity to remain relevant in these times of change. Action research offers a framework for research collaborations between scholars and practitioners, generating holistic and solution-oriented outcomes of value for science and practice. With the clear intention to induce change, action research starts with the reflection on practice with a view to improving it. This article argues for more action research in Digital Journalism Studies, elaborating on the opportunities for science and practice. A current action research project in Switzerland is introduced and evaluated to give an impression of this research culture. The remaining challenges derived from experiences in this project are also discussed.

Introduction

The internet, social media in particular, and the related transformation of user behavior have brought far-reaching change to journalism. Technological innovations induce simultaneous technological and social change processes, creating a complex environment for journalism practice and research. Journalists are confronted with evolving role concepts (Grubenmann, Meckel, and Fieseler 2014), additional skill requirements (Deuze 1999), new forms of teamwork (Lichfield 2012), and more service-oriented versions of journalism (Artwick 2013; Haik 2013). In turn, publishers and media organizations confronted with a changeable media ecosystem (Doctor 2015) find themselves in need of new, sustainable business models (Pavlik 2013). To overcome these challenges, journalistic organizations have to generate sustainable innovativeness (Pavlik 2013) and creativity. How can journalism studies support practitioners' pursuit of self-determined digital adaptation? How should we construct our research designs to foster problem-focused and solution-oriented outcomes? How can we give our research a holistic and long-term perspective in order to cope with a complex research environment? To answer these research questions, we introduce action research as a research culture that fosters closer collaboration between practitioners and scholars in order to overcome digital challenges in journalism. Action research is a framework for generating resolution-oriented (Stringer 1996, 10), local knowledge (Guba 1996, x) that science and practice value. As a methodology, action research offers a "participatory and collaborative" research approach and the reflection of practice "with a view to improving it" (McNiff and Whitehead 2006, 32).

To illustrate our arguments for more action research in Journalism Studies, we present our research collaboration with the editorial team of the Swiss daily newspaper *Neue Zürcher Zeitung*. The research questions guiding the project were:

RQ1: Why are this newspaper's journalists reluctant to become involved in the development of digital forms of news coverage?

RQ2: How can the editorial management and the involved scholars foster the implementation of digital journalism in the newsroom?

Our examination of journalists' attitudes and reservations showed their need for (protected) opportunities, separate from their daily business and time pressure, to deal with emerging forms of digital journalism. Based on the generated insights, we jointly developed the Innovation Ateliers concept. The ateliers provided the journalists and editorial team members with the opportunity to step back from their daily business and reflect on the industry trends and implications of these for the papers' digital news coverage. Journalists developed with our support brand-specific examples of digital storytelling. By presenting this action research application in the field of Digital Journalism Studies and evaluating its potentials for science and practice, we endeavor to foster the discussion and application of this methodological approach to the study of digital journalism practices in the research community.

In a first section of this paper, we introduce action research as a research culture by presenting the basic principles guiding the approach. In a second prefatory part, we elaborate on the potentials of Digital Journalism Studies and its practice. We subsequently present the above-mentioned action research project in Switzerland and discuss this study and its outcomes in the light of our arguments in the introduction. In a concluding section, we reflect on the remaining challenges for the further application of action research to study journalism's digital future.

Action Research as a Research Culture

Different researchers (depending on their discipline, the project at hand, their related values and attitudes) call action research a "remarkably inclusive methodology" (Cunningham 2014, 3), a "research culture" (Tacchi, Slater, and Hearn 2003, 4), a "collaborative approach" (Stringer 1996, 15), or simply a "tool" (Appelgren and Nygren 2014, 396) for inquiry. The motivation in these perspectives to induce change for "personal and social improvement" (McNiff and Whitehead 2006, 14) by taking "systematic *action*" (Stringer 1996, 15, italics in original) unifies them. In action research projects, members of communities become researchers—with or without the support of scholars, who act as enablers by contributing professional know-how and, in some cases, integrating their research questions. As a methodology that includes "a whole range of approaches and practices, each grounded in different traditions," it helps these researchers investigate their environment and gain knowledge about the problems confronting them (Reason and Bradbury 2001b, xxiv). Applied in professional contexts, action research offers practitioners an approach to improve their practice and adapt it to the changing environment.

Basic Principles of Action Research

The varying perspectives of action research listed above give us an impression of the "significant variations in how researchers, theorists and practitioners think about and define the action research process" (Hinchey 2008, 5). Ontological, epistemological, and methodological assumptions, as well as research's social purposes, characterize action research, just like other methodologies or research paradigms (McNiff and Whitehead 2006). Basic principles, which form a "frame" (Ladkin 2004, 536) for research activity, unify scholars from different fields and traditions. By presenting three basic principles, we endeavor to sensitize the reader to the peculiarities of this research culture.

First principle: the intention to change. Social groups' problematic situations (Stringer 1996), which are "puzzling, troubling, and uncertain," form the starting point for action research (Schön 1983, 40). Members of these groups evaluate their situations in terms of their values with the intention of changing them from *within* (McNiff and Whitehead 2006)—whether in private or professional contexts. By participating, scholars abandon their passive observing position and become actors with the explicit intention of *inducing change* (Ospina and Anderson 2014). It is this active attitude that distinguishes action research from other types of participatory research (Bergold and Thomas 2012).

Second principle: participatory and inclusive research. To maximize the usefulness of research outcomes for a particular community, they do not have to be generalizable, or replicable (McNiff and Whitehead 2006), but instead mostly *local* and *problem specific*. To develop valuable outcomes, researchers need "intimate knowledge of [the] local context" (Guba 1996, x). Local experts contribute their personal problem statement, their knowledge of the local reality, and their evaluation of the emerging resolutions. Consequently, "action research is only possible *with*, *for* and *by* [concerned] persons and communities" (Reason and Bradbury 2001a, 2, italics in original). As research facilitators, scholars are integrated if they can contribute methodological and theoretical know-how that are of value for the problem-solving process (Stringer 1996).

Third principle: developmental research process. The know-how on which action research projects build is the property of the involved individuals and, consequently, "subjective and biased" (McNiff and Whitehead 2006, 29). In research projects, stakeholders share their "diverse knowledge and experience" (Stringer 1996, 10) to find answers to community-relevant questions which do not pre-exist, but are created in negotiation with each other (a perspective shared by different forms of qualitative research; Schwandt 2000). Action researchers act on the epistemological assumption that knowledge is uncertain and ambiguous. Answers are always tentative and open to modification (Berlin 2000; McNiff and Whitehead 2006). There is no "one answer" (Berlin 2000, 5) but multiple possibilities, which the involved stakeholders have to negotiate. According to Reason and Bradbury (2001a, 2) "[g]ood action research emerges over time in an evolutionary and developmental process." Stages of action and reflection alternate in a process which is often messy, haphazard, and experimental (Atkinson 2006; Ladkin 2004; McNiff and Whitehead 2006; Schön 1983). Research processes are complex and ever-changing, necessitating taking one step at a time in order to find a way forward (McNiff and Whitehead 2006). Deviant opinions can hinder this process, but they introduce new perspectives to finding a solution (Bergold and Thomas 2012).

The introduced principles give us a first idea how practitioners might profit from this problem-focused and solution-oriented research approach in order to identify and develop their practice's required adaptations to digital challenges. The introduced principles help scholars develop a holistic, inclusive research perspective in a complex research environment. In the following section, we elaborate on these arguments.

Action Research for Digital Journalism Studies and Practice

Journalists and publishers find themselves in a "rapidly evolving [environment with] ever greater pressures and dilemmas" (Niblock 2007, 20). The internet's triumphant progress throughout society has triggered change processes in all social systems, with the media and communication system as one of the most affected industries. Legacy media are still struggling with the development of new, sustainable business models and innovative news offers to fight their demise (Carbin 2014; Knee, Greendwald, and Seave 2009; Lievrouw and Livingstone 2004; Pavlik 2013). For journalists, the ongoing transformations in a profession formerly characterized by its outstanding status, mass communication monopoly, and solid work conditions create a challenging environment that leads to role stress, identity conflicts, and overwork (Grubenmann, Meckel, and Fieseler 2013). In this increasingly digital and highly dynamic context characterized by "mind-blowing uncertainty" (Domingo, Masip, and Meijer 2015, 55) and instability, we argue for action research as an investigation approach with potential for practitioners' need for orientation (Ekdale et al. 2014) and innovativeness (Pavlik 2013), on the one hand, and for Journalism Studies in order to conduct research into vigorous and "complex meeting places where our human reality ... intersects with behavioral and technical systems" (Bradbury-Huang 2014, 666), on the other.

Innovativeness in Journalism Practice

In his paper on the future of journalism, Pavlik (2013, 190) defines innovation as "the key to the viability of news media in the digital age." To ensure long-term success, research, or "systematically gathered information designed to build knowledge," should guide innovation (187). We propose action research as a framework for *collaborative* research between media organizations and scholars in order to develop problem-focused and resolution-oriented outcomes fostering innovativeness in digital journalism. Action research serves these researchers as a framework to *reflect on developments and practice*, to *control their action*, and *improve their practice* from within. In collaborations with different Swiss editorial teams, we recognized that most journalists lack time and cognitive resources to truly engage in the industry developments, as they are fully occupied with news' content dimension. To be engaged in these kinds of questions on a meta-level, journalists need avenues of thought that allow them to step back and reflect on their practice. In action research projects, scholars can provide such avenues of thought as enablers and to support practitioners' self-reflection. As a framework, action research supports the systematic modification of practice by reflecting on it in a *conceptualizing* and *controlled* manner (Fendt and Kaminska-Labbé 2011). In these days of ever-evolving change, with insecurity hindering improvements to journalism practice

(Ekdale et al. 2014), the systematic analysis of ongoing developments can support practitioners' sense making and provide orientation by establishing understanding. However, research should not stop at reflecting on practice and systematic inquiry. Action research becomes a constructive process when the involved stakeholders create solutions to pending problems by combining their diverse knowledge and experience. Based on a collaborative, constructive approach, action research can be defined as a design science aimed at developing "solutions to real-life problems [by producing] artifacts that are innovative, novel to the world, and are for some reason preferred over existing ones" (Fendt and Kaminska-Labbé 2011, 224). Based on these characteristics, action research has the potential to bring scholars and practitioners together to focus on extant and future problems, thus improving their industry's innovativeness.

Digital Journalism Studies in a Complex Environment

Beside its mentioned capabilities in terms of journalism practice, action research also has the potential to strengthen Digital Journalism Studies as a discrete academic discipline by bringing theory and practice closer together. For this purpose, academics have to further align their research activities with the daily life of practitioners and their needs, thus bridging an identified relevance gap (e.g., Harcup 2011; Niblock 2007). Sarah Niblock (2007, 23) states that there is "tension between [the] theoretical approaches [and] everyday practice" in the field of Journalism Studies due to scholars' tendency to approach the research field with an outsider's limited perspective and focusing on journalistic output, while leaving a "range of territories" (28) (i.e., processes and decision making) uncharted. She further criticizes academics who tend to view the "news-making environment as somehow constant, seamless and unified," while news organizations see themselves as confronted with the challenge to adapt to rapid technological and social changes (23). To overcome this "clear gap in the current study of journalism" (28), we have to overcome the principles of distance and objectivity that characterize formal research processes (Stringer 1996) and bring theory and practice closer together by orienting research to problematic situations in practice.

To reach this goal, researchers need appropriate tools to conduct research in a complex environment and need to consider the "contexts and constraints" that practitioners face in their daily work (Niblock 2007, 23). Digital Journalism Studies are situated at the intersection of technological, social, strategic, and political dimensions providing a highly complex research environment. Information systems initiatives, as well as the introduction and maintenance of modern information and communication technologies in newsrooms, are dynamic and developmental processes requiring flexible and process-oriented research designs. Static, one-shot, positivist research with a limited focus on change processes' technical dimensions does not meet the complexity of this research setting (McDonagh 2014a, 2014b). Research needs to understand that digital journalism is not just a matter of ongoing technological change, but is simultaneously organizational change—a notion which has led to a constructivist-turn in Digital Journalism Studies (Boczkowski 2004; Weiss and Domingo 2010) and induced a wave of ethnographic studies over the past few years (Paterson and Domingo 2008; Steensen 2011). Action research follows this argumentation, but goes further by proposing a holistic, inclusive research culture that integrates different stakeholders and their perspective. It applies a process- and outcome-oriented perspective that is therefore also a long-term perspective. Together with the above-mentioned potentials to help practitioners systematically reflect on their practice and improve it from within, action research is a valuable framework for contributing to journalism's digital future—in science and in practice.

A Collaborative Research Project

In the following, we present our research collaboration with the editorial team of the Swiss daily newspaper *Neue Zürcher Zeitung* conducted between January 2013 and July 2014. After introducing the project, we evaluate its process and generated outcomes, providing arguments for more action research in Digital Journalism Studies and listing the principles characterizing this research culture.

In February 2013, myself and two research colleagues (Miriam Meckel and Christian Fieseler) from the University of St. Gallen in Switzerland had the chance (based on an existing business acquaintance) to meet Markus Spillmann, at that time the editor-in-chief of the *Neue Zürcher Zeitung*, for an informal talk about his worries regarding "losing" some of his journalists during the newspaper's ongoing convergence process. When we wanted to know more about his worries, he complained about his colleagues' lack of motivation and creative ideas when he announced his ambition to produce the first multimedia stories. As an editorial management member, he felt pressured to keep up with the international state-of-the-art digital news coverage, but simultaneously felt that his team did not back him. He asked us for support to identify the journalists' reservations and help the team gain ground in digital journalism. Interested in the research topic and the practice-oriented setting, we agreed to the collaboration, recognizing an opportunity for an interesting case study. Given this history, the research partner defined the participants and the research question for the case study. The research questions, which focused on local, case-specific insights, were: Why are this newspaper's journalists reluctant to become involved in the development of digital forms of news coverage? How can the editorial management and the involved scholars foster the examination and implementation of digital journalism in the newsroom? As scholars, we became participants in the research project due to our industry knowledge of the field of digital journalism and to contribute our methodological and analytical competences.

The Research Process

This action research project's starting point was the problematic situation of our practice partner. The collaboration goal was twofold. In a first step, we needed to identify the reasons for the journalists' reluctance to participate in the development of digital journalism projects. In a second step, we wanted to find a way to foster the examination of digital journalism and to determine what motivates journalists to implement their own digital projects. For our practice partner, the results of the second step had absolute priority. For us as scholars, the first element was a valuable opportunity to contribute to the emerging (scientific) research stream on convergence processes in journalistic organizations. Stimulated by the ongoing examination of the research context at hand, we expanded the research question to the following: How does journalists' professional identity influence their readiness to change? This adaptation added important theoretical objectives to the research project that drove the learning in this newsroom study.

To conceptualize and organize our research, a project team was chosen comprising four scholars (with Eliane Bucher as an additional member), two members of the editorial management, one journalist, and two members of the newsroom's lab-team (responsible for the exploration of potentials in the field of digital journalism). To learn more about journalists' attitudes and considerations, we decided to interview the editorial team members and discuss their perception of the convergence process. The editor-in-chief in particular helped the researchers compile a list of interview partners. A total of 34 of the 200-member editorial team were interviewed. Male and female journalists, journalists of different ages, and with different attitudes towards convergence and digital journalism were chosen for the talks. Two of the involved scholars (Stephanie Grubenmann and Eliane Bucher) and a student assistant (Lea Im Obersteg), who are experienced in qualitative interviewing, conducted the interviews which were subsequently transcribed and analyzed by all the involved scholars. At this point, the importance of the theoretical framework guiding the study became apparent. Even though the practitioners were not interested in the study's theoretical dimensions, it helped us as scholars to generate a far more detailed analysis of the interview data.

Conceptualization Based on Research Findings

After the insights from our research had been gathered, we discussed them with the project team. We identified several issues that hindered the convergence process and influenced the journalists' attitudes. We learned a great deal about the challenges in journalists' daily work due to the existing structures and conservative processes, and realized the significance of the cultural and leadership issues. These insights were of medium-term relevance for the editorial management, who would integrate them into future strategic decisions. Beside this, we drew implications for the second step of our project: the journalists had stressed the desire for hands-on experience with digital journalism in a protected environment separate from their daily business and time pressure. The differences between the journalists' experience with digital journalism, as described by the editor-in-chief at the beginning of the project, became apparent. Recognizing an opportunity to collaborate with scholars, the journalists identified specific areas in which they wished to benefit from insights based on international empirical studies and our industry knowledge. An important insight was the journalists' need for an explicit digital editorial strategy—a strategic issue that the editorial management had already postponed for months. The lack of editorial orientation seemed to constitute a basic challenge in the journalists' daily work. In these times of change, the journalists felt extremely uncertain about the paper's future and their personal situation. We realized that they not only needed an area—a kind of playground area—where they could examine digital journalism, but also an opportunity to discuss burning issues in an adequate context.

The gained insights gave us answers to our first research question by helping the project team to better understand the journalists' attitudes and corresponding behavior. This was the starting point to deal with our project's second goal—the "action" part of the collaboration. We developed a workshop concept which would provide the journalists with an opportunity to examine digital journalism and discuss pressing issues with their colleagues and the editorial management team—which were both opportunities that the journalists lacked in their daily work. Even though the lack of a digital editorial strategy was identified as one of the most urgent issues concerning the journalists' daily work, the editorial management team refused to implement one immediately. They argued that they would need more time for such an important task. When we insisted that this issue had to be approached, they agreed on the possibility of integrating the journalists in the development process: they would not only analyze existing examples of digital journalism, but would be allowed to develop brand-specific applications. This would make them reflect on the potentials of the digital storytelling they encountered that were in line with the newspaper's brand and would provide them with opportunities to influence the digital editorial strategy inductively. The conception and execution of the workshop concept was our (temporary) answer to the second research question. However, since the project team presented these workshops without afterwards systematically analyzing their effect on the journalists' attitudes and behavior, a concluding statement about their quantitative outcomes is difficult. We will return to this aspect in the discussion part of the paper, after having briefly described the implementation of the workshop concept.

The Implementation: Innovation Ateliers

The workshop format was called "Innovation Ateliers." Over a nine-month timeframe, eight ateliers were presented. In each atelier, the project team collaborated with between 12 and 14 journalists. All the journalists (even the correspondents) were invited to participate. More than 100 (out of 200) journalists participated in an atelier. The number of atelier presentations was increased until every interested journalist had had the opportunity to participate.

Each atelier lasted two days and consisted of three elements. In a first part, we presented an analysis of the current developments in the industry and introduced an international collection of state-of-the-art digital journalism. In the second part of the atelier, the journalists were divided into groups of three or four people to develop creative concepts for digital news coverage of a preliminary chosen atelier topic (e.g., foreigners in Switzerland), taking different digital journalism trends into consideration. The groups developed their concepts over two half-days by interacting with the project team members, who constructively challenged the emerging ideas. In a final session, each group presented its concept, which the participants then assessed. To complete the final session, the atelier allowed discussion and self-reflection: a short viewpoint that we had prepared, as well as the editor-in-chief's strategic outlook stimulated the discussion and self-reflection when the attendees were invited to ask questions. This opportunity was extensively used in each atelier, leading to lively discussions each time.

To link the atelier with journalists' daily work and to engage as many team members as possible, we also organized a digital poll after each atelier to determine which of the four developed concepts should be realized. After the first atelier, the editor-in-chief presented the idea of realizing the most popular concept of each atelier: he was excited about the quality and creativity of the developed ideas and wished to show his commitment. The editor-in-chief's decision thus intensified the developed projects' influence on the emerging digital editorial strategy. Several other minor adaptions were the result of the ongoing and intensive discussions with the participants and between the project team members. After the last atelier in June 2014, the project team members met for an intensive debriefing of the overall experience, the project outcomes, and other implications.

Discussion

In this section, we move from the project's research questions to this article's research objectives: How can Journalism Studies support practitioners' pursuit of self-determined digital adaption? How can we give our research a holistic and long-term perspective in order to cope with a complex research environment? To find answers to these questions, we discuss the project by referring to the advantages of action research for Digital Journalism Studies and journalism practice outlined in the first part of the article.

Evaluation from Practitioners' Point of View

To evaluate the research collaboration from the practitioners' point of view, we consider the formal and informal feedback talks with journalists after their participation in an atelier/workshop (which different project team members conducted), the project team's feedback sessions after every atelier, and the project team's debriefing after the last atelier.

Opportunity for reflection. The journalists perceived it as a very valuable opportunity to break out of their daily business, take a step back, and reflect on the changes in the industry and their influence on their newsroom practice. The journalists probably benefited most from the examination of international best practices and the meta-level discussions with colleagues from different departments. We were surprised that most of the participants had not examined leading international examples of digital journalism and trends before their participation in an atelier. Most of the journalists seemed to lack the resources and/or the motivation to follow these developments as part of their daily work. This conclusion led to the integration of avenues of thought, in the form of break-out sessions during lunchtime, into the newsroom's weekly routines as a project implication.

The workshop (and "action") part of the project was more akin to further education than research, and we acted more as consultants than as researchers (we signed a non-disclosure agreement as important strategic issues were the topic of some discussions). We provided space for the journalists to reflect on their practice and acted as enablers and supporters. In principle, it would have been possible to present the ateliers without our participation, but this would have resulted in a different outcome: the participants benefited from our outsider perspective, our industry knowledge, and the discussion with us.

Systematic improvement. What began as an issue of newsroom culture (the editor-in-chief's worries) developed into a collective reflection on the newspaper's digital news coverage and resulted in its systematic, collaborative improvement. A deliberate decision was taken to not leave the formation of practical knowledge in this important area of activity to chance, but to control its development. This decision was the result of the project's inclusive nature and is an example of emerging knowledge production over the course of the project. By involving journalists in the development of brand-specific digital storytelling and by contributing to the formation of the digital editorial strategy, the project process contributed to the organizational change and in turn made an important contribution to the newsroom culture. The journalists more than appreciated the opportunity to contribute to important questions regarding the newspaper practice and strategy.

Induce change. The starting point for the project was the clear intention to induce change—to go further than just describing and evaluating the current state. Even though the initiative for the project came from the editor-in-chief, what had to be changed and the direction in which this had to occur was the result of social knowledge construction (in cycles of observing, reflecting, planning, and acting) and, consequently, was an image of the editorial team's development. However, to measure the emerging knowledge production, or to capture the effects on journalists' practice would have been a difficult task. The project probably affected the cultural dimension most. The project team also refrained from measuring the quantitative effects on journalists' attitudes. This lack of a systematic evaluation of the ateliers' outcomes might be interpreted as contrary to the objective to improve practice in a *controlled* manner. However, their personal perception of the change was important for the practitioners—and distinguishable. In action research, we often find that "the process by which the project is undertaken is … as important, if not more important, than the 'result'" (Ladkin 2004, 538).

Even though just about half of the editorial team participated in an atelier, the project and its implications affected the whole team. Nevertheless, the following question is still relevant: Did the project reach its objectives of being inclusive and participative if only half of the editorial team and, for example, an interactive designer were involved in the "action" part? Certain values and principles are essential in the action research culture. However, certain researchers maintain that "[a]ction research is an aspiration, rather than a possibility" if one considers that action research theory assumes an ideal world (anonymous researcher, Peter, cited in Ladkin 2004, 547). Mostly, however, action researchers face a highly complex world rather than an ideal one. Researchers have to cope with never achieving a perfect action research process in the sense of considering all the principles fully. But they can make the best of a given opportunity to contribute to the "bettering of, or deeper understanding of, a situation" by respecting the local realities and action research's basic principles as a framework for their research activities (Ladkin 2004, 538).

Evaluation from an Academic Point of View

We evaluate the research collaboration from an academic point of view by considering the internal feedback session from the involved researchers, an internal debriefing after the project, and personal reflections during and after the project.

Holistic inquiry. A change process such as the convergence process in a newsroom constitutes a complex research setting at the intersection of the technological, social, political, and strategic dimensions combining technological and organizational change challenges. Researching such processes only delivers a snapshot, even if the research project endeavors to obtain an inclusive and long-term perspective such as the study at hand. However, it was the close collaboration with the involved practitioners, in the explicit sense of *working together* and not just having a joint project, that led to a deeper and holistic understanding of these journalists' situation in a changeable environment. In the course of the project, we were confronted with a variety of data: formal and informal talks, interviews, different types of artifacts generated in the ateliers (such as drawings, sketches, and written concepts), passive observation, and active discussions. Owing to different stakeholders' involvement, a variety of perspectives also characterized the data. All of the data allowed us to dive deeply into the journalists' life to explore their current issues and identify those on the horizon. However, we had to learn to deal with this amount and variety of data. In the project at hand, we missed several opportunities to systematically collect data, which appeared unexpectedly, or because we only realized the (scientific) value of a situation in hindsight. For us, an important lesson from the project was that, in action research, scholars have to anticipate and be prepared (their cognitive state and their equipment) for such unexpected opportunities. However, research is not only about systematic data collection, because interesting talks and observation can serve as a valuable inspiration and/ or trigger insights. But we have to accept that, in action research, scholars surrender some of the control that they normally try to maximize in more formal research. Action research projects are often messy and haphazard, which makes anticipatory planning and anticipating unexpected valuable occasions for data collection and conscious analysis (beside the planned ones) indispensable.

Action research literature (e.g., McNiff and Whitehead 2006) stresses the potential, even the responsibility, for scholars *and* practitioners to contribute to "the creation of theory from cycles of action and reflection," which is sometimes called action science (Ladkin 2004, 537). In the project at hand, we added a theoretical dimension to the project's first research question, resulting in more elaborated insights into the interview analysis and a theoretical contribution to the scientific community in the form of two conference papers (Grubenmann 2015; Grubenmann, Meckel, and Fieseler 2014) and one journal paper (Grubenmann and Meckel, forthcoming). This process illustrates that practitioners and the scientific community can benefit from action research projects. However, as mentioned above, we also missed a more systematic data collection and analysis opportunity in the second part of the project.

Relevance gap. The project offered us a very stimulating environment. Having an academic background and "one foot in practice" meant we had a valuable position from which to reflect on digital journalism practices and gain inspiration and knowledge for future research projects—not all of which will be realized as action research. The research objective to investigate cross-departmental teamwork in newsrooms as an innovative working format to cover "wicked problems" (Lichfield 2012) resulted from our experiences in the ateliers. An according explorative study has been realized in the spring of 2015 with the same research partner to investigate first experiments with cross-departmental newswork. Although this study did not comprise any "action," it was still of importance for the editorial management team already concerned with the next convergence issues. If we consider action research as a research culture (Tacchi, Slater, and Hearn 2003) or orientation (Reason and McArdle 2004) characterizing a closer co-existence between science and journalism practice, the two areas can provide each other with valuable stimulation: scholars can gain insights and inspiration for their theorizing and practitioners can profit from more practice-oriented and problem-focused research outcomes.

Conclusion and Remaining Challenges

In our argumentation, we introduce action research as a research frame for holistic inquiry dealing with highly dynamic and complex research settings—as in Digital Journalism Studies that lie at the intersection of technological, social, strategic, and political dimensions. It was the intensive examination of the involved stakeholders' situation that helped us to gain a (first) idea of the existing challenges, the related drivers, and the correlations. The developed approach may deliver a local, but only partial and temporary solution to some of the variety of existing (and persisting) challenges with which these journalists (and others) have to deal in digital journalism. It would be overconfident to assume that we can develop ultimate solutions, because digital transformation is developing very fast. Whenever we believe we have found a way of dealing with an issue and have improved our praxis, the next challenge is already looming on the horizon. The fast pace of change requires us to closely align our research objectives to practitioners' needs in order to generate problem-focused research outcomes. The principles on which action research is based help us design and realize flexible and adaptive research projects by centering the practitioners' situation—which may even change during longer collaborations. Despite, or because of, this flexibility, action research projects generate sustainable contributions for solving practitioners' problems.

The introduced project made it possible not just to contribute to solving practitioners' problems, but also to contribute to the scientific community. However, the presented approach is only one example of a research collaboration design. Others are possible, valid, and necessary. There is no such thing as *perfect* action research (Ladkin 2004). In every new project, the involved researchers have to find their own ways of aligning the participating and concerned stakeholders' interests. Further, researchers cannot fully respect all the presented principles in every stage of a research project, but their priorities have to be transparent and consciously determined. This is a learning process, which the researchers (practitioners and scholars) in the presented project had to learn. There are a few remaining challenges that researchers have to consider when studying journalism's digital future in action research projects.

The Search for a Reliable Partner

In action research, the project stakeholders share their "diverse knowledge and experience" to develop solutions for local challenges (Stringer 1996, 10). Different stakeholders gain the right to be integrated into such research through their personal involvement and/or by contributing their expert knowledge that is indispensable for solving the problem. Bergold and Thomas (2012) point to the difficulties with identifying the concerned stakeholders and criticize the lack of systematic procedures. Identifying such stakeholders is a complicated matter that most handbooks simply ignore in the relevant chapter. As a temporary alternative, Bergold and Thomas (2012) refer to examples of rather pragmatic strategies. In addition, not all of the identified stakeholders can become involved in research projects, or are willing to do so. Practitioners also have to decide if they do have a problem and require the support of scholars and, if so, which institution's scholars will meet their needs. If they cannot rely on established contacts, it can be a difficult task to identify and evaluate the relevant academic research institutions. Scholars face similar problems if they are looking for suitable research partners among practitioners—especially if they require a financial contribution to fund their research activities. However, successful projects can turn into trustworthy networks, which make new collaborations easier.

The Complexity of Action Research Projects

Digital Journalism Studies, which lie at the intersection of technological, social, strategic, and political dimensions, have to consider and integrate a variety of different perspectives. In our project, we recognized that even the integration of the three concerned stakeholder groups (journalists from different departments, members of the editorial management, and scholars) leads to resource and time-intensive research activities. Although it would have been very valuable to include interactive designers' or users' perspectives in the process to guarantee a holistic treatment, this would have exceeded the participants' capacity. In our project we thus decided to prioritize complexity reduction rather than a holistic examination. We believe that the complexity and dimension of inclusive action research projects are a fundamental challenge for the realization of this kind of research. Tanja Aitamurto (2013) integrates journalists' and users' perspectives in her study of co-creation in magazine journalism, while Appelgren and Nygren (2014) collaborate with seven media companies to learn more about data-driven journalism. Nevertheless, neither publication informs us about the challenges of handling such projects as a research facilitator. We argue for the further integration of process-related experiences into journal publications on action research projects to foster learning cycles and the development of adapted forms that take the field's specific peculiarities into consideration. What do we have to consider when integrating journalists' and users' interests in a research topic? How can we downgrade, or fragment, complex research issues? Researchers have to learn from each other how to cope most efficiently with these kinds of issues that action research raises.

Appropriate Quality Dimensions

"If an action research project does not *make a difference*, in a very specific way, for practitioners and/or their clients, then it has failed to achieve its objectives" (Stringer 1996, 11, italics in original). With this intention to induce change, action research harms traditional research standards of objectivity and validity. Researchers do not just change, but also *direct*, research outcomes with their purposeful intervention. To respect the basic principles of action research, we have to develop appropriate dimensions to evaluate the quality of such projects. Hilary Bradbury-Huang (2014, 667) offers seven "choice points" as a starting point for further quality discussions: relevance of the research objectives, the partnership and participation, the contribution to practice knowledge and/or theory, the actionability, reflexivity, and relevance beyond the immediate context. Herr and Anderson (2005) complement this list by postulating catalytic validity, process validity, and dialogic validity. Our discussion can build on this groundwork. However, to gain a further understanding of appropriate standards, we have to increase action research's visibility in the community and foster academic publications, even if the quality discussion has not been concluded as yet.

Scholars as Insiders and Outsiders

Another challenge when discussing the objectivity and validity in, and the quality of, action research projects is the issue of going native: the close collaboration with practitioners, the focus on local problems and solutions, and the alignment of scientific and the practitioners' research objectives make going native even more likely than in other forms of qualitative inquiry. Can research partners be too close? Or does the quality of action research outcomes increase the closer scholars and practitioners are? In our project, we certainly developed a more intense relationship with our project partner than we had experienced in other research projects. In action research, scholars do not just research the participants, but also collaborate with the practitioners, thus sharing their research objectives. However, our participation in the project probably generated the most value by contributing an outsider perspective. The editorial team wanted our *critical* analysis and feedback. They *expected* us to stay as impartial as possible. We did, of course, want to learn as much as possible about our project partner and often adopted the practitioners' perspective to provide local solutions. Self- and group reflection, as well as ongoing theorizing, specifically helped us gain valuable distance during the collaboration. We believe that the main challenge for scholars involved in action research projects is the requirement to simultaneously be an insider and an outsider.

The greater the number of action research projects realized and published, the faster scholars will learn to deal with such and similar issues. The extant action research publications in the field of Journalism Studies (Aitamurto 2013; Appelgren and Nygren 2014; Cochrane et al. 2013) reveal the openness of this research community to innovative approaches and attests to the connectivity between Journalism Studies and practice. It further shows that reflection on adequate forms of action research and quality dimensions for this field of research are already in progress. The field of Digital Journalism Studies in particular, a complex research environment at the intersection of technological, social, strategic, and political dimensions, holds considerable potential to invest further resources to leverage these efforts and contribute to journalism's digital future.

ACKNOWLEDGEMENTS

Special thanks go to our project partner for the trust shown and the inspiring collaboration. Further thanks goes to Jesse Bächler for his support in developing the concept of this contribution, to Miriam Feuls, bound to similar research values, and to Christian P. Hoffmann and Werner A. Meier for their constructive feedback. Earlier versions of this paper were presented at the annual conference of the Swiss Association of Communication and Media Research 2014. The author is grateful for comments received in the context of this presentation.

DISCLOSURE STATEMENT

No potential conflict of interest was reported by the author.

REFERENCES

Aitamurto, Tanja. 2013. "Balancing between Open and Closed." *Digital Journalism* 1 (2): 229–251. doi:10.1080/21670811.2012.750150.

Appelgren, Ester, and Gunnar Nygren. 2014. "Data Journalism in Sweden." *Digital Journalism* 2 (3): 394–405. doi:10.1080/21670811.2014.884344.

Artwick, Claudette G. 2013. "Reporters on Twitter." *Digital Journalism* 1 (2): 212–228. doi:10.1080/21670811.2012.744555.

Atkinson, Sue. 2006. "Rethinking the Principles and Practice of Action Research: The Tensions for the Teacher-Researcher." *Educational Action Research* 2 (3): 383–401.

Bergold, Jarg, and Stefan Thomas. 2012. "Partizipative Forschungsmethoden: Ein Methodischer Ansatz in Bewegung [Participatory Research Methods: A Methodological Approach in Motion]." *Forum Qualitative Sozialforschung* 13 (1): Art. 30, http://nbn-resolving.de/urn:nbn:de:0114-fqs1201302.

Berlin, Isaiah. 2000. *The Proper Study of Mankind: An Anthology of Essays*. New York: Farrar, Straus and Giroux.

Boczkowski, Pablo J. 2004. "The Processes of Adopting Multimedia and Interactivity in Three Online Newsrooms." *Journal of Communication* 54 (2): 197–213. doi:10.1093/joc/54.2.197.

Bradbury-Huang, Hilary. 2014. "Quality." In *The SAGE Encyclopedia of Action Research*, edited by David Coghlan and Mary Brydon-Miller, 666–669. London: SAGE Publications Ltd..

Carbin, Andy. 2014. "Welcome to Reported.Ly! a Global News Community with You at the Heart of It." *Reported.Ly*. https://medium.com/reportedly/welcome-to-reported-ly-3363a5fb7ea5.

Cochrane, Thomas, Helen Sissons, Danni Mulrennan, and Richard Pamatatau. 2013. "Journalism 2.0: Exploring the Impact of Mobile and Social Media on Journalism Education." *International Journal of Mobile and Blended Learning* 5 (2): 22–38. doi:10.4018/jmbl.2013040102.

Cunningham, Joseph. 2014. "Academic Discourse." In *The SAGE Encyclopedia of ACTION RESEARCH*, edited by David Coghland and Mary Brydon-Miller, 1–3. Los Angeles, CA: SAGE Publications Ltd..

Deuze, Mark. 1999. "Journalism and the Web: An Analysis of Skills and Standards in an Online Environment." *Gazette* 61 (5): 373–390.

Doctor, Ken. 2015. "Newsonomics: BuzzFeed and the New York times Play Facebook's Ubiquity Game." *NiemanLab*. http://www.niemanlab.org/2015/03/newsonomics-buzzfeed-and-the-new-york-times-play-facebooks-ubiquity-game/.

Domingo, David, Pere Masip, and Irene Costera Meijer. 2015. "Tracing Digital News Networks: Towards an Integrated Framework of the Dynamics of News Production." *Digital Journalism* 3 (1): 53–67. doi:10.1080/21670811.2014.927996.

Ekdale, Brian, Melissa Tully, Shawn Harmsen, and Jane B. Singer. 2014. "Newswork within a Culture of Job Insecurity." *Journalism Practice* published (January 2015): 1–16. doi:10.1080/17512786.2014.963376.

Fendt, Jacqueline, and Renata Kaminska-Labbé. 2011. "Relevance and Creativity through Design-driven Action Research: Introducing Pragmatic Adequacy." *European Management Journal* 29 (3): 217–233. doi:10.1016/j.emj.2010.10.004.

Grubenmann, Stephanie. 2015. "Journalists' Professional Identity: A Resource to Cope with Uncertainty?" Annual Conference of the International Communication Association. San Juan, Puerto Rico.

Grubenmann, Stephanie, and Miriam Meckel. Forthcoming. "Journalists' Professional Identity: A Resource to Cope with Change in the Industry?" *Journalism Studies*.

Grubenmann, Stephanie, Miriam Meckel, and Christian Fieseler. 2013. "Journalists as Innovation Agents: The Development of a Measure for Journalistic Role Stress." The Future of Journalism Conference. Cardiff, UK.

Grubenmann, Stephanie, Miriam Meckel, and Christian Fieseler. 2014. "Metaphors of Occupational Identity: Traces of a Changeable Workplace in Journalism." The 74th Annual Meeting of the Academy of Management. Philadelphia, PA.

Guba, Egon G. 1996. "Foreword." In *Action Research. a Handbook for Practitioners*, edited by Ernest T. Stringer, xi–xiii. Thousand Oaks, CA: SAGE Publications, Inc.

Haik, Cory. 2013. "Adaptive Journalism." *Cory Haik's Tumblr-Account*, May 6. http://coryhaik.tumblr.com/post/49802508964/adaptive-journalism.

Harcup, Tony. 2011. "Hackademics at the Chalkface." *Journalism Practice* 5 (1): 34–50. doi:10.1080/17512786.2010.493333.

Herr, Kathryn G., and Gary L. Anderson. 2005. *The Action Research Dissertation: A Guide for Students and Faculty*. Thousand Oaks, CA: Sage.

Hinchey, Patricia H. 2008. *Action Research. Primer*. New York, NY: Peter Lang Publishing Inc.

Knee, Jonathan A., Bruce C. Greendwald, and Ava Seave. 2009. *The Curse of the Mogul. What's Wrong with the World's Leading Media Companies*. Portfolio: London.

Ladkin, Donna. 2004. "Action Researchni." In *Qualitative Research Practice*, edited by Clive Seale, Giampietro Gobo, Jaber F. Gubrium and David Silverman, 536–548. London: SAGE Publications Ltd.

Lichfield, Gideon. 2012. "On Elephants, Obsessions and Wicked Problems: A New Phenomenology of News." *News Thing*, September. http://newsthing.net/2012/09/16/quartz-obsessions-phenomenology-of-news/.

Lievrouw, Leah A., and Sonia Livingstone. 2004. *The Handbook of New Media*. London: SAGE.

McDonagh, Joe. 2014a. "Information and Communications Technology and Organizational Change." In *The SAGE Encyclopedia of Action Research*, edited by David Coghlan and Mary Brydon-Miller, 439–440. London: SAGE Publications Ltd.

McDonagh, Joe. 2014b. "Information Systems." In *The SAGE Encyclopedia of Action Research*, edited by David Coghlan and Mary Brydon-Miller, 440–443. London: SAGE Publications Ltd.

McNiff, Jean, and Jack Whitehead. 2006. *All You Need to Know about Action Research*. London: SAGE Publications Ltd.

Niblock, Sarah. 2007. "From 'Knowing How' to 'Being Able'." *Journalism Practice* 1 (1): 20–32. doi:10.1080/17512780601078829.

Ospina, Sonia M., and Gary Anderson. 2014. "The Action Turn." In *The SAGE Encyclopedia of Action Research*, edited by David Coghlan and Mary Brydon-Miller, 19–21. London: SAGE Publications Ltd..

Paterson, Chris, and David Domingo. 2008. *Making Online News. The Ethnography of New Media Production*. New York, NY: Peter Lang.

Pavlik, John V. 2013. "Innovation and the Future of Journalism." *Digital Journalism* 1 (2): 181–193. doi:10.1080/21670811.2012.756666.

Reason, Peter, and Hilary Bradbury. 2001a. "Introduction: Inquiry and Participation in Search of a World Worthy of Human Aspiration." In *Handbook of Action Research. Participative Inquiry and Practice*, edited by Peter Reason and Hilary Bradbury, 1–14. London: SAGE Publications Ltd.

Reason, Peter, and Hilary Bradbury. 2001b. "Preface." In *Handbook of Action Research. Participative Inquiry and Practice*, edited by Peter Reason and Hilary Bradbury, xii–xv. London: SAGE Publications Ltd.

Reason, Peter, and Kate L. McArdle. 2004. "Brief Notes on the Theory and Practice of Action Research." In *Understanding Research Methods for Social Policy and Practice*, edited by Saul Becker and Alan Bryman, 114–122. Bristol: Policy Press.

Schön, Donald A. 1983. *The Reflective Practitioner: How Professionals Think in Action*. Avebury: Aldershot.

Schwandt, Thomas A. 2000. "Three Epistemological Stances for Qualitative Inquiry." In *Handbook of Qualitative Research*, edited by Norman K. Denzin and Yvonna S. Lincoln, 2nd ed., 189–213. Chicago, IL: SAGE Publications, Inc.

Steensen, Steen. 2011. "Online Journalism and the Promises of New Technology." *Journalism Studies* 12 (3): 311–327. doi:10.1080/1461670X.2010.501151.

Stringer, Ernest T. 1996. *Action Research. a Handbook for Practitioners*. Thousand Oaks, CA: SAGE Publications, Inc.

Tacchi, Jo A., Don Slater, and Greg Hearn. 2003. *Ethnographic Action Research: A User's Handbook*. New Delhi: UNESCO.

Weiss, Amy Schmitz, and David Domingo. 2010. "Innovation Processes in Online Newsrooms as Actor-networks and Communities of Practice." *New Media & Society* 12 (7): 1156–1171.

CONTENT ANALYSIS AND ONLINE NEWS
Epistemologies of analysing the ephemeral Web

Michael Karlsson and Helle Sjøvaag

In this article, we argue that digital media pose such challenges for analysing media content adequately that the established approach does not work as intended, reflecting underlying assumptions inherited from analogue media formats. We review two relatively new forms of the content analysis method—big data and liquid content analysis—and juxtapose these with established content analysis. In addition, we detail how these two methods tackle content analysis pillars such as mode of analysis, sampling, sampling size, variable design, unit of analysis, measuring point(s), access/capture/storing, conclusions/generalizability and the key agent doing the actual work. We summarize the article by arguing that established content analysis is insufficient for digital media but that common standards, protocols and procedures are yet to be developed for these new approaches to digital journalism research.

Introduction

The digitization and convergence of media pose fundamental challenges to the staple method of content analysis. However, the difficulties of conducting a content analysis of digital media are not, with a few exceptions (cf. boyd and Crawford 2012; Flaounas et al. 2013; Lewis, Zamith, and Hermida 2013), properly debated. Discussions tend to focus on issues raised by applying new methodology to digital news data, not on the issues that emerging forms of digital journalism in themselves pose for implementing new digital methodologies. In this article, we discuss why content analysis of online news remains a complex methodological issue, and outline conceptual aspects that scholars need to account for when assuming digital methodological approaches. To illustrate the discussion, we provide a taxonomy of approaches, juxtaposing the established content analysis method (e.g. Berelson 1971; Krippendorff 2013; Neuendorf 2002; Riffe, Lacy, and Fico 1998) with two contemporary approaches—*big data* and what can be termed *liquid content analysis*—and how they design, perform and infer from content analysis.

What we refer to as the established content analysis method is defined by Riffe and colleagues as "the systematic assignment of communication content to categories according to rules, and the analysis of relationships involving those categories using statistical methods" (Riffe, Lacy, and Fico 2014, 3). While content analyses can indeed be qualitative (as used, for instance, in rhetorical, discourse, critical or semiotic analysis; Neuendorf 2002, 5–9), established definitions of both the qualitative and the quantitative content analysis are grounded in space/time assumptions that resonate with analogue media, in general, and print media, in particular. Whether the content analytic technique used merely entails "objective" counting of manifest, quantifiable content, or if measures are inferred qualitatively from interpretive readings of latent content, methodological veracity is primarily bound to the continual affordances of analogue communication forms. As digital media are introduced, this approach to study content becomes problematic (Herring 2010; Karlsson 2012; Schneider and Foot 2004; Weare and Lin 2000). At the same time, the established method offers sound points of departure to study manifest content in a transparent and reliable manner. The taxonomy presented in this article aims to illuminate how two new approaches—big data and liquid content analysis—relate to central underpinnings of content analysis, how they derail from the standard method, and what the challenges of the digital nature of the data captured by these approaches entail for content analysis as a methodology for studying journalism in the digital age.

The Limits of "Content" Analysis

The great Canadian media scholar Harold Innis emphasized the connection between media, time and space, and society (Innis 1999). His central argument was that different media have different spatial and temporal biases—some media are better spread through space (e.g. ether media) while some are better as records durable over time (e.g. the newspaper)—aspects that impact on how societies are organized and power is distributed. These time and space biases also relate to dimensions of media and scientific method, more precisely content analysis. The logic of content analysis is to no small extent embedded in the affordances of analogue media, in general, and print, in particular. Therefore, a more apt description of content analysis would read, "a method that works very well quantifying texts printed on paper but loses its usefulness the further away from that scenario that it drifts".

These assumptions of content analysis are illustrated by the following four traits. First, content is assumed to be published according to successive pre-planned and recurring windows of publishing (Krippendorff 2013; Riffe, Lacy, and Fico 1998). This is essentially another way of saying that content is assemblages of news bundled in newscasts or newspapers, arriving at the convenience of the researcher. Second, and related, it is assumed that the data exist before the researcher wants to investigate them. "Typically, content analysts become interested in data only after data have been generated" (Krippendorff 2013, 46). It is also assumed that content is *preserved*, at least as far as text is concerned (Riffe, Lacy, and Fico 1998). Not only can the content analyst wait for the data to be created, it is also assumed that once it has been created it is a static one-dimensional entity that can be assessed, captured and measured (Berelson 1971, 18ff). Third, it is assumed that the researcher cannot affect this process as content analysis is an "unobtrusive, nonreactive, measurement technique" (Riffe, Lacy, and Fico 1998, 30; Krippendorff 2013) and that content is not affected by being watched. Fourth and finally, as "content" is assumed to have these inherent qualities it is up to the researcher to find the best way to plan, execute, record and reproduce their content analysis in a manner that makes it reliable and replicable. This scenario presupposes not only that it is possible to control how and when content is being produced, but also that content has the same basic qualities over different media platforms. Online, however, texts are fluid and ephemeral—difficult to pin down in space and time. Newscasts can take place at any time of the day, in any channel; news texts can be rearranged, edited or deleted, and users can add content or context. This ontological difference in production, distribution and consumption modes put new demands on researchers and their tools than those proposed by the authors of our methodology textbooks.

Because the content analysis is geared towards particular *kinds* of medium rather than *content*, changing affordances of the medium means that methods adjusted to one particular media are ill-suited as tools to investigate content as it shifts to a new medium. Whereas analogue media certainly come with their own, indeed very different, affordances—quantifying textual or visual elements from radio, television, film or advertising, for instance, requires tailored approaches to validly capture units for analysis—the boundaries of these units are nonetheless fixed in time and space. This is not to say that the established method is utterly incompatible with the content of the new medium, but that new or tweaked approaches have to be developed. Because digital media are absent of "proper" time and space, new problems and solutions are created. Indeed, this process is already taking place, presented here as a taxonomy (Table 1) of how three different approaches relate to and differ on central aspects of content analysis. We want to stress that the differences that are outlined here are principal and

TABLE 1

Overview of different approaches to content analysis of online news and their traits in relation to core conceptual aspects

	Established content analysis	**Liquid content analysis**	**Big data analysis**
Mode of analysis	Quantitative with qualitative elements	Quantitative with qualitative elements	Quantitative
Variable design	Deductive	Primarily inductive	Inductive/deductive
Scope/sampling size	Hundreds to thousands of news items	Tens of news items	Millions
Sampling procedure	Random	Purpose and somewhat inductive	"Census"
Unit of analysis	News item	"Floating" digital objects	Data structures
Recording/storage	Archiving crucial	Not necessary	Yes and no
Generalizability	Intermediary	Deep/limited	Shallow/encompassing
Key agent	Human	Human and computer	Computer
Analysis aim	Descriptive	Explanatory	Descriptive/predictive

Any given project will have limited resources and the researcher can utilize them by going wide or deep (not taking specific research questions/aims into account). This taxonomy presents a map of the principal choices one can make.

archetypical. In reality, it is still in all likelihood a viable option to conduct established content analysis of online media content, as many digital news stories will not display all the aspects of behaviours described here. Much of the content originally published in analogue forms eventually becomes archived in digital databases, illustrating that boundaries between platforms are not that definite. Regardless of these overlaps, and the continued viability of the established content analysis approach, there are fundamentally different logics at work that pose challenges for the content analyst.

Space, Time and Digital Content

Researchers interested in content have always been challenged and helped by spatial and temporal qualities of the medium to be able to sample, collect, measure and analyse content. Digital media is no different in this respect. Looking at previous studies of online news, discussions of methodological space/time issues primarily refer to these in practical terms. Digital news publishing does not follow the same recurring and pre-planned pattern embedded in analogue news publishing. Online news is not bundled in the same way as broadcast news or a printed newspaper. Instead, online news can be sporadic, appear in great chunks and can be largely aggregated. Naturally, when legacy media produce news for digital platforms, they follow an established production pattern that is reminiscent of analogue space/time media production, readership habits and standardized organization of labour. As such, news production still happens during normal working hours—with lower frequencies during evenings, weekends and public holidays. However, as newsrooms become smaller and increasingly digitized, the physical radius of news reporting moves closer and closer to the location of editorial offices (Ryfe 2012). Space/time dimensions in news production are therefore caught between the established analogue labour organization and the technical and economic pressures of digitization processes that make news gathering and dissemination more elusive. In the contemporary news ecology it becomes increasingly difficult to pin down where the news is produced, distributed and consumed as news appears in so many places—and comes in so many forms—at once.

First, because online news does not happen successively and recurringly, content analyses of online news largely need to be planned ahead of time. The data do not exist prior to investigation, but need to be collected continuously or in real time (e.g. Chadwick 2011; Keith, Schwalbe, and Silcock 2010). Internet archiving services are available (such as the WayBack Machine), however, these tend to be unstable and seldom offer fixed and frequent intervals of page sampling, nor provide complete archives (Karpf 2012; Keith, Schwalbe, and Silcock 2010). Most projects on online news priorities therefore perform data collection by doing image captures of the front pages at regular intervals (e.g. Groshek 2008; Kautsky and Widholm 2008). While these can be done automatically, they still have to be pre-planned. Automated image retrieval is clearly an advantage, however, only real-time observation can adequately capture developments as a story unfolds (Chadwick 2011), putting high demands on the content analyst.

Second, contrary to analogue analyses, *ex post* digital data collection is problematic because digital content is not necessarily preserved in the form it was published (Brügger 2009). This pertains primarily to news publishing on the Web platform. Indeed, analogue media forms can be published digitally—for instance, as digital renderings of the physical edition of a daily newspaper (such as pdf, iPad or e-paper versions). While some digital news formats (such as the e-paper) are digital merely in its distribution technology, online journalism as a particular publication format is digital in mode of communication. Analogue media formats such as printed newspapers, magazines, feature films and news broadcasts are "frozen" entities with a set beginning and end. Journalism on the Web, on the other hand, is an elastic mode of communication that stretches in space and time—across sites as quotes, across domains as links, across formats as social media posts, and across time as permanently searchable and retrievable objects. Space/time limitations for digital data collection therefore stand in stark contrast to analyses of linear media. Whereas significant breaking news stories can be surveyed in full—from beginning to end—on printed or recorded platforms, the required continuous data collection online presupposes a certain level of planning, to the extent that capturing all relevant content is unfeasible, as no one knows when a big story might break. Because Web-based news is not static, data gathering after the fact can be faulty, and is subsequently rare.

Third, digital data collection is neither non-reactive nor unobtrusive. The fact that data processing of digital media content is performed by programming and can be stored on computer hardware puts greater demands on the researcher to be in possession of the tools that enable data protection and processing. Fourth, who is in control of the content becomes increasingly contentious. Data structures are not neutral, nor are they necessarily transparent, creating black boxes where "Data go in, 'facts' come out" (Stavelin 2013, 80). Unlike analogue media formats, digital data can go missing, automatic collection can be interrupted, systems can be hacked and news organizations can erect digital walls around content—putting new demands on the tools needed to conduct reliable analyses. Due to the capacity to individualize what information is presented to different users (Pariser 2009; Tewksbury and Rittenberg 2012), researchers can also not be sure their data collection is replicable in another setting, even if the exact same approach is used.

New approaches to tackle these problems are already in development—approaches that *differ* from traditional demands of content analysis in fundamental areas. Two such approaches are *big data* and *liquid content analysis*—an archetypical comparative overview of which is presented in Table 1.

Big data analysis involves the introduction of a computer (and code) to collect and process data from online news sites to a scale not feasible for human coding. Whereas big data refers to volume of information, big data analysis is the systematic processing of big volumes of data (Lewis, Zamith, and Hermida 2013, 34). When used for content analytical purposes, the computer runs one or several scripts written to the specific publication template, designed to "assemble, filter and interpret" (35) from the data manifest content either embedded in the code of the published story or in the news text. This process can render large amounts of structural data about news publishing online, as well as extract stylistic and semantic properties of the content (cf. Flaounas et al. 2013). Big data methods allow the researcher to store potentially millions of news items (collected either continuously as they are published or *ex post* from the publisher) that can later be subjected to information extraction through data mining.

The benefit of big data analysis is not only scale and scope—computational power facilitating larger longitudinal and comparative studies (cf. boyd and Crawford

2012; Leetaru 2012)—it is also that the computer is able to both extract information "hidden" from plain view (such as links, file names, time stamps, etc.), as well as textual elements facilitating a larger-scale analysis of news topics, sources, links and interactive features embedded in online news items (e.g. Flaounas et al. 2013; Lewis, Zamith, and Hermida 2013; De Maeyer 2013; Sjøvaag and Stavelin 2012). Once algorithms are written for data extraction, the corpus can render quantitative data on all manifest values in the codebook design, provided missing data are accounted for. The advantage of big data analysis of online news is that there is essentially no need to randomize or stratify sampling procedures (cf. Neuendorf 2002) to reduce the size of the corpus to a manageable size. However, as Lewis, Zamith, and Hermida (2013) point out, while algorithms can help reduce large data-sets into thinner slices of data, computerized content analysis tools also deliver only surface-level analyses, and do so at the expense of nuanced context (see also boyd and Crawford 2012; Flaounas et al. 2013).

Liquid content analysis is not an established term but offered here as a collection name for several studies that have tried to map and approach digital media on its own terms using a mix of quantitative and qualitative lenses. The use of the nomenclature "liquid" here refers to the general ephemeral character of digital content (Schneider and Foot 2004; Weare and Lin 2000) and, in particular, to the concept of "Liquid Journalism" as proposed by Deuze (2008). Liquid journalism has, in theory, no clear boundaries between different contents, drafts of news items, media outlets or producers/consumers. In order to track, capture, illustrate and analyse this kind of liquid news, new methodological approaches have been developed. One thing that unites studies that have tried to capture the dimensions of liquid journalism is the will or necessity to track content, in a very broad sense, as it develops or recreating this development—in contrast to traditional content analysis working under the assumption that the content analyst can wait for the static content to be created (Krippendorff 2013). In essence, therefore, they can also be labelled micro longitudinal studies (Chadwick 2011; Kutz and Herring 2005). A range of studies have explored how content in news items changes (Karlsson 2006, 2012; Kutz and Herring 2005; Lim 2012; Saltzis 2012), or how front-page news items change over time (Karlsson 2006; Karlsson and Strömbäck 2010; Kautsky and Widholm 2008). Similarly, Steensen (2013) has developed and proposed a method to study journalist–user interaction on news sites also requiring evolving content (in a broad sense) to be tracked over time. However, this approach is so far hampered by heavy manual labour demands and, as yet, not capable of providing larger and representative samples.

Although these two new approaches are dissimilar both to each other and to central aspects of established content analysis techniques, they both relate to the changing time/space dynamics of digital media where big data approaches primarily try to explore the spatial dimension and liquid content analysis works more along the temporal dimension. However, all three approaches are united in their assumptions that manifest content is important and can be systematically measured according to certain protocols of sampling and data analysis. As such, the essential components of content analysis as an established method of scientific enquiry remain the bedrock of liquid and big data investigations. These new approaches are both quantitative and summarizing, and aim at generalizability. It is where they differ from the analogue content analysis design that they reveal the significant challenge that the digital poses to scientific enquiry. As big data and liquid content analyses are necessarily more inductive in their approach to the research object (as digital news is an ever-changing environment), they cannot necessarily apply *a priori* coding schemes (cf. Neuendorf 2002), predominantly look for measuring points rather than units of analysis and, to a large extent, defy replicability. Moreover, there is a dire shortage of agreed-upon protocols in the newer methods, which have to be innovated and developed to establish "high standards of conceptual clarity, systematicy of sampling, and data analysis" (Herring 2010, 13).

Demarcation, Unit of Analysis and Sampling

Traditional content analysis stresses the need to set up limits for the study—the size of the population and sample and the unit of analysis (words, sentences, news items or something else). Usually, content analysts limit themselves to study one or two randomized/constructed weeks of news stories/items. These rules of thumb do not necessarily apply in digital media although the *news content* may be very similar or even identical. An analysis aiming to capture the specifics of online news in comparison and contrast to linear news also needs categorization schemes that can capture the impact of new technological solutions on news content.

In the established content analysis approach, *sampling* involves selecting "a subset of units for study from the larger population" (Neuerdorf 2002, 83). With big data analysis, this process is not necessary to enable manageable data-sets that can be coded by a human. Rather, the computer may be the *key agent* doing the actual work. Moreover, linear television formats and printed newspaper texts represent a standardization of the limits that exist between elements that carry with them an implied understanding of their specific syntactic structure. Digital content analysis differs from this in fundamental ways. Web production entails nonlinearity, something that "obscures the boundaries and environment of messages and involves more complex semantics" (Weare and Lin 2000, 280). The challenge from this realization is one chiefly concerning the *unit of analysis*. Weare and Lin noted in 2000 how the size and chaotic structure of the internet "complicate efforts to select representative samples of messages for analysis" (273). While online news research entails augmentation in terms of the *scope of sample* that can be collected for analysis, amplifying the scope of extraction (as big data can deal with millions of items) can also entail complications. Because, say Weare and Lin, categorization schemes involve specific theories regarding the characteristics of messages from particular publication technologies, appropriate categorization schemes for online journalistic output requires a clear understanding of the syntax, semantics and logics of the media under investigation (284–286). This is in order to capture adequately the *measuring points* required for big data analysis, and in turn to facilitate analysis of an aggregation of these points.

When *sampling* content for analysis using big data methods, the data are not "merely there" to access—researchers have to make informed decisions about where to draw the line around a data-set. Using continuous extraction of new URLs published, for instance, requires a starting point (if not necessarily an end point), to set the boundary of the corpus. Because journalists are bound to update news texts published before a given start date—rendering these included in the sample—rules are necessary to decide valid time of publication. Is it when first published, or when last updated?

Because news items can be endlessly updated, the most sensible operationalization is the original publication time—a definition that requires "weeding out" stories with earlier publication from the sample.

While traditional content analysis has rather strict rules for *unit of analysis* and *sampling*, this is by necessity more complex in liquid content analysis. In traditional content analysis everything is ultimately about meaning (Krippendorff 2013), but this meaning is derived from content, in the form of raw data, which is assumed discriminate and static (Berelson 1971; Krippendorff 2013; Riffe, Lacy, and Fico 1998). As we have argued above, not even raw data can be pinned down online. Hence, the meaning has to be derived from moving targets (McMillan 2001). Additionally, how these thousands, if not millions, of targets move or might move (position on the front page/website and relation to each other), change (versionality) and are contextualized (comments, hyperlinks) also affect the meaning that can be derived from their study. Consequently, there cannot, in principle, be a preferred *unit of analysis* beforehand, as the analyst would not know what limitations would be meaningful. From this follows that liquid content analysis needs several *measuring points* and a greater qualitative *mode of analysis* than the other two forms. This will help the analyst carve out a *narrative*, or a thematic meaning as Herring (2010) puts it, as the news story unfolds—drawing from both content and context. This in turn suggests that *sampling* has to be, at least to a certain extent, purposive (to weed out narratively irrelevant information) and inductive (since it is impossible to know beforehand exactly what is going to happen). While this narrative-guided procedure might seem very different from the established content analysis approach, it still draws from the "logical associations" (Krippendorff 2013, 57) that must guide any selection process. However, the selection process is, due to the spatial and temporal challenges of digital media, very different. This is an area where liquid content analysis could be said to have an advantage over big data analysis, as the issue of "meaning" is a problematic matter in the latter (Mahrt and Scharkow 2013), while its disadvantage is that it cannot cover as many news stories.

Finally, this procedure, entailing a great deal of manual labour throughout the process as opposed to the other approaches, also implies that the *scope of analysis* or *material/sampling size* will be low due to the resources inevitably consumed, unless options emerge that can replace or complement human with machine thinking.

In a sense this method encourages and makes it possible to "follow the white rabbit" and see what happens with a news story over time. Here, the dependency of the human mind represents a strength as it is better at understanding information in the deep compared to more mechanical approaches (Lewis, Zamith, and Hermida 2013). Although perhaps counter-intuitive to the ways of traditional content analysis, this is merely another way of "making" the data that content analysis has always done (Krippendorff 2013). However, the circumstances in which these data are made have changed due to the characteristics of digital media. With this approach, it might be necessary with *more* rather than *less* human intervention as content moves online (boyd and Crawford 2012). Here, the *key agent* will be the human, but heavily aided by the use of computers to capture data and document the process.

Variable Design

According to Neuendorf (2002, 98), identifying the critical features of the medium used to design variables for traditional content analysis "is both painstaking and creative". This implies using a mixture of theory and past research in combination with an "emergent" approach to identify universal and medium-specific variables. Because the object of online news analysis keeps changing, big data analysis needs to assume an *inductive approach*. When designing content analyses to study journalism on the internet quantitatively, coding schemes used for analogue news are not necessarily directly transferable to the world of online news (cf. Kautsky and Widholm 2008; Keith, Schwalbe, and Silcock 2010; McMillan 2001; Quandt 2008; Sjøvaag and Stavelin 2012; Weare and Lin 2000, 282). Big data methods necessarily need a *deductive vantage point*, but it is also important to pay detailed attention to the particularly inductive angle needed when approaching online formats.

For the analogue-based content analysis, *variables* must be not too large, nor too small, in order to capture content in a way that can render a productive analysis (Weber 1990). Big data analysis, while allowing for great detail in the coding, faces the same problem. Certain values that can easily be extracted are not necessarily appropriate to the analysis—paragraph counts, for instance, or stable features of the template design—while some elements that required manual coding in the past can now easily be computer coded—bylines, for instance. Hence, computer-coding schemes should be designed with reducing the human labour as much as possible in mind.

Whereas news priorities in print and broadcasting follow a standardized format—usually in a sinking order of importance in televised broadcasts, and in a sectioned order in print—online news production is not organized in the same way. Online news production caters to a different user situation, addresses a different advertising market and faces different competitive situations than linear media. Content found towards the back of newspapers—such as sports, travel and consumer features—are usually placed further up the hierarchy in online news. The online platform also tends to label news more explicitly, in order to facilitate easy browsing (Hågvar 2012). News broadcasts and printed newspapers tend to speak to broad audience groups at a particular moment in time—either at deadline, or at the scheduled broadcasting slot, presenting a highly edited version of today's (or yesterday's) most important events, whereas online news publishing is continuous. Online news also carries more elements of news aggregation and assemblage. Time/space issues ensure greater disparity, greater disruption and less treatment of journalistic content online. This is why immediacy and disruptions are such staple features of online news. Hence, when designing variables for online news analysis, the *scope of values* available needs to account for this growing disparity between linear and online news publishing.

Concerning liquid content analysis, the issue of variables is, at best, points of departure that should be constantly reconsidered rather than a grid that can be superimposed. As everything in or around a news item can change—sources, framing, authors, etc.—this needs to be acknowledged, particularly whether the first, last or archived version is used. Different versions of the same news item can be treated as the same item, as different items and/or as linked items. Diverging weight can be given to the distinct versions of a news item depending on time of exposure, placement on the page, publication hour (due to the day-parting tendencies) and most read/shared listings. Another dimension that needs to be accounted for is whether the news item is published onsite or embedded third-party material, for instance from YouTube—i.e. the news site as an assemblage of many and qualitatively different sources. In any case, the online environment provides new and yet-to-be-solved problems.

So far much of the research in this area has focused on demonstrating how elusive the Web is rather than providing research tools or protocols that can be used on the Web. However, emerging research displays movement towards a systematic approach in liquid content analysis that could be built on. Regular capture intervals, consideration of the placement of news items and considerable downtime during the night (Karlsson and Strömbäck 2010; Saltzis 2012; Widholm 2015) seem to be staple parts of the approach—and a path towards establishing protocols. Saltzis' (2012) research demonstrates that news stories in general do not change much after the first initial hours of publication. This means that it is possible to establish cut-off points for when news stories no longer have to be monitored with varying degrees of certainty. Hyperlink analysis, counting comments and monitoring social media sharing might similarly give an idea about the salience of the news story. Common practices are indeed emerging, both in liquid content analysis and in big data approaches. While these allow for a certain degree of comparison, it is important to stress that protocols for big data and liquid content analysis need to assume as baseline the inductivity of doing research on digital news media. Methodological flowcharts therefore require validity checks more in the planning and execution of data collection, in how data are stored and are sorted than in the deductively based procedures and rules of variable design in the analogue-catered content analysis.

Access, Collection and Storage

Proponents of traditional content analysis demand that researchers create "durable and analyzable records of otherwise transient phenomena" (Krippendorff 2013, 85), allowing the researcher, once this archive is created, to compare content across time and replicate analysis. It is also assumed that "Written text is always recorded" and "is re-readable" (Krippendorff 2013, 85), that content "has a life beyond its production and consumption" (Riffe, Lacy, and Fico 1998, 31) and that "recorded information is a must" (Krippendorff 2013, 268). Thus, it is crucial for the researcher to have access to, and be able to collect and store the raw data in order for a proper content analysis to be possible.

Using *big data* methods for content analysis of online news implies first of all that the material is *accessed digitally*. Analogue media are procured and stored as physical objects, either in archives, through libraries, as printed newspapers, or as tapes, discs or files containing audio/visual content. Whereas analogue media formats today can be accessed as digital renderings in digital archives, the content is still in static form. Web-based journalism is more akin to a flowing river that Web scrapers or algorithms can step into at a fixed point in time. Big data analysis can access and store data online, on a computer or server, meaning the material is available for processing any time or place, by more than one researcher at once. With computational methods, tools are available that can sort through this vast and essentially messy material in systematic ways. But whereas systematic approaches to analyse digital media have primarily been developed for social media content (e.g. Bruns and Burgess 2012), few common guidelines have been established for digital news analysis.

Another aspect is the potential increase and velocity in the *volume of data* accessible online (cf. Kahn et al. 2014). Depending on how big the data are, server space could imply a cost issue. On the other hand, as the material for digital news analysis is also available in its original form online, storage is only necessary when objects need to be "frozen" to allow for analysis at a certain point of extraction. Digital boundaries, however, complicate matters when data access is reliant on user identification. Digital subscription solutions, paywalls and micropayment models introduce further issues of cost and access to online news analysis. As such, it is often the case that real data, such as the full output of the Twitter-verse, costs money (cf. Driscoll and Walker 2014). Also, even though these data can be bought, these services are often provided by commercial companies that do not disclose their methodological procedures in collecting and processing data—essentially rendering this part of the process a black box. Using data without knowing what it represents is very problematic and definitely a no-no (boyd and Crawford 2012; Mahrt and Scharkow 2013). In many cases this may be the best available option, reflecting the dilemma of doing it the right (established) way or not at all. This problem illuminates just how resource-demanding big data analysis can be. For methodological veracity, researchers should ideally command both the access, collection and storage of digital news data. As tailoring code, acquiring access and purchasing storage for each project is costly and time-demanding, it is imperative that researchers share their computational solutions with other researchers. Moving towards protocols for big data analysis therefore requires greater attention to the labour of preparing and running digital data collection and analysis. The original contribution aspect of this part of content analysis research is something that should inspire scholars to publish more widely on the process of inductive method design rather than merely disseminating results from the analysis.

Because *liquid content analysis* collects data as the analysis is under way, this implies that data can be reliably recorded through various means—pdfs, screenshots, notes and different software—utilizing both human and computer as *key agent*. As with big data, this material can be stored locally or globally in databases accessible to other researchers. As this method is inductive, and agreed-upon protocols and procedures are so far lacking, documenting used approaches and best practice becomes imperative, both for transparency, reliability and method development. Although it is possible to document and archive the process of on-going online news, to "freeze the flow of online news" (Karlsson and Strömbäck 2010), one may question if this is the right approach after all. The Web is constantly moving. Any attempt to capture and store it would be against its nature and, as time shifts, any sample will be increasingly unrepresentative of how the Web looks and looked. A river cannot be stored in a fair manner. Therefore, liquid content analysts will probably have to use themselves as a tool—in a manner that has more in common with qualitative approaches than with traditional content analysis.

The Depth/Generalizability Trade-off

Traditional content analysis uses theory to interpret an aggregate of words, texts or signs into more abstract categories. As "quantitative data do not speak for themselves" (Weber 1990, 80), research results must be translated into the appropriate theoretical language. Generalizing from a few thousand manually coded news items is seen as problematic if not adequately representative of the population in general (Neuendorf 2002, 89). For traditional content analysis, manageability is key to completing projects in a timely fashion. Big data approaches to news content do not suffer from the same limitations, but there is a trade-off. When the data consist of millions of items, there is real danger that analytically valuable information gets lost in the sheer noise of volume. If two weeks is sufficiently representative to conclude about a news organization's annual output in traditional content analysis (89), the question becomes what do we actually gain from collecting the entire annual output digitally. The fact is that having big data, and using big data methodologies, can also disclose patterns, consistencies, habits and organizational factors of news production that would otherwise be lost with traditional sampling procedures.

The populations from which samples are drawn for big data analysis can be different in a number of respects, which makes *comparisons* troublesome. Comparing different online news ventures may encounter problems of inferring analysis from theoretically formed questions measuring news produced within different socio-political, professional, market and even technological contexts. Comparing online and offline versions of news comes with its own challenges, particularly in terms of defining the units of analysis, and especially when comparing between manual and computational coding, with different agents doing the coding. It even creates problems in defining the borders of the units of analysis, relevant also to the aspect of links—serving as context, background or additional information for the reader to explore—raising the question of where the story really ends. This point extends to social media sharing of journalistic content, which creates an additional challenge to the question of textual boundaries. When Web media "outsource" discussion of editorial content in this way—especially to large commercial and international operators such as Facebook and Twitter, the question no longer pertains just to boundaries; it also becomes one of editorial reach. Whereas newsrooms are legally responsible for the content published on their own domains, social media sites fall under a different jurisdiction.

In addition to the problems shared by liquid content analysis and big data, generalizations are difficult as the trade-off is to sacrifice depth and meaning in few news stories. As opposed to other modes of content analysis, it is virtually impossible to *draw generalizable conclusions* with liquid content analysis. On the other hand, the method is fairer to the nature of digital media and the content published here as it plays by its spatial and temporal rules.

Discussion

The problems of transferring the established content analysis to the digital news environment outlined in this article may be overstated as they relate to the practice of news enterprises that have not changed as much as digital media allows, but there are nevertheless interesting and important principle matters at stake. The two emerging approaches we have detailed bring something new and different to the table. They are currently, paraphrasing Karpf (2012, 642), "messy but productive" solutions, while established content analysis is well thought out but does not cover new scenarios.

When contrasting big data methods with the traditional content analysis, their space/time discrepancies imply that new doors are opened. Big data drastically expand the potential scope of analysis, but this also requires greater analytical efforts. Sampling *units of one* for quantitative coding to enable an aggregate understanding of news production online means that the deep understanding of the medium in question attained from analogue-tailored content analysis is, to some extent, offset by the *shallowness* of big data analysis. Human coding is arduous, yes, but the detailed attention required to attain veracity in the analysis of a few thousand news items also means that human agents are able to move closer to the material. Machine learning that can tailor programmed coding based on manual coding may offer future solutions to this problem. As yet, however, few efforts at automated content analysis are able to attain accuracies beyond the statistically random (e.g. Mahrt and Scharkow 2013). The rewards of the arduous manual nature of analogue content coding lie in the deep knowledge and understanding that can be achieved when researchers engage with the units of analysis on a one-to-one basis. Big data analysis means we lose this kind of intimacy with the object at hand. Looking at millions of data points can also obscure potential objects for analysis. Even as digital news content is conceptualized as the sum of its parts, it still consists of many parts—each an individual measuring point. Hence the critical question to be asked of big data analysis is what we gain from having millions of units, and what we lose with this type of analytical scope.

When accessing news content as digitally encoded material, we must realize that what we are studying is not news items as they appear on the screen. Digital news objects cannot be studied in the form that they appear, but must be broken down to enable quantification—to again be aggregated to allow for analysis. The Web is a dynamic form of content production, and "freezing" this form for analysis also entails a reduction of the Web-publishing format. Hence, big data analysis of online news is not exactly an analysis of *the medium* in which news appears. Part of the reason why this gap appears is that big data news analyses are designed based on a methodology adjusted to the analogue news format. Here, liquid content analysis offers a way out, or at least a supplementary approach, as it allows for tracking the life cycle of a news item from its birth on the front page, how its content changes, how it is intertwined with other current and past news—and user engagement—how it loses pace and inevitably sinks lower on the front page to rest eventually in the sediments of the archive, here it can form context for a new item or be reanimated if stumbled upon and found timely and relevant by journalists or an influential (group of) user(s). The limit of this approach is evident as it, currently, consumes a lot of resources and only allows for tracking a few news stories.

All methods will have their benefits and deficiencies, obviously dependent on the research questions asked, but what we hope is evident is that there cannot be one approach to quantitative analysis of online content. Naturally, the established content analysis method—honing its tools for at least 60 years—is more developed, but falls short of capturing all dimensions of online content. Our aim here has been to illuminate some of the challenges we have to be aware of when conducting content analysis of digital journalism based on analogue methodological training and practice. When pointing out the difference between traditional content analysis and emerging digital methods, our intent is not to provide recommendations for new methodological procedures, but to illustrate the points at which methodological veracity has to be re-examined when digital methods are used and the epistemologies underlying the different approaches. We would encourage other researchers to put effort into developing similar tools, keep protocols and publish procedures to further new approaches, especially concerning new online forms of collaboration and evidence/storing as the new methods are resource intensive. At this point, improving and standardizing the procedural aspects of digital content analysis entails original contributions to the field that deserve the attention of the scholarly community. This would not only further discussions about how best to approach content online but also help scholars to conduct research on content that is increasingly becoming the main news diet for the citizens of the world.

DISCLOSURE STATEMENT

No potential conflict of interest was reported by the authors.

REFERENCES

Berelson, Bernard. 1971. *Content Analysis in Communication Research*. New York: Glencoe.

boyd, danah, and Kate Crawford. 2012. "Critical Questions for Big Data." *Information, Communication & Society* 15 (5): 662–679.

Brügger, Nils. 2009. "Website History and the Website as an Object of Study." *New Media & Society* 11 (1–2): 115–132.

Bruns, Axel, and Jean Burgess. 2012. "Researching News Discussion on Twitter: New Methodologies." *Journalism Studies* 13 (5-6): 801–814.

Chadwick, Andrew. 2011. "The Political Information Cycle in a Hybrid News System: The British Prime Minister and the 'Bullygate' Affair." *International Journal of Press/Politics* 16 (1): 3–29.

De Maeyer, Juliette. 2013. "Towards a Hyperlinked Society: A Critical Review of Link Studies" *New Media & Society* 15 (5): 737–751.

Deuze, Mark. 2008. "The Changing Context of News Work: Liquid Journalism and Monitorial Citizenship." *International Journal of Communication* 2: 848–865.

Driscoll, Kevin, and Shawn Walker. 2014. "Working Wihtin a Black Box: Transparency in the Collection and Production of Big Twitter Data." *International Journal of Communication* 8: 1–20.

Flaounas, Ilias, Olar Ali, Thomas Lansdall-Welfare, Tijl De Bie, Nick Mosdell, Justin Lewis, and Nello Cristianini. 2013. "Research Methods in the Age of Digital Journalism". *Digital Journalism* 1(1): 102–116.

Groshek, Jacob. 2008. "Homogenous Agendas, Disparate Frames: CNN and CNN International Coverage Online." *Journal of Broadcasting & Electronic Media* 52 (1): 52–68.

Hågvar, Yngve Benestad. 2012. "Labeling Journalism: The Discourse of Sectional Paratexts in Print and Online Newspapers" *Nordicom Review* 33 (2): 27–42.

Herring, Susan. 2010. "Web Content Analysis: Expanding the Paradigm." In *International handbook of Internet research*, edited by J. Hunsinger, L. Klastrup and M. Allen, 233–249. Dordrecht: Springer.

Innis, Harold. 1999. *The Bias of Communication*. Toronto: University of Toronto Press.

Kahn, Nawsher; Ibrar Yaqoob, Ibrahi abaker Targio Hashem, Zakira Inayat, Waleed Kamaleldin Mahmoud Ali, Muhammed Alam, Muhammed Shirazand Adhullah Gani. 2014. "Big Data: Survey, Technologies, Opportunities, and Challenges". *The Scientific World Journal* Vol. 2014: 1–14.

Karlsson, Michael. 2006. *Nätjournalistik. En explorativ fallstudie av digitala mediers karaktärsdrag på fyra svenska nyhetssajter* [Online Journalism. An Explorative Case Study of Digital Characteristics on Four Swedish News Sites]. Lund: Lund studies in media and communication.

Karlsson, Michael. 2012. "Charting the Liquidity of Online News: Moving towards a Method for Content Analysis of Online News." *International Communication Gazette* 74 (4): 385–402. doi:10.1177/1748048512439823.

Karlsson, Michael, and Jesper Strömbäck. 2010. "Freezing the Flow of Online News: Exploring Approaches to the Study of the Liquidity of Online News." *Journalism Studies* 11 (1): 2–19.

Karpf, David. 2012. "Social Science Research." *Information, Communication & Society* 15 (5): 639–661.

Kautsky, Robert, and Andreas Widholm. 2008. "Online Methodology: Analyzing News Flows of Online Journalism." *Westminster Papers in Communication and Culture* 5 (2): 81–97.

Keith, Susan, Carol B. Schwalbe, and B. William Silcock. 2010. "Comparing War Images across Media Platforms: Methodological Challenges for Content Analysis." *Media, War & Conflict* 3 (1): 87–98.

Krippendorff, Klaus. 2013. *Content Analysis. an Introduction to Its Methodology* (3rd ed.) Los Angeles, CA: Sage.

Kutz, Daniel O and Susan C. Herring. 2005. "Micro-longitudinal Analysis of Web News Updates". In Proceedings of the 38th Hawaii International Conference on System Sciences Vol. 00: 1–10.

Leetaru, Kalev. 2012. *Data Mining Methods for the Content Analyst: An Introduction to the Computational Analysis of Content*. New York: Routledge.

Lewis, Seth C., Rodrigo Zamith, and Alfred Hermida. 2013. "Content Analysis in an Era of Big Data: A Hybrid Approach to Computational and Manual Methods." *Journal of Broadcasting and Electronic Media* 57 (1): 34–52.

Lim, Jeongsub. 2012. "The Mythological Status of the Immediacy of the Most Important Online News. an Analysis of Top News Flows in Diverse Online Media." *Journalism Studies* 13 (1): 71–89.

Mahrt, Merja, and Michael Scharkow. 2013. "The Value of Big Data in Digital Media Research." *Journal of Broadcasting & Electronic Media* 57 (1): 20–33.

McMillan, Sally. 2001. "The Microscope and the Moving Target: The Challenge of Applying Content Analysis to the World Wide Web." *Journalism and Mass Communication Quarterly* 77 (1): 80–98.

Neuendorf, Kimberly A. 2002. *The Content Analysis Guidebook*. Thousand Oaks: Sage.

Pariser, Eli. 2009. *The Filter Bubble*. What the Internet is Hiding from You. London: Penguin.

Quandt, Thorsten. 2008. "(No) News on the World Wide Web? A Comparative Content Analysis of Online News in Europe and the United States." *Journalism Studies* 9 (5): 717–738.

Riffe, Daniel, Stephen Lacy, and Frederick G. Fico. 1998. *Analyzing Media Messages Using Quantitative Content Analysis in Research*. Mahwah: Lawrence Erlbaum Associates.

Riffe, Daniel, Stephen Lacy, and Frederick G. Fico. 2014. *Analyzing Media Messages. Using Quantitative Content Analysis in Research*. 3rd ed. New York: Routledge.

Ryfe, David. 2012. *Can Journalism Survive? An inside Look at American Newsrooms*. Cambridge: Polity.

Saltzis, Kostas. 2012. "Breaking News Online." *Journalism Practice* 6 (5-6): 702–710. doi:10.1080/17512786.2012.667274.

Schneider, Steven M., and Kristen A. Foot. 2004. "The Web as an Object of Study." *New Media & Society* 6 (1): 114–122. doi:10.1177/1461444804039912.

Sjøvaag, Helle, and Eirik Stavelin. 2012. "Web Media and the Quantitative Content Analysis: Methodological Challenges in Measuring Online News Content." *Convergence* 18 (2): 215–229.

Stavelin, Eirik. 2013. *Computational Journalism: When Journalism Meets Programming*. Dissertation for the degree philosophiae doctor (PhD). Department of Information Science and Media Studies, University of Bergen.

Steensen, Steen. 2013. "Conversing the Audience: A Methodological Exploration of How Conversation Analysis Can Contribute to the Analysis of Interactive Journalism." *New Media & Society* 16 (8): 1197–1213. doi:10.1177/1461444813504263.

Tewksbury, David, and Jason Rittenberg. 2012. *News on the Internet. Information and Citizenship in the 21st Century*. Oxford: Oxford University Press.10.1093/acprof:osobl/9780195391961.001.0001

Weare, Christopher, and Wan-Ying Lin. 2000. "Content Analysis of the World Wide Web: Opportunities and Challenges." *Social Science Computer Review* 18 (3): 272–292.

Weber, Robert Philip. 1990. *Basic Content Analysis*. 2nd ed. Newbury Park: Sage University Paper.

Widholm, Andreas. 2015. "Tracing Online News in Motion: Time and Duration in the Study of Liquid Journalism". *Digital Journalism*, doi:10.1080/21670811.2015.1096611.

Index

Note: **Bold face** page numbers refer to figures and tables. Page numbers followed with "n" refer to endnotes.

a priori coding schemes 183
access to content 186–7; *see also* content analysis
access to people's media use 5; *see also* audience research
account logins 118
action research 160–1; from an academic point of view 169–71; challenges 171–3; complexity of 172; conceptualization based on research findings 166–7; deeper and holistic understanding of 170; developmental research process 162; for digital journalism studies and practice 163–5; implementation 167–8; intention of inducing change 162; issue of going native 173; journalists' attitudes of 161, 166–7, 169; literature 170; participatory and inclusive research 162; from practitioners' point of view 168–9; quality dimensions 172–3; as a research culture 161–3, 171; research process 165–6; stakeholders of 171–2; systematic, collaborative improvement 169; in terms of best practices 168
active audience 126–7
Agarwal, Amit 111
Aitamurto, Tanja 172
algorithms 46; bisecting k-means 84; clustering 84; Linguistic Inquiry and Word Count (LIWC) 12, 18n2; search *see* search algorithm; SentiStrength 12
alpha hyper-parameter 95, 104n2
Amazon Mechanical Turk 12
AmCAT 95–6
analogue-based content analysis 185
Anderson, Gary L. 173
Appelgren, Ester 172
Application Programming Interfaces (API) 108, 111
archived website 29

ASAP (as soon as possible) culture of online journalism 27
Ashley, Seth 132
audience activity, interpretations of 127–8; active 126–7; passive 126; productive activity 127–8; in relation to news content and device **130**; selective activity 127
audience research 142–3; audience data 142–3; explanatory factors and response distribution 152–4, **153**; implications for journalism 143–4; media habits and media attitudes **150–1**, 154–5; methodology and data 146–8; mode effects 143–4; mode of 143–5; non-response rate 144, 149, 152, 154–5; results 148–54, **150–1**, **153**; theoretical views and research questions 144–6
automated content analysis (ACA)/text analysis 8–9; benefits of 8–9; of boilerplate content 78; classification of **10**; co-occurrence analyses 80; corpus comparison 80; deductive and inductive approaches 10–11, 76; dictionary-based techniques 12; identifying and overcoming obstacles 16–17; implicit framing analysis 10; of keywords in context 80; need for 75–7; of normalized text 78; overview of **76**; of pre-defined categories 80–3; preparation of data 77–9; recommendations and discussion 85–6; sentiment analysis 11–12, 77; stemming 79; of stopwords 79; supervised machine learning 13–14, 77; text statistics 79–80; understanding of datasets 79–80; unsupervised methods 14–16; visibility analysis 10–11; of visualizations 80; when categories are unknown 83–5
Automated Data Collection Terms (ADCT) 59
auto-mated semantic network analysis 16

bag-of-words representation of text 11
Barnhurst, Kevin 52
Baumgartner, Felix 113, 115, **116**, 117
Bayes classifiers 13

INDEX

Bayesian nonparametric topic model 85
Bergold, Jarg 172
big data 56, 177, 181–2, 186, 189
bisecting k-means algorithm 84
Blei, David 85
Blei, David M. 85
boilerplate content 78
Bradbury-Huang, Hilary 173
breaking news 27, 32, 36
British news sites, study of 28–9
Brügger, Niels 29, 112
Burscher, Björn 13, 15, 83

Carpentier, Nico 126, 128
Chronicle 50
citation 42, 50–1
Claes H., de Vreese 83
classifier, assessment of a 14
click behaviour 112, 118, 121
cluster analysis 15
CNN effect 27
code literacy 17
collocations 80
commercial links 42, 51
communication channels, contemporary 9
computational journalism 9
computational methods in journalism research 2, 55; analysing data from the warehouse 64–5; automated methods 3–4; automatic *vs* manual data gathering 60; collecting and analysing digital journalism data 2–3; content-centric data of the links 68; escalated activity of likes, shares and comments 68–70, **69–70**; event-centric data of the links 68; examination of news flows 68–70; exploratory automated method 2–3; Facebook data collection 57–9; guiding principles for methodological innovation 4; hybrid nature of 3; issue-attention cycle perspective 65–8, **67**; necessity of clarifying data and creating a data warehouse 62–3, **63**; post-related shares, likes, comments and comment likes 65–9, **66–7**; push-stream and pull-stream views on data retrieve 61–2; searching and retrieving data from public interfaces 61; semi-automated methods 3; *see also* Facebook
computer-assisted reporting 9
contemporary journalism 1
content analysis 5, 177–8; access, collection and storage 186–7; analogue-based 177–82, 185; assumptions of 178; big data analysis 181–2; demarcation, unit of analysis and sampling 183–4; depth/generalizability trade-off 188; different approaches to **179**; discussion 188–90; limits of 178–80; liquid 182–3, 185–7, 189; logic of 178; qualitative and the quantitative 178; space, time and digital content 180–3; static approach 32; variables for 185–6
content-analytical tools, traditional 9
content-centric data 64
Couldry, Nick 126, 128, 130
counting method 11
Craft, Stephanie 132
cross-sectional model 112–13
Crowdynews 52
Cushion, Stephen 27
custom-made tools 17

Danish Web archive 113, 121n5
dark data 59
data journalism 9, 56
data warehousing 62–3, **63**, 71; Bill Inmon's 3NF model (Third Normal Form) 63; push-stream-based event data-centric model 63, **64**; Ralph Kimball's star schema 62–3
De Graaf, Rutger 15
deductive techniques 9–11, 13, 15, 76–7
depth/generalizability trade-off of content 188
Deuze, Mark 26, 182
developmental research process 162
dictionary-based techniques 12, 82; limitations 16
digital data collection 180–1, 187
Digital Footprints 58
Digital Journalism Studies 163–5
digital journalistic content, availability and volume of 8
directly observable variables 19n3
document clustering 77, 83–4, 86
document similarity, assessment of 11, 15–16
domain of a link 47
Domingo, David 27
Dougall, Elizabeth 31
Douglas, S. J. 133
Downs, Anthony 57
dynamic topic models 85

editorial setting, digital challenges in 5
ensemble learning approach 83
e-questionnaires 145
event-centric data 65
event-driven news 27, 34
ex post digital data collection 180–1
Excel software 11

Facebook 3, 42, 44, 46, 50, 52, 56, 58, 71, 80, 120; application programming interfaces (API) 57–60, 62; computational approach to retrieve data 57–8; data gathering on 58–9; data-centric research approaches for studying 59–65; event data-centric star schema of tables and their connections **64**; key concepts **64**; main concepts and their explanations **60**; news flows and exposure to news in 56–7; Platform Policy (FPP) 59;

INDEX

"Principles" and "Statement of Rights and Responsibilities (SRR)" 58; push-stream and pull-stream views on data retrieve 61–2; Query Language (FQL) 61; searching and retrieving data from public interfaces 61; titles and functions of data warehouse tables **63**
Facepager 58
factor analysis 91, 93, 95, 103n1
feature selection 93
Flaounas, Ilias 83
focused interview 1
fragment portions 47–8

Gamson, William A. 95–6, 99
Gans, Herbert J. 26
garbage in, garbage out 76
George, Karypis 84
Gillespie, Tarleton 52
goodness-of-fit measure 104n3
Google Search 4, 107, **111**; business model of 111; case of Red Bull Stratos *see* Red Bull Stratos, working of algorithm; Scraper 111
Google Trends 111, 114–15
granularity 100, **101**
Grimmer, Justin 9, 12, 14, 84, 89

Haddon, Leslie 132
Hall, Stuart 127
Helsingin Sanomat 68
Hermida, Alfred 182
Herr, Kathryn G. 173
Herring, Susan C. 25
Hester, Joe Bob 31
hidden topic Markov models 85
Hillard, Dustin 83
HTML language 42
Human Dimensions of Wildlife 12
Humphreys, Lee 132
hyperlink/hyperlinking 41–2, 81, 186

"idea transition" rules 12
implicit framing analysis 10
inductive techniques 9–11, 15–16, 76, 102, 167, 182–5
Innovation Ateliers 167–8
innovativeness in journalism practice 163
internet and social media 56
issue-attention cycle of online news 56–7, 65–8, **67**, 71; stages of 57

Java Programming Language 82
journalism: arrival of the internet and 27; in digital online era 26; professional ideology 24; research 1
journalism toolkit (Jot) 2, 47
journalistic production practices 24
JPGs 29–30

Kammer, Aske 29
Karlsson, Michael 26, 28
Karnowski, Veronika 132
Karpf, David 189
keywords in context, study of 80
Kilgarriff, Adam 80
King, Gary 84
Kumar, Vipin 84

labelling of news stories 35
Lafferty, John 85
Latent Dirichlet Allocation (LDA) 4, 77, 85, 89–90, **91**, 92, **94**; best practices 101–3, **102**; issue "nuclear power" in the news, illustration of 96–100; perplexity of **94**, 94–5; setting up 92–3; tool support for 95–6
laurendo.wordpress.com 42
learning classifier 82–3
lemmatization 92–3
Lewis, Justin 27
Lewis, Seth C. 182
Leydesdorff, Loet 15
lifespan of a news article 32–3
lifetime of a link 48
Lim, Jeongsub 27
linear news models 24
Linguistic Inquiry and Word Count (LIWC) algorithm 12, 18n2
liquid content analysis 182–3, 185–7, 189
liquid journalism 25–6, 182; *see also* online news
liquid modernity 26
liquid news 24, 26; defined 26; from a methodological perspective 28–9; study of 26; as a theoretical concept 26
live news reporting 27
Livingstone, Sonia 127–30
log likelihood 11
longitudinal model 113
Loughran, Tim 82
Lucas, Christopher 90

Maksl, Adam 132
MALLET software 95
Markham, Tim 130
Matthews, Dylan 50–1
McDonald, Bill 82
McMillan, Sally J. 28
measurement of online news 31–5; event-driven news 33–4; lifespan of entities 32–3; publication time and content variations 34–5, **35**; in terms of allocated airtime 32–4, **33**; in terms of static entities 32; in terms of subject entities 32–4, **33**, 37
media audience, financial implications of 142–3
media user 128–9
mercurynews.com 42
meta-medium 130

INDEX

Michael, Steinbach 84
Michael I., Jordan 85
micro-archiving 112
mobile news 131, 147, **150**, 152, **153**
mode effects 143–7, 152, 154–6
Modigliani, Andre 95–6, 99
Mohammed, Saif M. 12
Moores, Shaun 136
Morley, David 136
MOTUS project (Modular Time Use Survey) 135, 137, 138n1

named entity recognition 10, 16
native advertising 48
navigation link 42, 48–9, 51
Nerone, John 52
Netvizz 58
Neue Zürcher Zeitung 161, 165
Neuendorf (2002, 98) 185
New York Times 48–9, 83, 92
news audience 125–6; active audience 126–7; interpretations of audience activity 127–8; *see also* media user
news geography 34–5
news links, study of: analysis of general categories 42; automating link analysis 46–9; basic purposes of links 46, 49–51; in context of content 43; domain of a link 47; fragment portions 47–8; issues related to navigation and social links 51–2; lifetime of a link 48; linking practices 51; maximizing the value of the link 51; methodology 41; path of a link 47; query string 47–8; strategy for discerning categories of meaning 43–4; structure and content of a link 48; in terms of algorithms 46; 5-Ws taxonomy of news link 42–9, **45**
news use, conceptualizing 129–33; guiding principles for methodological innovation 133–4; news literacy and domestication 131–2; news production and creation 132–3; news repertoires 130–1; openness and representativeness 137; time use research in 135–7
Ng, Andrew Y. 85
Niblock, Sarah 164
NodeXL 58
normalization of text 78
Nygren, Gunnar 172

online immediacy 27, 29, 127; connection between publication routines and 35–7, **36**
online journalists and their audiences, research on 5
online news 42–3, 185; "ASAP" (as soon as possible) culture of 27; breaking news 27, 32; British news sites, study of 28–9; content analysis of 28; event-driven news 27; issue-attention cycles of 56–7; live news reporting 27; measuring 31–5; Oslo terrorist attacks, real-time coverage of 29; publication cycle of 27; real-time reporting and construction of immediacy 35–7, **36**; Swedish online news, explorative study of 28; *vs* offline versions of news 29; measurement of online news; *see also* content analysis
Opgenhaffen, Michael 130
Opinion Crawler 58
Oslo terrorist attacks, real-time coverage of 29

Papacharissi, Zizi 133
paper-based questionnaires 145
participatory and inclusive research 162
part-of-speech tagging 16
passive mass-media audience 126
path of a link 47
Pavlik, John V. 163
people-centric data 64–5
Political Analysis 17
political communication research, machine learning approach in 14
pre-defined categories, analysis of 80–3; dictionary-based techniques 82; rule-based approach 81–2; supervised machine learning 82–3
predictability of deadlines 26
pre-processing of text 10
principal component analysis 15
printed *vs* online tabloids, non-response rate for 149, **150–1**
prosumers 70
public data 59
Pulitzer, Joseph 24
pull-stream data 61–2
Purpura, Stephen 83
push-stream data 61–2
Python Programming Language 17, 82, 86

Quandt, Thorsten 27
query string 47–8
questionnaires 145
Quinn, Kevin M. 84, 90

R Programming Language 17, 86
Reason and Bradbury (2001a, 2) 162
Red Bull Stratos, working of algorithm 113–19; endogenous factors 114–18; exogenous factors 120; experimentation and randomisation 120; keywords 114–15; language settings and IP address 115–18, **116–17**; Web history, click behaviour, account logins 118
Regular-Interval Content Capturing method (RICC) 2, 25, 34; content analysis 31; data collection and variables 29–31, **30**
Rens, Vliegenthart 83

INDEX

repertoires 130–1
retrieving data: from public interfaces 61; push-stream and pull-stream views on 61–2
Reuters Institute Digital News Report 129
rewards, for journalism studies and communication research 1
Roberts, Margaret E. 85
Rogers, Richard 118
rolling news 27
Rosen, Jay 126
Rosen-Zvi, Michal 85
Ruby program language 29
rule-based approaches 76–7, 81–2

Saltzis, Kostas 28, 186
sampling content for analysis 183–4
Scharkow, Michael 13, 83
screen dumping 29, 112, 114
search algorithm 108; factors in 109–10; Red Bull Stratos, case of 113–19; relationship between endogenous factors and exogenous factors 110; retrieving and archiving rankings for 111–13; way forward 119–20
search engines 81, 107–9, 120–1
search results, models for: cross-sectional model 112–13; longitudinal model 113; short burst model 113
Semenov, Alexander 58
semi-public data 59, 71
sentiment analysis 11–12, 77, 82; aim of 11; application of 11–12; level of sophistication of 12; of political communications 12
SentiStrength algorithm 12
sfgate.com 42, 47, 49, **50**
Shanoff, Dan 137
short burst model 113
Silverstone, Roger 132
Sjøvaag, Helle 81
Social and Cultural Planning Bureau (SCP) 135
social links 42, 50–2
social media data analysis 58
social network sites (SNS) 56, 71; data catgorization 59
SocialMediaMineR 58
SOM survey (Society, Opinion, Media) 146–7
source code 17
space/time dimensions in news production 180–3, 189
SPSS software 11
Stanford corenlp suite 95
Stata software 11
Stavelin, Eirik 81
Steensen, Steen 182
stemming 10, 79
Stewart, Brandon M. 9, 12, 15, 89
stop-clock culture 26
stopwords, removal of 10–11, 79

storage of content 186–7
structural topic models 85
structure and content of a link 48
subject entity, defined 32
supervised machine learning 13–14, 77, 82–3; advantages 13–14; human coder's decisions, importance of 13; rules for coding 13
support vector machines 13
Sveriges Radio (SR), content analysis of the online news flow 26, 28, 30, 32, 35; attention on domestic issues 34; event-driven news 33; in terms of immediacy 35–7, **36**; thematic distribution of the news stories 32
Swedish online news, explorative study of *see* Sveriges Radio (SR), content analysis of the online news flow

temporality of practices 25
text statistics 79–80
tf–idf (term frequency–inverse document frequency) scheme 18n1
The Onion Router (TOR) 116
Thomas, Stefan 172
tokenization 92–3
tool development for digital journalism research 3
topic modeling 15, 77, 84–6; best practices 101–3, **102**; choosing parameters 93–5; defined 90–2; feature selection 93; granularity 100, **101**; issue "nuclear power" in the news, illustration of 96–100; lemmatization 92–3; perplexity of **94**, 94–5; setting up LDA model 92–3; tokenization 92–3; tools 95–6
Tuchman, Gaye 26
Turney, Peter D. 12
Twitter feeds 42, 44, 46, 50, 52, 56, 58, 80

unsupervised methods 14–16

Van Atteveldt, Wouter 16
Van Damme et al. (2015) 131
van der Vossen, Robert 15
variables for content analysis 185–6
Vector Space Model 84
virtual private network (VPN) servers 116
visibility analysis 10–11; simple form 11
visualizations 80
Vlieger, Esther 15
Von Pape, Thilo 132

Wallach, Hanna 85
Weare and Lin 2000 183
Web 2.0 128
Web crawler 78
Web history 112, 118, 121

INDEX

Web surveys 5, 143–5, 147, 152, 154
Web-based questionnaires 145
Web-mail mixed-mode 145
Wilkerson, John 83
WinHTTrack Website Copier 29
wonkblog.com 50
5-Ws theory of media effects 42–9, **45**

YLE (Finnish National Public Service Broadcasting Company) 68
YouTube 114, 120, 186

Zamith, Rodrigo 182